Maps of Englishness

Maps of Englishness

Writing Identity in the Culture of Colonialism

Simon Gikandi

COLUMBIA UNIVERSITY PRESS

NEW YORK

Columbia University Press
Publishers Since 1893
New York   Chichester, West Sussex
Copyright © 1996 Columbia University Press

Library of Congress Cataloging-in-Publication Data
Gikandi, Simon.
Maps of Englishness : writing identity in the culture of colonialism / Simon Gikandi.
p. cm.
Includes bibliographical references (p.) and index.
ISBN 0-231-10598-3 (cloth : alk. paper). — ISBN 0-231-10599-1 (pbk. : alk. paper)
1. English prose literature—19th century—History and criticism.
2. Travelers' writings, English—History and criticism.
3. Literature and society—Great Britain—Colonies—History—19th century.
4. British—Travel—Great Britain—Colonies—History—19th century.
5. National characteristics, English, in literature.
6. Nationalism—England—History—19th century.
7. Group identity in literature. 8. Imperialism in literature.
9. Colonies in literature. 10. Narration (Rhetoric) I. Title.
PR778. T45G55 1996
820.9'358—dc20   96-26173
CIP

Casebound editions of Columbia University Press books
are printed on permanent and durable acid-free paper.
Printed in the United States of America
c 10 9 8 7 6 5 4 3 2 1
p 10 9 8 7 6 5 4 3 2 1

To Juandamarie, *nyiina wa aandu akwa*

Contents

Preface

I began this book as an attempt to answer some questions that had been troubling me since my student days at the University of Edinburgh in the early 1980s: Why did formerly colonized people, many of whom had spent generations fighting against colonial domination, seem to invest so much in cultural institutions—such as the school, Shakespeare, and cricket—that were closely associated with imperial conquest and rule? And why was it that here in Great Britain, in the heart of civilization itself, the nature and destiny of the country were being discussed in terms previously reserved for the former colonies? Why was it that here in Edinburgh, in the center of the imperial religion that had controlled and shaped my family's destiny for three generations, I found myself attending forums on the crisis of Scottish identity, the problems of underdevelopment on the Celtic periphery, and the nature of usable pasts in the context of contested histories? And why was it that here, in the place where—as far as my families and neighbors back in East Africa were concerned—civilization began, the most popular book at that time was titled *The Break-Up of Britain: Crisis and Neo-Nationalism?*[1] For someone like myself, who had come of age in the shadow of colonialism, the notion of a British state in twilight, or even of English nationalism in crisis, was hard to countenance.

Since this was before the advent of postcolonial theory and cultural studies, attempts to understand this crisis in British culture were hampered by the absence of a grammar that could conceptualize the metropolis in terms of crisis, decline, or disintegration. The discourse of nationalism in Africa, Asia, and the Caribbean had given me paradigms for understanding how colonial cultures were established in moments of crisis and how new narratives of identity had emerged to diagnose and represent the colonial condition, but none of the writers I had read on this issue—Aimé Césaire, Frantz Fanon, and George Lamming—had considered the ways in which the terms they used to describe the colonial periphery could be applied to the imperial center itself.[2]

And so, unable to deal with what Tom Nairn described as "the twilight of the British state," I retreated into the past in an attempt to understand how notions of cultural crisis might apply to Britain itself. And it was in reading the literature produced in response to the "condition of England" question—Carlyle's "Signs of the Times," Dickens's *Hard Times*, and Mrs. Gaskell's *North and South*, to mention just a few titles—that I began to engage with the notion of an English identity in crisis and to think of some of the ways in which Englishness was itself a product of the colonial culture that it seemed to have created elsewhere. The critical possibilities here were provided by the early works of Raymond Williams: in reading *Culture and Society*, for example, I could sense some of the significant ways in which the central moments of English cultural identity were driven by doubts and disputes about the perimeters of the values that defined Englishness—the nature of civil society, subjectivity, the meaning of the past, and the structure of feelings.[3] The sets of oppositions around which Williams had structured his book—Burke and Cobbett, Newman and Arnold, Richards and Leavis—appeared to be determined not purely by ideological or intellectual traditions but also by important foundational disputes about the meaning of Englishness itself:

> To put together the names of Burke and Cobbett is important, not only as a contrast, but because we can only understand this tradition of criticism of the new industrial society if we recognize that it is compounded of very different and at times even directly contradictory elements. The growth of the new society was so confusing, even to the best minds, that positions were drawn up in terms of inherited categories, which even then revealed unsuspected and even opposing implications.[4]

If Williams's majestic diagnosis of the condition of England question did not lead to a clearer understanding of the "twilight" of Englishness that

I was witnessing in the major cities of the realm—many of them plagued by massive unemployment and racial riots in the 1980s—it was because he, like Burke and Cobbett, had fallen back on the categories he had inherited from the nineteenth century. The most delimiting category was his postulation of foundational disputes about Englishness as essentially differences of opinion, differences whose implications needed to be contained for the sake of a common culture. Thus Williams was to conclude his book by asserting that in spite of the "disintegrating pressures" faced by different generations of English writers and intellectuals, and in spite of their different positions on the major issues of the day, their postulations were subordinated to a self-evident ethic of community and solidarity.[5] It was this ethic, I suspected, that seemed to retard Williams's attempts to extend his diagnosis of the English past to the present, or from the metropolis to the colonies. And since I myself was unable to understand this ethic—or to relate to it in any significant way—I did not find Williams's critique of Englishness useful in my attempt to come to terms with the twilight of imperial British culture.

But there was another, more serious reason that Williams's book could not address the questions generated by Britain's postimperial decline, the very crisis that had motivated his work in the first place: beneath the majestic analysis of the crisis of Englishness from which *Culture and Society* derived much of its authority, there lay a faulty conception of culture not simply as "an abstraction and an absolute" but also as a general response that did not take account of colonialism as the event that structured the integers—industry and democracy—that Williams considered imperative to understanding Englishness.[6] As a student of Englishness, I too seemed unable to comprehend the extent to which colonialism had shaped the character of the domestic space; colonialism had dominated every facet of my life and experience, but it was not something one associated with the culture of Great Britain or with its monumental literary works. Indeed, when it came to the organization of knowledge and literary culture, the common practice was to separate the Great Tradition of English literature from the new body of writing that had been produced in the former colonies. The idea of culture that informs colonial and postcolonial studies today—the idea that "culture was what colonialism was all about" and that "culture is a colonial formation"[7]—would perhaps have not made sense to the early Williams or even some of his associates and students—

cultural and literary scholars such as Stuart Hall and Terry Eagleton—who were products of colonized cultures or imaginations. For me, then, reading *Culture and Society* had ended up creating an interpretative impasse: the book had suggested, in some powerful ways indeed, that crisis was a central category in the definition of English identities in the nineteenth century, but it had not indicated how this crisis was intricately connected to colonialism and, by extension, to the decline of the British state in the period after decolonization.

In retrospect, I can now see how I wrote *Maps of Englishness* as an attempt to overcome this impasse—to read Englishness as a cultural and literary phenomenon produced in the ambivalent space that separated, but also conjoined, metropole and colony. But bridging the gap between the culture of colonialism and metropolitan debates about the condition of England was not the most urgent thing on my mind when I began researching and writing this book. Indeed, when, almost ten years after my intellectual encounter with Williams, I returned to some of the questions that had troubled me in the 1980s, my primary intention was not to explain the ways in which English identities had been shaped by the colonial experience. On the contrary, my intention was to intervene in what appeared to be an intractable debate on colonial discourse and the status of postcolonial theory in contemporary cultural studies. In reflecting on what it meant to exist at the historical juncture between colonial rule and decolonization, I found myself caught between critical theorists who insisted that the cultures created by the colonial experience had undergone an epistemic rupture and a group of influential writers and social critics who argued that behind the mask of decolonization lay the powerful political and economic structures established by colonialism and strengthened by decolonization.[8] While my political sympathies lay with the latter group, it was evident to me that the culture of colonialism had undergone some radical transformations since decolonization, that we could not continue to discuss this culture in the framework of progress and continuity that it had established.

In these circumstances, I believed that I could prove my hypothesis, as it were, by tracing the central narratives established by colonial culture—narratives about selfhood, nation, identity, and history—from their supreme moments in the high imperial period (1840–1880), through their decline before and after World War I, to their atrophy and transplantation in the period of decolonization. By tracing the colonial narrative of identity from its moments of triumph and celebration, especially in the travel narratives of official historians such as Charles Kingsley and James Anthony Froude, to its decline in the modernist narratives of writers such as Conrad and Greene, I hoped to show that the postcolonial condition had emerged in the spaces of colonial failure. Narratives of nationalism that had emerged from the decolonized polis and the postcolonial narratives that migrant writers were producing in the heart of the English metropolis were to serve as the clearest signs of the ways in which the colonial narrative had been supplanted by new stories of Englishness. The authority of my argument, it seemed, would depend on my ability to find—and then read—a narrative or discursive moment that could be considered to represent the break from colonial to postcolonial narratives.

Like most other scholars in this field, I assumed, as Gyan Prakash has put it so succinctly, that modern colonialism had instituted such "enduring hierarchies of subjects and knowledges" that the ideological antagonism between colonial and postcolonial narratives and ideologies could not be blurred.[9] I also assumed that when the colonized produced discourses within colonial culture, these were bound to be connected, in one way or another, to the project of resistance against colonial rule. In this respect, I subscribed to what amounted to a creed, or at least an act of faith, in the field of colonial studies—that one of the most fascinating aspects of colonial rule was its uncanny generation of narratives that refused to fit into the hierarchies of colonial government and rule, narratives that dislocated the colonial project itself or called its central assumptions into question.[10] But I assumed, at the same time, that in spite of what appeared to be their artfulness, their bricolagic function, or even what Homi Bhabha has characterized as their subversive mimicry, such narratives still functioned within the epistemology established by the dominant culture of colonialism.[11] For this reason, I assumed, these narratives could not be conceived as postcolonial if we considered that term to refer to a system of knowledge—and its narratives—that lay beyond the colonial enterprise.

In carrying out my research in the colonial library, however, I began to encounter writers located within imperial hierarchies who, nevertheless, produced narratives that seemed to exist both inside and outside the central doctrines of Englishness. These writers seemed to position themselves squarely within colonial Englishness and to affiliate themselves with a set of identities and values that were considered to be the very condition of existence of colonialism itself—civilization, progress, literacy, and civility. At the same time, however, these writers took their local histories and traditions for granted and assumed that whatever Englishness had brought to the colonized had not supplemented such histories and traditions; indeed, they assumed that what made their cultural moments and identities unique was the simple act of social hybridity. In the narratives of such colonized writers as Mary Seacole, J. J. Thomas, and Ham Mukasa I encountered a surprising conjunction between the ideals promoted by metropolitan Englishness and local identities and histories that seemed to call such ideals into question.[12] These little texts, often produced without much publicity or fanfare in the metropolitan center, came to provide me with what I consider to be the defining occasion and function of postcoloniality.

Consider, for example, the circumstances in which J. J. Thomas was to produce his book *Froudacity*. This little text, which appeared soon after the publication of James Anthony Froude's famous narrative of his travels in the British West Indies, has to be considered an example of the ways in which the colonized subject fashioned itself by both questioning and appropriating the civilizational authority of Englishness. For if Froude's narrative was an attempt to assert the undisputed authority of empire in the West Indies and to insist on the paramount rights of white settlers in the period after emancipation, Thomas's work has to be read not only as a direct rebuttal of this claim to the doctrine of inalienable empire—and white supremacy—but also as a subtle affiliation with the culture that colonialism had created in the West Indies. In other words, Thomas's book was neither a discourse of resistance, which was to become popular in the postcolonial world in the period after World War II, nor a narrative of self-vindication in the field of empire; it was both these things. It was a narrative of resistance because it systematically set out to debunk "the ghastly imaginings" of Froude's text; it was a discourse of self-vindication and affiliation with Englishness because Thomas's powerful critique of imperial historiography depended on his appropriation and discursive use of the grammar he had inherited from colonial culture.[13] This identification with the culture of Englishness did not, however, seem to negate the specific and local institutions that had shaped the lives of the colonized; if many of them saw their destiny as a variation on the culture inherited by colonialism, it was because they also assumed that they had been instrumental both in the making of this culture and in its redefinition.

When the Ugandan writer Ham Mukasa stood outside the University of Cambridge Library in 1902, one of the significant sources of his pride in this monument of English culture was the fact that it contained not only "every kind of book" but also the books written by Sir Apolo Kagwa, the man whom he served as amanuensis. In calling Cambridge "the tutor of the world," Mukasa was also claiming it for himself. In this respect, instead of locating himself in a marginal position in relation to this tradition, Mukasa was reading it in relation to the central institutions of his own Buganda culture and the primary referents it provided.[14] And yet—and this was to become a central concern of my project—one could not seriously argue that England (the colonizer) and Buganda (the colony) existed in a state of cultural reciprocity or political equivalent. As a colonizing power, England had systematically emasculated Buganda's power or transformed it into an agency of colonial expansion; the kind of Buganda culture that Mukasa used as his point of reference had either been rewritten in terms that were more acceptable to the colonial inventors of tradition or simply subordinated to the narrative authority of the Bible. From a political perspective, then, the colonial space was marginal.

But what were the cultural implications of this marginality? Unconvinced by many attempts to valorize marginality as a kind of cultural value in postmodern social theories, I began to ponder on ways in which cultures produced on the margins of a dominant discourse might actually have the authority not only to subvert the dominant but also to transform its central notions. I wanted to be able to argue that colonial cultures had been central in the transformation of English identities without discarding the claim that colonialism was, as a system of power and authority, responsible for the radical displacement of the colonial world and its narratives. How could a space in which traditional authority had been relegated to the margins of the dominant ever have the authority to transform the center? How could what appeared to be the minor narratives of empire play a constitutive role in the remaking of Englishness? The answers to these questions were to be found, surprisingly enough, in a group of theoretical and historical texts that were trying to diagnose the crisis of Englishness in the decade defined by the cultural politics of what Stuart Hall has called "Thatcherism."[15]

Clearly, while many intellectuals from the postcolonial world were busy trying to figure out how the concept of postcoloniality could be applied to the nation-states that had succeeded British imperialism, leading scholars of Englishness were already deploying the techniques and ideologies of postcoloniality in their diagnosis of the crisis of modern Englishness. Indeed, one could argue that not until they began to link the crisis of English culture with the decline of empire were students of modern British society able to find the appropriate grammar for representing the crisis of Englishness. In his 1964 essay on the "origins of the present crisis," for example, Perry Anderson began with a familiar refrain: "British society is in the throes of a profound yet cryptic crisis, undramatic in appearance, but pervasive in its reverberations. So much everyone agrees. But what kind of crisis is it? What kind of outcomes to it are likely? Anyone who looks for an answer to these questions in the spate of recent books on the 'condition of England' is likely to be disappointed."[16] The cryptic nature of this crisis—and the failure of established attempts to understand it—arose because the critique of English culture refused to, or was unable to, confront its colonial antecedents and to see this crisis, in the way it was being articulated in the former colonies, as a crisis of the national state itself.

In an important retrospective moment of self-critique, Anderson was to put his finger on the problem in ways that other scholars of Englishness have been forced to emulate:

> In my case, it was not the nation but the state which formed the principle object of subsequent reflection. The result was a work of the same period centred on absolutism, rather than nationalism. There were a number of reasons for this difference of interest. One was no doubt personal background. Active Scottish origins were more likely than residual Anglo-Irish ones to produce a sharply critical but sympathetic understanding of the ambiguities of popular nationalism; although the example of my brother's work shows that post-colonial aftershocks could yield their own insights here.[17]

Several points in this observation were to turn me in other directions as I sought paradigms to link the crisis of Englishness with the problems that seemed to plague the postcolonial traditions and literatures I was reading.

First, it was obvious that prior attempts to examine the nature of English culture in absolutist and universal terms, be they neo-Marxist (Perry Anderson, Raymond Williams, and Stuart Hall) or conservative (Margaret Thatcher and Enoch Powell), were being retarded by their inability to come to terms with colonialism in its absence. Second, it was easier to diagnose Englishness in terms of absolutism (class, history, and hegemony) rather than the ambiguous consequences of postimperial decline (the emergence of racism, industrial decay, and the transformation of the national body). Third, so long as "personal background" was repressed in the critique of Englishness, readers could not understand where the insights and pressures in this debate were coming from. Simply put, if Benedict Anderson's small text, *Imagined Communities*, has come to have more resonance in recent studies of identity formation in the British Isles and in Britain's former colonial possessions than the monumental works by his brother, it is not merely because it located the problem of the nation at the very heart of modern identity but also because it called attention to the different ways in which the national imaginary was generated by personal and collective desires whose authority was derived from the narrative and historical forms that they assumed.[18]

It is not perhaps a great exaggeration to say that if Williams's and Hall's readings of the crisis of English culture in their early works remained incomplete, it was because they had not recognized the extent to which the authority of their narratives depended as much on their training as it did on their location on the periphery of Englishness. For me this recognition was important because, as I will explain later, the main argument I make in this book—that it was in the incomplete project of colonialism that the narratives of modern Englishness and postcoloniality were produced—could not have been possible if I had not reread Williams's book *The Country and the City* as a meditation on the function of peripheries in the making of cultural hegemony.[19] It was in this book that I discovered the extent to which the versions of Englishness that I had inherited as a child of colonialism, the Englishness of F. R. Leavis, an Englishness in which the national culture found its untroubled refuge in the works of its great writers (Shakespeare and Milton), were the result of a false totality.[20] From Williams's book, I began to see how Englishness, far from emerging from a body of stable value and shared experiences, had been produced by a continuous conflict between the center and its Celtic and colonial peripheries.

Out of this conflict was to emerge the culture of colonialism, a culture of mutual imbrication and contamination. The invention of Britishness, as Linda Colley has asserted in *Britons: Forging the Nation, 1707–1837*, was the quintessential case of identities constituted in difference: "The sense of a common identity here did not come into being, then, because of an integration and homogenisation of disparate cultures. Instead, Britishness was superimposed over an array of internal differences in response to contact with the Other, and in response to the conflict with the Other."[21]

My claim in this book goes a step further: that this other was a constitutive element in the invention of Britishness; that it was in writing about it that the metropolis could be drawn into the sites of what it assumed to be colonial difference and turn them into indispensable spaces of self-reflection. By the same token, I argue that the colonized cannot continue to be conceived as victims of a triumphant Englishness imposing its rule and civility on its radical other; on the contrary, the colonial space was to reconstitute itself in response to the imposition of Englishness; in inventing itself, the colonial space would also reinvent the structure and meaning of the core terms of Englishness, including Shakespeare and cricket. My book is on the textual implications of these two processes. While I work within the purview of the cultural questions generated by the debates on Englishness in the face of postcoloniality, and while I often borrow from the techniques and tools of other disciplines, including anthropology and history, my approach is deliberately textual. My interest is in the relation between the texts of colonial culture and the larger contexts in which they were produced, but my emphasis is always on the production and the meaning of these texts.

The attention I pay to the textualization of the colonial scene should not, however, be construed as an attempt to "aestheticize colonialism"[22] as a way of either containing its political effects or negating the mechanisms by which imperialism was an exercise in power. I am eager to theorize and textualize colonialism for two main reasons. First, while it is true that many studies of colonial culture in the Euro-American context suffer from what Nicholas Thomas has called "the aspiration of theorizing globally," the situation in the former colonies seems to want to resist theory either because it threatens the nativism that underwrites the national culture or because it calls into question established colonial constructs such as history, aesthetics, and, of course, Shakespeare.[23] While many critics of colonial theory in Europe and America have attacked it for its failure to consider the particularities of its objects of analysis, theory is renounced, in the postcolonial world itself, for calling into question what empire ordained as true and unchanging. Second, my textualization of colonial culture is the recognition that texts were important and indispensable weapons in the imposition of rule and governance; and as I will show in the course of my discussion, texts provided the medium through which the crisis of both colonial and domestic identities were mediated.

There is, however, a more personal reason for this predilection toward texts. I was born in the shadow of colonialism, under a state of emergency in Central Kenya. My earliest memories are dominated by insignias of colonial rule at its most dramatic moment of crisis and power: images of barbed wire fences, watchtowers, the Royal Scottish Fusiliers in red berets, and guard dogs. But against these images of colonial terror, I can vividly recall the other side of colonial culture, represented by the hospital, the school, and the church at the Church of Scotland Mission at Tumutumu, where I grew up. At this center of Presbyterianism in East Africa, I was part of a distinct group of African Christians who defined themselves not in terms of their Christian beliefs or their affiliation with colonial culture but in terms of the books they read. They called themselves *Athomi*, people of the book, and you could tell them apart from those they had proclaimed to be their others not only by their European dress and European-style houses but also by their books, the books they held religiously on their way to church on Sunday, the books that filled their living rooms, the musty, yellowed textbooks in which they recorded their private lives and professional experiences.[24]

One of the things that puzzled me about my people—and this ultimately is an indirect subject of this book—is how strongly they detested colonial rule, which they fought tooth and nail, often ending up in prison, and how passionately they believed in the efficacy and authority of colonial culture. For many of them, this was not a contradiction: the reason they were fighting colonial rule was not because they wanted to return to a precolonial past (in spite of the nationalist rhetoric gesturing that way) but because they wanted access to the privileges of colonial culture to be spread more equitably, without regard to race and creed. They wanted African children to be taught English so that they could have access to the institutions of colonialism, so that they could read Shakespeare in the original instead of having to rely on translations and adaptations.

Such claims were, of course, anathema to my generation when I went to the University of Nairobi in the late 1970s. Indeed, the major intellectual debate under way when I arrived at the university in 1976 was to complete the abolition of the English department by debunking the "presumed centrality of English" in the humanities curriculum.[25] From this high nationalist pedestal, the *Athomi's* desire for more Englishness could only be treated with contempt. But that was because we did not know that the desire to abolish the English department was driven by the same paradigms and assumptions that had generated Leavis's desire to make English criticism the center of national life. For though Leavis had argued that literature was the vessel of an organic community and an essential English past, those who advocated the abolition of the English department at the University of Nairobi wanted to reject the primacy of English literature and culture—but not the epistemology of literary studies inherited from colonialism: "The primary duty of any literature department is to illuminate the spirit animating a people, to show how it meets new challenges, and to investigate possible areas of development and involvement."[26] Postcoloniality is perhaps the interpretative moment when the complicity between such colonial and nationalist moments is recognized without guilt or recrimination.

The critical cartography of this book—its reflection on discrete moments of Englishness—has been across a cultural landscape that stretches from East Africa to Scotland and Michigan, and I owe special thanks to the different people I have encountered in the process of writing *Maps of Englishness*. To the *Athomi* of Tumutumu, including my parents, who insisted on the primacy of the text in cultural discourse, and my teachers at the Universities of Nairobi and Edinburgh, I owe special thanks and fond memories. This book owes its character to the support I have received from the University of Michigan, and I would like to thank Bob Weisbuch, who, first as chair of the department of English and later as interim dean of the Rackham Graduate School, provided me with tremendous personal and intellectual support. The completion of the book was aided by a summer research grant from the Rackham Graduate School at the University of Michigan. I have continued to benefit from the generosity of Martha Vicinus, who has supported this project both institutionally, as the chair of the English department, and through her keen reading of the manuscript; she helped me avoid many errors and forced me to rethink some important issues. Numerous corridor discussions with Lemuel Johnson and George Bornstein on the second floor of Haven Hall have shaped this book in ways that the two may not have suspected.

The central arguments of this book were also shaped by students in my seminars on colonial culture and modernism, and I want to take this opportunity to thank them for having taught me so much about modernism and empire. Susan Friedman read an early draft of chapter 5 and provided me with important insights on modernism and late colonialism. I owe Abiola Irele a special debt for intellectual support at crucial moments in my career. And in the midst of the tedium of research and writing, Natasha Barnes shared her expertise on the Caribbean and also provided warm friendship.

An earlier version of chapter 3 appeared in a special issue of *Nineteenth-Century Contexts* dealing with colonialism, and I thank Greg Kucich, the editor of the journal, and Gordon Breach Publishers for permission to reprint. A version of the same chapter was presented as the keynote address at the annual Conference of Interdisciplinary Nineteenth-Century Studies (University of Arizona, Tempe, 1993), and I would like to thank Julie Codell for providing the opportunity to present the argument of the book publicly for the first time. I am grateful to Jennifer Crewe, my editor at Columbia University Press, for supporting this project during some trying moments.

More than any of my other works, this book has been written in the midst of the pleasures and pressures of fatherhood, and I would like to thank Edwin and James Middleton, Tasha Taylor, and Christine Davies for heeding my calls for relief. My greatest debt is to my partner, Juandamarie, who has lived with this book perhaps longer than I wanted, patiently listened to its arguments in the midst of coparenting, and provided the love to sustain it through some difficult times.

Maps of Englishness

⋖ I ⋗

Colonial Culture and the Question of Identity

For the ex-colony, decolonization is a dialogue with the colonial past, and not a simple dismantling of colonial habits and modes of life. Nowhere are the complexities and ambiguities of this dialogue more evident than in the vicissitudes of cricket in countries that were once part of the British Empire. In the Indian case, the cultural aspects of decolonization deeply affect every domain of public life, from language and the arts to ideas about political representation and economic justice. In every major public debate in contemporary India, one underlying strand is always the question of what to do with the shreds and patches of the colonial heritage.

Arjun Appadurai, "Playing with Modernity"

A government centred upon Westminster which aims at preserving the United Kingdom needs to think long and hard about the nature of "British identity." That there is confusion in high places emerged in Mrs. Thatcher's speeches when she happily intermingled "British" and "English" history. There was also uncertainty in the setting up of a national history curriculum, which turned out to be not "national" in the sense of "British" but more narrowly national in the sense of Welsh, English and "Northern Ireland." Scotland was not even included. Small wonder if immigrants from Pakistan or Bangladesh are confused about their identity if the British people have not yet made up their minds.

Hugh Kearney, "Four Nations or One?"

The subject of this book is the relation between writing, identity, and colonial culture. This relation may not appear to be difficult to ascertain, especially given the voluminous number of cultural texts that emerged from the British imperial experience and in its aftermath, but as my opening epigraphs suggest, reading identities constituted in the field of empire, or in the aporia that separates the imperial past from the enunciative moment of decolonization, is not easy. We may be privileged to be able to read the grand narrative of empire from the vantage point of decolonization, as Edward Said has argued in a famous essay on Kipling, but we labor to develop mechanisms for understanding and deconstructing an identarian schema whose logic and history have always sought to affirm the radical difference between the metropole and its colonies.[1] And thus one is almost obliged to begin by calling attention to the unstable zones and contested boundaries that conjoin and divide metropolitan cultures and colonial spaces, to the frontiers in which the dialectic of imperialism is played out, and to that ill-defined space in which the experience of empire and its long past seem to cast an aura—which is also an anxiety—over contemporary culture.

Throughout this book, the frontier, the boundary, and the field of alterity will be read as important signifiers of ambiguous cartographic moments and amorphous temporalities, but they will also provide the topology for reading the relation between colonial pasts and decolonized presents, imperial cultures and their postimperial sites of crisis. As insignias of difference and identity, these boundaries, frontiers, and spaces will be read as constant reminders of the ways in which British and colonial identities are staged as radically different and yet inherently similar. What I have in mind here, of course, is the now familiar dialectic of identity and difference. But while a sizable body of theory exists to affirm this dialectic, a dialectic that could be said to be an enabling condition for the project of postcolonial studies, it has never been clear where the identity between colonizer and colonized ends and the difference between them begins.[2] As the quoted passages from Appadurai and Kearney clearly indicate, the temporality of our postcolonial moment is defined by an inevitable conjuncture between the desire for decolonization and the reality of the colonial archive: in the former colonies, as the example of cricket and other forms of public discourse in India, Africa, and the Caribbean illustrates so well, the large issues that plague the decolonized polis are mediated through the institutional, ideological, and aesthetic "shreds and patches" of the British colonial heritage.[3] In Britain, in the meantime, the former imperial center seeks to understand its unraveling (in the aftermath of empire) using the cultural grammar (nationalism, tradition, and usable pasts) inherited from its former colonies.[4]

This situation presents readers of postimperial culture with a paradox: they hear, on the one hand, proponents of colonialism and the imperial ideal insisting on the common identity—the Pax Britannica—between colonizer and colonized; on the other hand, however, they are subjected to a nationalist rhetoric, in both the former metropole and its colonies, that insists on the radical difference between imperial centers and colonial margins. Indeed, it is in this paradox that the debate on postcoloniality and its texts has been shaped; this paradox is also the source of intense debates—and doubts—about the exact nature of the relation between empire and colony (in the past) and the metropolis and the postcolony (in the present). In turn, this debate, which will be examined in some detail in this introductory chapter, emanates from continuous confusion about the temporal and spatial relations between Britain and its former dominions: for if nation and colony are linked in fundamental ways, as many practitioners of postcolonial theory insist, why have they developed such elaborate temporal devices and ideological schemes to conceal their mutual genealogy, cultural interest, and agency? And why do questions that decolonization was supposed to have settled—questions about cultural affiliations and citizenship, for example—continue to overdetermine the conjugation of identities in both Britain and its former colonies?[5]

It seems logical to explain the resurgence of colonialism in the debate on the nature of modernity and modern society by arguing, as Frederick Cooper and Ann Laura Stoler have done, that the great categories that came to define the modern age—race and citizenship, civility and authority, for example—were haunted, from the start, by the colonial question. At the twilight of the modern age, then, an examination of the function of colonialism in the shaping of modernity is not an act of theoretical reversion; on the contrary, it is an attempt to name—and thus come to terms with—the hitherto invisible specter whose presence we have felt around us, whose effectivity we have encountered in the texts of our identity, but whose logic we could not name until now.[7] The significance of this problem—the ghosting of colonialism, as it were—will be appreciated by those readers who may recall that, until recently, the relation between the imperial center and its colonial margins was characterized by a denial of what Johannes Fabian calls temporal coevalness.[8] For in the face of decolonization, especially in the period after World War II, both the postimperial nation and the decolonized state sought to cast their mutual pasts—and their narratives of identity—as autonomous of their colonial heritage. Identity and alterity were written as mutually exclusive entities. Thus the desire of a former colonial power such as Britain to represent its national history as immanent, and its geography as essentially insular, was matched by the drive, in the decolonized polis, to promote nationalism as the radical alternative to imperialism.

The questions that emerged in this situation of geographical and temporal disclaimer—questions about usable pasts, literary traditions, and contested communities—have come to dominate the politics of culture and identity in both Britain and its former colonies. Such questions have, indeed, become inevitable in our search for mechanisms for reading the narratives that emerge when colonized peoples encounter European events and institutions and for explicating the discourses produced when Europe thematizes its colonial other as a figure of its own desires and a symptom of its temporal dislocation. Who reads the imperial past and its narratives? Who bears testimony to the identities constituted in the encounter between Europe and its others? The answers to these questions are presented—too often, perhaps—as a consequence of theoretical reorientation in the postmodern age and, thus, as an effect of our critical anti-ethnocentrism.[9] The assumption here is that if the texts of what I will be calling the culture of Englishness now seem to produce meanings other than those imputed to them by proponents of the "Great Tradition," this new situation primarily reflects a change in readership rather than a transformation of the epistemological condition in which such texts were produced.

And yet, as Ross Chambers argues in *Room for Maneuver*, literary discourses do not simply produce change through their reading; "they *are produced* also in historical circumstances whose features the text necessarily takes into account."[10] It seems to me that while postcolonial theorists have expended a lot of time on how readers mediate colonial and postcolonial texts, the work of figuring the conditions of possibility of these texts is only just beginning. My argument, then, is that to understand the historical and "communicative circumstances" that produced these texts, we have to move beyond the politics of canonicity—the desire for equal access to knowledge and the curriculum.[11] I am not, of course, suggesting that issues of literary canons and the location of readers are unimportant; but I worry that a careless incorporation of the "other voice" into a literary tradition can, if it is only appendative, function simply as a mechanism of covert marginalization. But then, the claim I make in this chapter—that the postcolonial reader needs to establish a certain affiliation with the texts of Englishness—may be seen in some literary quarters as a surreptitious subordination of various national literatures to the Great Tradition. Nevertheless, if we are to recognize the instrumentality of colonial spaces and subjects in the production of modern Englishness, this is a risk we must be willing to take.

I am, then, in general agreement with Edward Said's thesis (in *Culture and Imperialism*) that colonized peoples and imperial spaces were crucial ingredients in the generation and consolidation of a European identity and its master narratives; that the imperial map of the world was to thread its way into the cultural products of the West and become a vital part of its "texture of linguistic and cultural practice."[12] This argument will underwrite much of my reading of colonial spaces in the texts of Englishness. But my primary concern will be with what I consider to be some unanswered questions in postcolonial theory in general and Said's project in particular. Beyond an astute proffering of alternative interpretations to the canon, what is the usefulness of this rereading of the texts of Englishness? If self-willed acts of rereading the canon pluralize the culture of Englishness, as Barthes would say, do they serve any purpose in the ex-colonial space itself?[13]

The most apt response to this question is probably contained toward the end of V. Y. Mudimbe's *The Invention of Africa*, where the author argues that an African invention of Europe—through a "critical reading of the Western experience"—is both a mastery of its techniques and an "ambiguous strategy for implementing alterity"; therefore, for ex-colonial subjects to master the instrumentalities of Western discourse is to posit the ways in which Europe can be positioned as the "other" of its former dominions.[14] The question that awaits an answer, however, is whether postcolonial theory, having brilliantly exhibited its mastery of Western techniques, can displace the uneven cartography in which the texts it reads have been produced. Faced with the possibility that this mastery of Western techniques is just another homage to European dominance, one might be tempted to follow Aijaz Ahmad's lead and dismiss the whole theoretical enterprise as a diminution of politics, an ascension, as it were, to Western hegemony.[15] But as I will argue in this introductory chapter, postcolonial theory is most useful in its self-reflexivity, especially its recognition that the colonized space was instrumental in the invention of Europe just as the idea of Europe was the condition for the possibility of the production of modern colonial and postcolonial society.

The best postcolonial theory, I will argue, is one that both analyzes the discourse of "the other" and reads empire as the cultural formation in which, through the writing of the colonial landscape and its subjects, the provincial concerns of several European countries assumed a universal normativity, one that seeks to understand, conversely, how imperial ideologies came to be reverted into what Dipesh Chakrabarty has called the "collective origin-myths" of the decolonized state.[16] My point here is that, contrary to Ahmad's view, any theoretical reflection on the epistemic gestures through which Europe came to be constituted as a universal force must, given its "real-life" consequences, be read as political.

And yet, if a concerted reconceptualization of—and critique of—the epistemology of colonialism has become the raison d'être of postcolonial theory, it presents particular difficulties to a postcolonial reader like myself. What does it mean to read the culture of empire from the vantage point of what Ahmad has called "the structures of metropolitan hegemony"?[17] Is it possible to promote a system of knowledge that simultaneously acknowledges the constitutive power of empire at home and abroad and yet devalorizes its totalizing claims? And if rereading an imperial past implies immersing ourselves in it, as Mieke Bal has suggested, can we transcend the topography of imperialism or must we always relive its trauma?[18] Above all, what is the relation between colonial narratives and their objects of knowledge? On what epistemological grounds are we to invoke a postcolonial mode of cognition and what techniques of reflection are demanded by that space of "reciprocal exclusivity" in which colonial cultures and peoples encounter European events and stories?[19]

These questions are certainly not new in literary and cultural studies; on the contrary, they were central to the analysis of the colonial situation in the works of such nationalist theorists as Aimé Césaire and Frantz Fanon. My contention, however, is that the analysis of the relation between metropole and colony in the works of such theorists—an analysis prompted by the desire for an autonomous national culture—was premised on the belief that, given the proper circumstances and institutions, the colonial infrastructure could actually be liberated from doctrines of imperial power, racism, and Eurocentrism. And thus the critique of imperialism in nationalist theory came to be driven by the need to sever the link between the imperial center and its colonies, even when it seemed condemned to reproduce the values of the culture of colonialism.[20] But after several decades of independence in the former colonies, it has become evident that the nationalist desire for a radical rupture from the colonial past has failed, that nationalism cannot seriously be considered to be the alternative to imperialism that it was once thought to be; indeed, some postcolonial theorists have begun to suspect that the rush from imperialism has been, in paradigmatic terms, part of the problem rather than its solution.[21]

A certain ghost, nevertheless, haunts the works of these theorists. How do we read the relationship between metropole and colony as conjunctive when our ideological desire is the inscription of their uneven temporality and their inherent heterologies? How can we advocate a diachronic approach to, let's say, English and Indian cultures, and at the same time argue that the imperial experience that created these cultures in the modern period was a synchronic event? The conceptual problem involved in addressing what Cooper and Stoler have aptly called "the contingency of metropolitan-colonial connections" is indeed difficult, for it requires interpretative strategies that insist, on the one hand, that Europe's colonies provided the theater in which modern European identities were shaped and revamped but that call attention, on the other hand, to how this shaping of identity was predicated on the invention and exclusion of the colonial subject as a figure of alterity.[22] In short, if the ideals of modern bourgeois society were framed and justified within the theater of colonialism, colonial society was often written as the space deprived of, or undeserving of, such values as individualism and citizenship. Furthermore, in a situation in which cultural formations were marked and generated by an undesirable political event—European imperialism—the most urgent questions in colonial and postcolonial studies came to be centered, not surprisingly, on the problem of mediating cultural crisis and the conjugation of identities consolidated in spaces of alterity.

My focus in this book is on the function of narratives of identity and alterity in the constitution of English identities in the imperial and postimperial age. Like many other scholars in the field of postcolonial studies, I draw many of my illustrations from narratives of travel and novels informed by the notion of journeys into the space of the other. My premise here is that the trope of travel generates narratives that are acutely concerned with self-realization in the spaces of the other, that the European excursion (and incursion) into the colonial space is one of the most important vehicles by which, to paraphrase Nick Dirks, Europe and its others are re-created.[23] My critical method—and selection of primary texts—are intended to explore how colonial spaces entered the discourse on Englishness in the modern period, and how British colonies functioned as indispensable ingredients in the institution of English identities in certain specific moments and circumstances.

I am also interested in exploring the ways in which the cultural documents of colonialism provided the parameters within which Englishness was defined by simultaneous acts of inclusion and exclusion. For one of the most amazing aspects of the high culture of Englishness, as it was articulated by leading liberal intellectuals such as John Stuart Mill and Charles Kingsley (see chapters 2 and 3), was the extent to which its inclusionary intentions were underwritten by what Uday S. Mehta has defined as exclusionary effects:

> One needs to account for how a set of ideas that professed, at a fundamental level, to include as their political referent a universal constituency nevertheless spawned practices that were either predicated on or directed at the political marginalization of various people. More specifically, one must consider if the exclusionary thrust of liberal history stems from the misapprehension of the generative basis of liberal universalism or if in contrast liberal history projects with greater focus and onto a larger canvas the theoretically veiled and qualified truth of liberal universalism. Despite the enormous contrariety between the profession of political universality and the history of political exclusion, the latter may in fact elaborate the truth and ambivalence of the former.[24]

Not all aspects of colonialism were defined within the liberal paradigm, but liberalism promoted the best elements of colonial Englishness, the kind of values that colonized people aspired to and were to try to realize in the moment of decolonization. In these circumstances it is imperative that we consider how colonial culture was premised on a universal identity that, nevertheless, was predicated on systematic modes of exclusion. Like the liberalism that defined its affirmative character, colonial culture would continue to be defined by its generative contradictions. One of my major arguments in this book, then, is that it is within these contradictions that we have to read the effects of colonial culture; we have to consider how colonialism was a project of power and control, of domination and racial exclusiveness that, nevertheless, provided the context in which modern identities were constituted.

The corollary to this argument is that the crisis of Englishness in the present period is symptomatic of the incomplete project of colonialism, for it calls attention to the fate of powerful cultural categories forced—by decolonization and the demise of empire—to exist outside the historical conditions that made them possible. Indeed, one of the central claims of my book is that the persistence and enforcement of colonial categories in their moment of disappearance points us in two related directions: in the formerly colonized space itself, we encounter the foremost insignias of colonial culture overdetermining the making of what were supposed to be decolonized identities; in the metropolis itself, we see these same categories returning, in their phenomenality and ghostliness, to call into question the axioms of Englishness.

Let us examine this problem using one of the most exemplary cultural and aesthetic categories inherited from colonialism—the game of cricket. As numerous scholars have noted, cricket was considered, in both Victorian England and its colonies, to be the perfect expression of the values of bourgeois civility, Anglo-Saxon ethics, and public school morality. And if cricket was valued as a national symbol, it was because, in Keith Sandiford's words, "it was an exclusively English creation unsullied by oriental or European influences" and was hence further proof of the Victorians' "moral and cultural supremacy."[25] And it was precisely because of the affinity between cricket and Englishness, between the game and the idea of nationhood, that nationalists in India and the Caribbean were to posit their entry into the field of cricket as the mark of both their mastery of the culture of Englishness and their transcendence of its exclusive politics. The resulting apotheosis of nationalism and decolonization was to be presented in its most lyrical form in C. L. R. James's memoir, *Beyond a Boundary*, where Frank Worrell's captaincy of the triumphant West Indian cricket tour of Australia in 1961 was discursively conceived as both a break from the colonial past and an entry into the universal value system denoted by "global" cricket. Here are James's memorable final words on the Worrell tour of Australia:

> I caught a glimpse of what brought a quarter of a million inhabitants of Melbourne into the streets to tell the West Indian cricketers good-bye, a gesture spontaneous and in cricket without precedent, one people speaking to another. Clearly their way with bat and ball, West Indians at that moment had made a public entry into the comity of nations. Thomas Arnold, Thomas Hughes and the Old Master himself would have recognized Frank Worrell as their boy.[26]

In James's view, what was striking in this Australian embrace of the West Indian team that had beaten them was not so much the simple fact that it had been captained by a black man (although this is what ultimately made it a nationalist occasion) but the idea of mutual comity on display in the streets of Melbourne, the idea that the game that had been intended to mark the radical disjuncture between the values of the colonizer and the colonized had become, on the contrary, the emblem of shared values.

What James had missed in his celebration of cricket as the colonized subjects' paradigmatic entry into Englishness, however, was the very ambivalence of the terms of inclusion. For even as the colonized were touting cricket as an example of their simultaneous mastery and transcendence of Englishness, they were well aware of the extent to which the game had become what Orlando Patterson calls "a byword for all that is most English in the British way of life," and hence the symbol of a difficult, if not embarrassing, colonial grammar:

> The vocabulary of cricket is a standard pool of stock images for Tory statesmen. No better symbol of English culture could be found. Yet, this is the game which West Indians have usurped, have come to master. What the former colonial subject has done is to literally beat the master at his own game. But, more important, he has

beaten him symbolically. Here all the ambivalence of the black lower-class West Indians towards English culture can be played out.[27]

But Patterson's notion of cricket as the ritual in which colonial ambivalences toward the master culture of Englishness is played out fails, like James's theory of colonial mastery, to see the extent to which the game, by acquiring a different character in its colonial and postcolonial situations, had worked its way out of this ambivalence. For what now seems so remarkable about postcolonial cricket is not the axiomatic fact that colonized peoples beat the English at their own game but their radical reinvention of the terms of play. In other words, cricket was no longer thought of as the game that signified the core values of Englishness; it was viewed as the mode of play and ritual that has been redefined by Indian and West Indian players well beyond its original configuration.

In fact, as early as 1950, when the West Indies defeated England in the second test at Lords, the essence of English cricket culture itself was being transformed in unprecedented ways. In the words of one commentator, "The Lords test was the scene of the first 'cricket carnival' in England. The ground exploded in dance, song and bacchanal, West Indian style, and signalled the beginning of a tradition that was to shape the culture of cricket crowds in England."[28] The important point, then, is that the indigenization of cricket in the colonial and postcolonial sphere was transforming the nature of the game and its culture in England itself; indeed, after the "blackwash" of the English cricket team by the West Indies in the 1984 "world series"—and subsequent defeats by India—cricket clubs in England had no choice but to adopt the "African" and "Indian" characteristics of the game if they were to remain serious competitors.[29] But even more fascinating is the extent to which this most colonial category, this game that was supposed to represent the triumphant moral character of Englishness, has now come to derive its energies—and innovative forms—from localities that are far removed—by race and class—from the centers of middle class civility and restraint represented by the Kensington Oval (figure 1.1). It is through the aesthetic forms of cricket that the beaches and back streets of the West Indies enter the national gallery of Englishness (figure 1.2).

FIGURE 1.1

Playing street cricket in Barbados.

Courtesy of National Library of Barbados.

FIGURE 1.2
William Bowyer's action portrait of the great West Indian batsman Viv Richards,
who led the West Indies to major victories against England in the 1980s.
Courtesy of National Portrait Gallery, London.

And so in this book I read colonial categories such as cricket (and literature) as the mark of the incomplete project of colonialism, as the institutions that allow formerly colonized peoples to hallow new spaces of
identity and self-expression and provide the metropolis with the alibi to
reinvigorate its cultural traditions. After all, would cricket have acquired its

intellectual and aesthetic force—or its universality, for that matter—if it were not the most popular game in India and the West Indies today? Isn't it ironic that the imperial sport is more important in the cultural politics of the Caribbean and the Indian subcontinent than it is in England itself?[30]

For me, the survival and efficacy of the colonial moments represented by categories such as cricket are the true marks of postcoloniality. For while most critical literature has focused on the problems posed by the concept of postcolonialism, especially when it posits itself as a mark of a certain kind of paradigmatic transcendence of the colonial situation, I use the term *postcolonialism* as a code for the state of undecidability in which the culture of colonialism continues to resonate in what was supposed to be its negation. My book thus takes the controversial notion of "postness" in colonial studies as the cultural sign not of transcended political states but of their intractableness, of their hegemonic presence and theoretical frailness. I invoke the *post* to describe a condition in which colonial culture dominates the scene of cultural production but one in which its face has been changed by both its appropriation by the colonized and the theoretical oppositionality it faces in the decolonized polis.[31] It is, thus, worth making some distinctions here: the argument that colonialism has been transcended is patently false; but so is the insistence that, in the former colonies, the culture of colonialism continues to have the same power and presence it had before decolonization.

But since the charge that the trope of postcoloniality sustains the delusion of historical rupture will not go away, it demands a careful response. Let us consider, for example, the position taken by Ama Ata Aidoo, the eminent Ghanaian novelist, whose abrupt dismissal of postcoloniality— "colonialism has not been 'post'-ed anywhere"—provides opponents of postcolonial theory with their most dramatic epigraph. Aidoo's position is succinct: "Applied to Africa, India, and some other parts of the world, 'postcolonial' is not only a fiction, but a pernicious fiction, a cover-up of a dangerous period in our people's lives. For unlike 'neocolonial,' for instance, 'postcolonial' posits a notion of *something finished*. (And 'post' definitely is not 'ante.')"[32]

It is not difficult to see why this statement strikes such a powerful chord among literary theorists in the former colonies: for people who live the practical effects of colonialism, imprisoned in its decaying infrastructure and incomplete postmortem, it is hard to make a case for any significant temporal shift from an imperial past, especially when its ideologies appear to have been legitimated by decolonization. If postcoloniality has been defined as the transcendence of imperial structures and their histories, such a definition is obviously contradicted by the everyday experiences and memories of the people in the ex-colonies. But the assumption that the lives and experiences of people in so-called Third World countries are wretched because they are perpetual victims of their colonial past similarly needs to be questioned. For whether we consider decolonization as a successful or an arrested factor, we cannot deny the power of the social and cultural projects that have sought to transcend the imperial legacy and the "states of mind" they have generated.[33] If such "states of mind" seem hard to categorize, it is because even as ex-colonial subjects reject the culture of colonialism, they also refuse to be contained within the discourse of official nationalism. One of the most compelling reasons for a postcolonial theory, then, is the desire, among the formerly colonized peoples themselves, for historiographies and cultural instruments that might help demythologize the ideology of nationalism—especially the claim that the nation-state in Africa, the Caribbean, or the Indian subcontinent represents a political and interpretive moment in which colonialism is finally transcended.

I want to argue that the postcolonial paradigm is most useful as a strategy for rereading the convergence of structural continuity in the face of temporal disruption, of understanding entrenched memories in the midst of reconfigured desires. *Postcoloniality* is thus the term for a state of transition and cultural instability.[34] Indeed, if we accept the premise that all contemporary culture in the fin de siècle is marked by a state of doubt and crisis, we have to argue, contrary to Aidoo's trenchant suggestion, that *postcoloniality* is a term for a state that does not exist, that postcolonial theory is one way of recognizing how decolonized situations are marked by the trace of the imperial pasts they try to disavow.[35] Thus, if postcolonial historiography and theory are generated by the imperative to "provincialize" the European narrative, as Chakrabarty has argued, we cannot dismiss its attempts to deconstruct the terminology—and thus the ideologies— through which colonized peoples sought, and still seek, to escape their repressive pasts and presents.[36] Yes: Aidoo is right when she says that colonialism has not been " 'post'-ed anywhere" and that it "survives in many forms,"[37] but to read the persistence of the imperial past and to understand the continuing presence of colonial structures of domination where they are supposed to have disappeared, we have to question the rhetoric that advocates historical rupture in the name of the new nation and its antiquity.

Mine, then, is a simple claim for the power of the discursive agency that lies hidden beneath the rhetoric of postcolonial theory, a theory that is driven, in spite of its overt intentions, by the antinomies of colonialism. And if we are to grasp postcoloniality as what Fredric Jameson called (in a different context and in reference to postmodernism) "a symptom of the deeper structural changes in our society and its culture as a whole," we have to begin by acknowledging that the central antinomy here is how the postcolonial project seeks, unconsciously perhaps, to complete the project of colonialism.[38]

What seems immanent, amid all the debates on postcoloniality, is the fact that postcolonial theory—like many of its practitioners—is situated at the "uncanny crossroads" where metropolitan culture is simultaneously affirmed and subverted, where its ideological concerns are shown to be both global and local. I agree with those critics of postcolonial theory who continue to insist that questions of modernity and nationalism have uneven histories and modalities, and that the meaning of theory has to be adjudged by the cultural forms it mediates, but I also believe that the whole teleological movement promoted by the imperial experience needs to be subjected to a rigorous act of theoretical inversion.[39] In other words, narratives of empire and decolonization need to be reexamined in the light of their historical and cultural demise, but that interrogation must confront the ways in which colonialism triumphs—as we saw in the example of cricket—in its moments of failure.

And if we are looking for ways in which this historical and paradigmatic failure cuts across both the former metropole and the colony, we need not look further than the troubled status of the concept of the nation and ideals of national identity. For if what made British and postcolonial identities most secure in their moment of separation was the idea that both entities now constituted independent and autonomous nations with separate historical memories and genealogies, both have come to confront the postcolonial period as a state of awakening to the realization that the ideality of the nation and the identities it secured were very tenuous. But before we rush to demonize the idea of the nation and the topology it embodies, we need to understand its cogency and appeal in both metropolis and postcolony. We need, in particular, to recognize the investments that both empire and nation used to make—and still make—in the ideals of modernity and modern temporality. These ideals are, in essence, crucial to the functioning of nationalist discourse and its oppositional desire.

In Fanon's seminal work on national consciousness, for example, the absurd drama of colonialism is cast in what Patrick Taylor aptly calls "irreconcilable antinomies" in which the colonizer's drive to subjugate the colonized is counterweighted by resistance.[40] Colonial modernity would thus appear to be pitted against nationalist desire: "In the colonial context," says Fanon, "the settler only ends his work of breaking in the native when the latter admits loudly and intelligibly the supremacy of the white man's values. In the period of decolonization, the colonized masses mock at these values, insult them, and vomit them up."[41] In Fanon's thought, furthermore, the consciousness of freedom reveals itself in the narrative and historical form of the decolonized nation, which functions, in Taylor's words, "as the symbol of the totality of freedom in a temporal and spatial dimension."[42] And thus the politics of culture came to be structured by a simple Manichaean equation: empire equals domination and the culture of silence; nation equals freedom and the culture of liberation.

What would not become apparent until the process of decoupling metropole and colony was under way was the extent to which the categories that were cast in the above radical binaries were imbricated in their production and deconstruction. Simply put, when the process of decolonization failed to yield total freedom, the foundational histories of both the metropolis and the decolonized nation, and the categories that defined them, would begin to unravel in unexpected ways. This unraveling was, however, already written into the genealogy of both empire and nation. For while the nationalist dissociation of nation from empire often depended on an essentialist appeal to precolonial histories—ancient India or Africa, for example—it also justified its authority by claiming to be the true agent of modernity and modernization, a function it sought to wrench from the metropolis itself.

Under the circumstances, it would, indeed, be a fatal analytic error to forget that in the discourse of the "founding fathers" of the decolonized nation, what is often attacked is not the process of modernity—or what many of them call Europeanization—but imperial domination. The scandal of nationalism, it seems, is to be found in this discursive dissociation, or abstraction, of the ideal of modernity from the imperial experience that engendered it in the first place.[43] But since, in Chakrabarty's words, "the question of European imperialism cannot be separated from the problem of [postcolonial] modernity," we should no longer be scandalized by what Vincente Rafael calls the postcolonial "critique not only of the universalizing claims of modernity but also the naturalizing demands of nationality."[44] Our task, then, is to develop a critique of our inherited modernity and its dominant categories.

One way of clarifying this argument is to suggest that instead of reading metropole and colony as oppositions, we should see them as antinomies connected through the figure of modernity.[45] My assumption here is that the "founders" of the new postcolonial nations legitimated their authority by claiming the agency of pure modernity (even as they sang praise songs for precolonial traditions) not because they were attracted to the imperial project per se but because they had no real access to modes of knowledge outside the horizon of expectations established by empire.[46] In Jomo Kenyatta's monumental work *Facing Mount Kenya*, for example, the future "father of the nation" sees his ethnography as driven by the need to preserve Gikuyu traditions as a counterculture to British imperialism. Kenyatta is quite insistent that his access to Gikuyu traditions is what makes his ethnography different from that of his European contemporaries, including his teacher, Bronislaw Malinowski. But he is also clear that the political function of his work depends on its valorization of the precolonial culture as a means rather than an end, as a prerequisite for the nationalist future, rather than a return to tradition qua tradition. A return to the past is thus only the first step in the search for (an African) path to modernity: "If Africans were left in peace on their own lands, Europeans would have to offer them the benefits of white civilisation in real earnest before they could obtain the African labour which they want so much."[47] Yes: colonial subjects will resist imperialism because it is a system of domination and conquest propelled by brute force and naked self-interest; but imperial structures will survive colonialism because, within the context of modernity, they have a universal appeal.

My contention here is that postcolonial theory has helped us question the universality shared by the imperialists and their nationalist opponents.

And thus what C. L. R. James once called "the postcolonial prerogative" becomes both a discursive engagement with the postimperial state (Britain) and its ex-colonies and a process of "reinterpreting and rewriting the forms and effects of an older colonial consciousness from the later experience of migration, diaspora, and cultural displacement."[48] This prerogative is driven, ironically enough, by the much-maligned process of decolonization, which we now need to read as the uncanny moment that was intended to consolidate national boundaries but ended up opening them even more. In this spatial and temporal reversal is to be found what Said has identified as the retrospective and heterophonic hermeneutics of decolonization: it proffers a privileged moment of closure that allows us to read the narratives of the imperial period and the culture of empire within a framework mapped by "their affiliations with the facts of power which informed and enabled them."[49] From a purely interpretative perspective, then, my evocation of postcoloniality is not intended to valorize postcolonial theory as a paradigm or strategy for negotiating moments of historical translation or of mediating disputes on the meaning of colonial spaces in the politics of contemporary culture. On the contrary, I want to read postcoloniality (and postimperial testimony) simply as the symptoms of a disjunctive moment in which imperial legacies have come to haunt English and postcolonial identities, their cultural formations, and their modes of representation.

But an understanding of how English identities are constituted in the spaces of imperial alterity remains incomplete in the absence of a serious examination of how colonized peoples themselves represent the imperial center both within and outside the infrastructure of colonialism. How do colonial subjects write their identities within the cultural totality established by imperialism? If power still resides in the metropolitan center, even after empire, what is the meaning of a reversed gaze at the culture of Englishness? What vehicles do the colonized use to represent England as a space of desire that is also the other? We can, in fact, rephrase one of the questions raised earlier—what does it mean for a formerly colonized subject to read the culture of Englishness?—by asking what it means to read the culture of colonialism inside and outside Englishness, to gaze at Englishness gazing at you, to read the Great Tradition simultaneously as the vector of the same and the other?[50]

Colonial and postcolonial theorists have spent a lot of time analyzing how Europe constitutes itself as a subject gazing at the other, but rarely have they examined how the other gazes at Europe. For the great irony of the relationship between self and other is not that spaces of identity and totality are relative and unstable but that even in their spaces of cultural confinement, such as expositions and exhibitions, the colonized are always able to cast a long gaze at their colonizers. Colonial culture is as much about the figuration of the metropolis in the imagination of the colonized themselves as it is about the representation of the colonized in the dominant discourses of the imperial center.

This book's concern with the intricate production of colonial culture in the space between colony and metropole is prompted, ultimately, by my own location (or dislocation) in relation to both Englishness and colonialism. As a native of a former colony, I am a product of the imperial experience and a subject in the European story it valorizes. My authority as a reader depends not only on my mastery of European literary traditions and techniques but also on the simple fact that once upon a time my parents decided to break away from the traditions of their people and embrace the modern culture of colonialism, a culture that seemed to guarantee them new spaces of self-inscription in the narrative of modernity. For this reason, among others, I want to understand the logic behind the imperium's engagement with its colonial subjects, but also I want to come to terms with the colonized subject's self-willed entry into the imperial realm. I want to probe how the British rewriting of my culture and peoples, and their subordination to the master narrative of imperialism and the Enlightenment, are, at the same time, the enabling condition for modern subjectivities not only in Africa but also in England and its Celtic periphery. Reading imperial and postimperial texts is my way of coming to terms with my identity in the alterity of Englishness.

In the Shadow of Englishness

Living in the shadow of Englishness, even in our postcolonial moment, demands that one begin to come to terms with not only the legacy of empire but also the "presentness" of the culture of colonialism even in the discourses and political practices that negate it. It also demands that we recognize the mutual imbrication of both the colonizer and the colonized in the making of modern social and cultural formations. But what are the political and cultural implications of this epistemic imbrication? And how are we to make use of a past whose practical and theoretical consequences were often negative and destructive—a past that casts such a long shadow over our present moment that many of us still reel from its trauma? If the answer to these questions is hard to come by, it is because empire has meant different things to colonizer and colonized and has come to be deployed in ways that are as differentiated as they are contested.

If, for example, it took what appears to be a long time for sustained opposition to imperialism to emerge in Britain (it was probably not until the publication of J. A. Hobson's *Imperialism* [1902] that imperialism acquired its most powerful negative connotation), it was because official discourse always rationalized colonial cultural practices in terms of their ideality (the modernizing mission) and the name of the metropolitan national interest (the "greatness" of Great Britain). Now, after trying to sustain colonial authority in the guise of a commonwealth of independent nations, official Englishness has (at least since the 1970s) dressed itself up in imperial nostalgia, as a way of restaging its lost identity. Indeed, this presencing of an absence is central to what has come to be known as Thatcherism, a political discourse that seems to be generated by the need to take stock of that which no longer exists. Thatcherism, as Stuart Hall has observed, derives its success from its performance of patriotism and imperial nostalgia; but the performativity is also a mark of the crisis that has gripped the postimperial English nation.[51] In graphological terms, if the figure of Elizabeth I sits on top of the world (and Oxfordshire) in Marcus Gheeraerts's famous portrait, that of Elizabeth II, the monarch who oversaw the dismantling of empire, gazes into the cartographic emptiness of the postimperial realm, tortured by the idea of a commonwealth that is an empty shell of the imperium it was or would have liked to be (figures 1.3 and 1.4).[52]

But if the disappearance of empire has left Great Britain with nothing more than imperial nostalgia and the signs of postimperial atrophy—the decaying industrial infrastructure, racism, and cultural hysteria—it has also generated questions about colonialism's surreptitious function in the forms of British identity. Nowhere is the linkage between colonial pasts and English presents as marked as in the debate surrounding the so-called Rushdie affair, a cultural debate that has become a dispute not only about the blasphemy of one author and his controversial novel but also about

FIGURE 1.3

The Ditchley portrait (circa 1592) of Elizabeth I standing on the map of the world.

Courtesy of National Portrait Gallery, London.

FIGURE 1.4.
Pietro Annignoni's controversial portrait of Elizabeth II (1969).
Courtesy of National Portrait Gallery, London.

what it means to be English or British. For if Rushdie's novel had irreverently raised this question by contaminating Englishness with its colonial frame, the debate surrounding his book has revolved as much around his radical critique of English identity as it has around the threat that both the Tory government and liberal opinion have come to detect in the actions of British Muslims outraged by the novel. Talal Asad has framed this threat most succinctly:

What exactly was the danger sensed by the Tory government and "liberal opinion" in Britain? It was a perceived threat to a particular ideological structure, to a cultural hierarchy organized around an essential *Englishness*, which defines *British* identity. There were already worrying developments that threatened that identity—integration into the European Community (dominated by its defeated enemy, Germany), the demands of Welsh and Scottish nationalists, and the unresolvable civil war in Northern Ireland between two collective religious identities. It was too much to be confronted in addition by immigrants from ex-colonies (a vanished empire) trying to politicize their alien traditions in England itself. Thus, the Rushdie affair in Britain should be seen primarily as yet another symptom of postimperial British identity in crisis, not—as most commentators have represented it—as an unhappy instance of some immigrants with difficulties in adjusting to a new and more civilized world.[53]

What is important to note here is that while the Rushdie affair did not create the crisis of English identity, it helped crystallize it more than any other cultural event in the 1990s. It did so by valorizing the place of the alien threat in the politics of Englishness and by destabilizing the terms by which English identity was conceived and performed. In other words, the disappearance of empire has made what used to be purely colonial issues—such as the grievances of Muslims—a domestic affair and thus turned the colonial event into probably the most cogent force driving the demand for new histories and narratives of identity in the metropolitan space. Thus while imperial Britain used to be defined intrinsically—as a pastoral ideal or racialized body—the dissolution of empire has forced students of British history and culture to explore the ways in which "Britons defined themselves against a real or imaginary Other" in the past and in relation to a larger European idea in the present; some of these scholars have come to acknowledge what was suspected all along—that "Britain is an invented nation, not so much older than the United States."[54]

Now, we cannot understand the radical implications of this idea of an invented British nation unless we read it against the most persistent and powerful of English moments of origination—the myth of William the Conqueror. This myth, as students of Englishness will recall, derives its power and resonance from its innate capacity to repress its historicism for the sake of its specularity. As Benedict Anderson notes,

> English history textbooks offer the diverting spectacle of a great Founding Father whom every schoolchild is taught to call William the Conqueror. The same child is not informed that William spoke no English, since the English language did not exist in his epoch; nor is he or she told "Conqueror of what?" For the only intelligible answer would have to be "Conqueror of the English," which would turn the old Norman predator into a more successful precursor of Napoléon and Hitler.[55]

Every nation needs a myth to sustain its sense of antiquity, but the myth of William the Conqueror appears more bizarre than others not only because, as Anderson notes, the founding father of England is French, but also because colonial subjects are invited to invest in it against all logic and common sense. When we first encounter this myth in the colonial textbook, for example, it strikes us with all the powers of a phantasmagoria: here the colonized are asked to consume the foundational narrative of Englishness—in order to identify with it—but not to understand it well enough to question its pseudo-historicism or false cartography. Cast in a colonial situation, this narrative does not merely generate a series of ellipses but also performs the role of that modern mythology whose function, according to Roland Barthes, is to turn "culture into nature" and "the social, the cultural, the ideological, the historical into the natural."[56]

But what has postcolonial theory done to these mythologies of English beginnings? It has, for one thing, provided English cultural historians with a grammar of demystification: armed with the knowledge that we can deal with alterity in other ways than irrational idealization, that our foundational fictions need not always appeal to a ratio, students of Englishness have even begun to read the Norman conquest of England as a traumatic imperial event. It is my contention that this concern with the problematic beginnings of Englishness is clearly connected to the crisis of the postimperial nation. As Ann Williams notes in *The English and Norman Conquest*, her concern with the conquered rather than the conquerors in this period of English history is justified by the way the subject "touches closely upon the question of English national identity": "At a time when the submergence of England in Europe is once more a subject for impassioned debate, to 'surmise about the present from the past, the future from the present' may not be entirely irrelevant."[57] We have truly come far from the colonial myth that the civilizational authority of Englishness was derived from a Norman heritage.

But this does not mean that the myth of conquest and its civilizational authority have been dissipated. After all, the reason the Norman conquest of England was to function as the inaugural moment in colonial histories was that, in quite insidious ways, it alienated the colonized from their immanent history by performing a palatable narrative of imperial conquest. In the following example from George Lamming's *In the Castle of My Skin*, Barbadian schoolboys are involved in a heated debate on colonial historiography in which two versions are in contention: the slavery experienced by their grandparents and the imperial mythology promoted by the colonial textbook:

> The idea of ownership, One man owned another. They laughed quietly. Imagine any man in any part of the world owning a man or a woman from Barbados. They would forget all about it since it happened too long ago. Moreover they weren't told anything about that. They had read about the Battle of Hastings and William the Conqueror. That happened so many hundred years ago. And slavery was thousands of years before that. It was far back for anyone to worry about teaching it as history. That's why it wasn't taught. It was too far back. And nobody knew where this slavery business took place. The teacher had simply said, not here, somewhere else. Probably it never happened.[58]

Here, colonial discourse has turned the foundational myth of Englishness into a palpable reality and, in the process, elided local histories of slavery and enslavement.

Now, as readers of the novel will recall, Lamming's narrative response to such moments of historical elision and amnesia takes two forms: first, he narrates the moment of nationalism as one in which the founding mythology of imperialism loses its credence as colonial subjects learn how to read the signs of history and historiography that surround them; second, the new consciousness (represented by Trumper, the schoolboy who has returned from the United States) acquires its authority by finding a detour around institutionalized colonial histories. Trumper's capacity to understand his own experiences—to come to terms with his race and its repressed past—is possible only because he has realized that "Hist'ry ain't got no answers" (297). Throughout the novel, however, Lamming has also problematized such resolutions: the Fanonist idea that the nation is the space in which the consciousness of freedom is revealed is called into question by Slime's betrayal of the village's collective investment in nationalism; Trumper's belief in an existential identity unencumbered by history is limited by the possibility that his revelation might be an untransferable individual moment, that his insights might not be discovered or shared by others (299). It is on this cusp between the knowable—but now discredited—colonial past and the unknown future that postcolonial identities begin to be articulated.

Postcolonial subjects seem, however, to face an intractable problem here: even when the mythology of Englishness is displaced by alternative national histories, the imperial myth still continues to have a sacred presence, if not in the colonies themselves, then at "home" in England. For this reason, as many postcolonial writers and critics have recognized, the task of decolonization must be taken to the metropolis itself; the imperial mythology has to be confronted on its home ground, where it must be denied its "sacred" language.[59] Salman Rushdie provides us with a tantalizing example of this process in *The Satanic Verses*:

> I know what a ghost is, the old woman affirmed silently. Her name was Rosa Diamond; she was eighty-eight years old; and she was squinting beakily through her salt-caked bedroom windows, watching the full moon's sea. And I know what it isn't, too, she nodded further, it isn't a scarification or a flapping sheet, so pooh and pish to all bunkum. What's a ghost? Unfinished business, is what. . . . Come on, you Norman ships, she begged: let's have you, Willie-the-Conk.[60]

Instead of seeking to question the logic of the founding mythology of Englishness, the postcolonial writer revels in its aphoristic instances; misrepresenting the sacred communication of the nation through dementia, he reveals its ghostly presence; but the ghostly is also that mode of representation that exercises its surreptitious power in its absence, in its lack of substance.[61]

Some critics might argue that such a postcolonial deriding of metropolitan mythologies has only a minimal effect on the English national narrative. Some readers might even be wary of the claim that the semiotic instabilities we read in Rushdie's novel constitute an epistemological rupture. Nevertheless, it is precisely this kind of contestation of English history in the domestic realm that has forced us to question the forms of British identity itself. For if Englishness used to be represented to the colonized as the sign of a dynastic presence, the existence of narratives that deconstruct and secularize this presence has forced the British to be more self-reflective of their identities and subjectivities.

Let us consider the case of Raymond Williams, one of the most astute scholars of British culture and society in the imperial age. In his discussion of his Welsh boyhood in *Politics and Letters*, Williams speaks of his peripheral relation to England in ways that will be recognized, later in this book, as the enabling condition of postcoloniality. He begins by speaking of Wales as the mark of an absence, as a place that has lost its language, in which other affiliative institutions—such as education and religion—are propelled by an English orientation "which cut one off thoroughly from Welshness." He then goes on to observe that the result of this alienation was "a rejection of my Welshness which I did not work through until well into my thirties, when I began to read the history and understand it."[62]

Williams's journey from negation to disalienation is a familiar one among colonial and postcolonial writers, but it presents problems and prospects that are both constructive and dissembling. For if a writer like Williams cannot initially be grounded in his Welshness, does he read the imposed English identity as a substitute for the erased Welsh self or as a self-willed entry into the culture of the imperial power? When asked by his interviewers whether the Welsh communities of his childhood considered themselves British, Williams provides an answer that is both revealing and enigmatic: "No, the term was not used much, except by the people one distrusted. 'British' was hardly ever used without 'Empire' following and for that nobody had any use at all, including the small farmers."[63] What is intriguing in this response is not the debatable fact that the Welsh might not have had any use for empire, but how the category *British* lacked validity without the imperial tag.

We will return to Williams's cultural dilemma later. For now, let us note that revisionist historians of Britishness—Linda Colley is the most prominent member of this group—have argued that British patriotism became an important category of identity when there was a need to counterpoise local experiences and notions of self against the Catholic, French, or colonial other. Drawing on the works of such postcolonial theorists as Edward Said, Colley has convincingly shown how the sense of an Eastern or African empire came "to embody an essential quality of difference against which Britishness could emerge with far greater clarity."[64] But there is an important need to underscore the multiplicity of Britishness, for while the English proper might perhaps take their identity for granted, those who existed in the margins of this identity—the Scots, the Welsh, and the Irish—could only be integrated into the emerging discourse of conquest and imperial expansion through the invention of a British identity, an identity that, in turn, depended on imperial possession. As a figure of shared desires, empire was the cultural and political entity that sustained the core of a common British identity against the pressures of nationalism on the fringe. It was perhaps because its relationship to the core was ephemeral that the English periphery—the Celtic fringe, and even the emerging lower middle classes—came to have a greater emotional investment in an invented British nationalism than the old aristocratic classes did.

This desire for empire as a supplement for nationalism is exemplified in Sir David Wilkie's famous painting *Chelsea Pensioners Reading the Gazette of the Battle of Waterloo* (figure 1.5). This painting, as Colley aptly notes, is a performance of Britishness as an invented community, invented—in terms that Anderson has popularized—as "a deep horizontal comradeship."[65] Sir David Wilkie, born on the fringes of Englishness, recenters himself in his portrait of Britain by focusing not on the event that generates his painting (the triumph of the British over the French at Waterloo) but on the receptionality of this event, on the act of reading whose goal is to harmonize what might otherwise be antagonistic regional and class relationships. In effect, the painting rewrites potential antagonisms as sources of imperial affinities; reading, in turn, triggers deep sentiments that compel the readers to forget their differences—their Scottish, Welsh, Irish, and black identities—and to valorize their common Britishness. The emphasis in the portrait, then, is on the horizontal nature of Britishness—"the

FIGURE 1.5.

Sir David Wilkie, *Chelsea Pensioners Reading the Gazette of the Battle of Waterloo.*

Courtesy of the Trustees of the Victoria and Albert Museum.

existence of a mass British patriotism transcending the boundaries of class, ethnicity, occupation, sex and age," according to Colley.[66] And as Anderson would say, such imagined identities exist in a space of "homogeneous, empty time."[67]

But Wilkie's portrait also points to something missing in Anderson's notion of the nation as an imagined community—the close connection between the figures of nationness and empire. For if a modern British nation cannot be imagined outside the realm of empire, then imperialism becomes the raison d'être of Britishness itself. Indeed, one of the greatest ironies of modern British history is the extent to which the loss of empire has forced the imagined community to unravel—witness the rise of Welsh and Scottish nationalism—but has also generated a new discursive space in which the imagined character of the nation can be understood. It is not by accident that Peter Scott's conclusion cited earlier (that Britain is an invented nation) makes sense in the face of colonial atrophy and its cognates—imperial nostalgia and postimperial industrial decline. In such a situation, the nature of Britishness comes to be represented in a melancholic tone and with a sense of historical belatedness:

> Even if there were time to paint a portrait it would be difficult to know where to begin. The outline has been lost. The images of Britain from which these outlines were derived have faded away. Britain is no longer a great imperial or industrial power. It has shared in the secular decline of the West. Our national identity cannot be imagined in terms of a manifest destiny to spread British civilisation around the world—Shakespeare and Milton, Parliamentary democracy and the rule of law.[68]

The point of all this is that while Spivak is right when she asserts that "empire messes with identity," one needs to add that it messes with the identity of both the colonizer and the colonized.[69] This assertion, however, presupposes a time when empire secured identities and provided the mythology and framework in which metropolitan centers and colonial localities functioned as parts of what Anderson would call a "dynastic realm."[70] The more immediate question, however, is whether we can recognize a historical period in which the British empire provided its citizens and subjects with a secular version of a community of language and expectations, a community in which, to quote Anderson, "ontological reality is apprehensible only through a single, privileged system of re-presentation"—the "truth language" of colonial culture?[71]

Identity in the Field of Empire

From one perspective—the historical and economic—the dynastic nature of the culture of colonialism seems indisputable: the great age of empire, as Eric Hobsbawn has argued, was the age of economic totalization, of the "conquest of the globe by the capitalist economy," and thus of the rationalization of the world "in the historically specific forms of bourgeois society in its liberal version."[72] It is imperative to understand the emergence of bourgeois society as one of the major cultural factors linking metropole and colony in the nineteenth century for two closely related reasons. First of all, the most attractive and persistent ideals of colonial culture, as far as the colonized were concerned, was the idea of bourgeois civility and identity; it was what marked the colonized as modern subjects who had broken with outmoded or "tribal" traditions. Second, whatever disputes we may have about colonialism as what Ann Laura Stoler has called a "unified bourgeois project," we cannot ignore the affinity between colonization and the making of—or desire for—middle-class sensibilities.[73] The age of empire was the period in which the rest of the world came to be written into the dominant European narrative, a narrative that defined itself in categories—modernity and a bourgeois identity—which even the colonized came to admire and emulate.

And once modernity and bourgeois culture had been established as the ethical and political norm, the narratives of the colonized world would come to be perceived as peripheral to the imperial narrative, *petits récits* in the grand narrative of capital and the Enlightenment. Our first interpretative problem, then, is how to read the grand narrative of imperialism when it has lost its authority and legitimation. Do we read it, within its dominant mythology, as the confident imposition of the European narrative (civilization) over historically belated local narratives (barbarism)? Or do we read the imperial story, within its contradictions, as a trajectory haunted by a sense of its doom, as the story of "bourgeois liberalism advancing towards what has been called its 'strange death' as it reaches its apogee, victim of the very contradictions inherent in its advance?"[74] Or do we read the imperial story as a dialectic in which the confrontation between the culture of colonialism and local resistances to its hegemony have generated interdependences "which give rise to a new configuration, a global transformation which can no longer be described in terms of either one of these perspectives"?[75]

If the first priority of postcolonial theory is, as I suggested earlier, to recover the circumstances that produced colonial and postcolonial cultures and texts, then we need to figure out ways for reading empire within the following triad: (a) within its founding mythologies (which need to be demystified); (b) from the perspective of its inevitable end (its apoplectic moment of closure); and (c) in relation to the dialectical configuration of metropolitan identities after empire, a process that is driven by the realization that Britain can only be comprehended in relation to its colonial others (and that those colonial others can only be read in relation to the imperial center). In all three cases, then, we are dealing with the consequences of incomplete colonialism, which we are forced to define both by its negation (in the postcolony) and by its nostalgic valorization (in the metropole).[76]

There is, however, a second interpretative problem: when we examine the totality and hegemony of empire from an identarian perspective (i.e., the so-called politics of identity), we discover a very unstable framework and a series of questionable axiologies. Our working hypothesis so far has been that empire (and its collapse) provide the infrastructure within which both the colonizer and the colonized have had to reinvent themselves. Within this infrastructure, we have argued, local loyalties, knowledges, and even identities came to be subordinated to the epistemology of empire and imperial ideologies. Clearly, as Colley has noted, the invention of a British identity did not obliterate older loyalties (those of Scottish Presbyterians, for example) but proffered a conduit through which such loyalties could be synthesized and, indeed, legitimated, by the civilizing mission embedded in doctrines of conquest and rule.[77] Thus, to be Scottish in the service of colonialism was to belong to a larger, more compelling and authoritative narrative, one made possible by the imperial mission. To be a colonial subject was, by the same token, to become an active agent in the same narrative of bourgeois civility; through the culture of colonialism, the dominated came to be positioned, ironically, within the most powerful institutions in the modern world—the school, the nation, the metropolis.

It was through the historical encounter between the agents of the imperial mission and the colonized that new subjectivities were constituted
both at home and abroad. Out of such encounters, as the following example illustrates, were to emerge the colonial readers of my grandparents'
generation:

> In 1909 the Scottish missionaries spread further north to Nyeri,
> where Arthur Barlow founded a station at Tumutumu. Before long,
> an increasing band of mission adherents learned the three "Rs" and
> a variety of skills which qualified them as "readers," who spread the
> Gospel, manned clinics and taught basic literacy in the "bush
> schools."[78]

To become readers, the colonized were required not only to acquire literacy but also to adopt Western values, vocations, modes of dress, and a
"European demeanor" (figures 1.6 and 1.7).[79] For my Gikuyu ancestors,
then, the acquisition of literacy and civilization became one and the same
thing. The new readers were called *athomi*. The literal meaning of the word
athomi is "one who reads," but the word quickly came to connote a whole
configuration of identities: those who could read were now defined as "the
civilized ones," radically distinguished from their non-Westernized kins-
men and kinswomen as much by their new colonial identities as by their
literacy and Christianity. As a leading Gikuyu theologian and minister has
succinctly observed, literacy was the mark of conversion, the sign of a radical rejection of the past; conversion, in turn, was inconceivable except in
relation to the act of reading and writing: "conversion to Christianity was
referred to as *Guthoma*, which literally means 'to read' or to 'become a lit-
erate' to backslide was referred to as *guthomoka*, i.e., to revert to illiteracy."[80]
But this reconfiguration of identities was not a one-way street. From
1909 on, the destiny of the Scotsman Arthur Barlow and that of the
Gikuyu people of Tumutumu—including my own family—became
entwined. Gikuyu Christians would "Africanize" the Scotsman's name
(turn *Barlow* into *Baaru*) and name their children after him; he in turn
would acquire their language and translate important aspects of their culture into English. Above this mutuality, however, empire was to hover as a
superperspective ensuring that the encodement of identities was ultimately uneven. In other words, the Scottish missionary would secure his

FIGURE 1.6.
Turning the colonized into modern subjects. Early industrial training
at Tumutumu. Courtesy of Church of Scotland

British identity in the service of empire (his disciples always assumed that
Scotland and England were the same thing), but the Gikuyu "readers"
could consolidate their imperial identity only by reading their local narratives not as stories about an autonomous African past but as minor and
sometimes undesirable events that had now been transcended by a colonial
destiny and whose previous authority had been nullified by imperialism.
Henceforth, the history of the peoples of Central Kenya, like the histories of colonized peoples elsewhere, would be interpreted from the vantage point of the greater imperial narrative. Thus, Muriuki's *History of the*

FIGURE 1.7.
Catechists at Kikuyu Mission (circa 1914).
Courtesy of Church of Scotland.

Kikuyu, 1500–1900, from which the above quote comes, begins with the origins of the Gikuyu people on the East African coast and ends with their incorporation into the European story; this story now functions as the historical cusp on which ancestral traditions are transcended and European modernity is inaugurated.

But an important qualification is called for here: such narratives of imperial mutuality, historical rupture, and closure were bound to face multiple complications and contradictions not least because of the unevenness that defined imperial identities and stories. The desire for an all-encompassing imperial identity was also often in conflict with the realities encountered or engendered in the field. The Scottish missionary at Tumutumu was simultaneously—though not always visibly—"a citizen of Edinburgh, a Lowlander, a Scot, and a Briton"; but such identities did not necessarily all carry the same weight. The new Christian "readers" would be simultaneously Gikuyu, Kenyan, and African, but they were also British subjects, wards of the empire, not its citizens. In addition, the stories read by both the colonizer and the colonized assumed the superiority of the European narrative and its informing ideologies of progress, reason, and conversion. After all, what made the African readers *athomi* was not merely their newly acquired literacy but also their willingness—and capacity—to renounce their previous identities and narratives to enter an imperial future in which—many of them were to complain later—they were still marginal.

The new subjects of empire were thus located at a destabilizing epistemological juncture: their past identities and narratives could not disappear entirely, nor could they remain central to their lives—hence the paradoxical claim by African historians that colonialism barely scratched the surface of African cultures but radically altered their socioeconomic institutions.[81] The new Africans functioned on a temporal plane that was authorized by neither the past they had renounced nor the future they desired. It was in their attempt to mediate this unstable epistemological position that cultural nationalists in the colonial world came to rewrite the history of African (or Indian) identities as a self-willed return to a precolonial past, now read as a first step toward a decolonized modernity.

My focus here, however, is not on such nationalist rewritings of the past. Rather I concentrate on the colonial subject's uneasy identification with—and representation of—the metropolitan center. A major concern of this book, then, is the nature of peripheral identities in a hegemonic field and the uneasy mediation—through writing and discourse—of colonial relationships. As I have already suggested, a study of the culture of colonialism that simply adjudicates such relationships in terms of centers and margins, of the dominant and the dominated, of conquest and resistance, will not take us very far. For when we look beyond the metaphorical and mythological binarism promoted by empire, we discover that notions of margins and centers are conflated and often reversed; such binarisms are sometimes sustained by the colonized themselves, sometimes rendered meaningless by their experiential situation. Margins, boundaries, and peripheries are not muted spaces in which the dominated act out their resentment or even resistance; on the contrary, they are key ingredients in the making of the implosive center itself.

The relation between the metropolitan center and the colonial periphery can be read through a paradigm developed by Peter Sahlins in his examination of how local societies in the Pyrenees were active ingredients in the shaping of French and Spanish national identities:

> States did not simply impose their values and boundaries on local society. Rather, local society was a motive force in the formation and consolidation of nationhood and the territorial state. The political boundary appeared in the borderland as the outcome of national political events, as a function of different strengths, interests. . . . But the shape and the significance of the boundary line was constructed out of local social relations in the borderland.[82]

If there is any political motivation behind my book, it is the absolute rejection of the popular image of the colonial borderland as a victimized margin, one without a voice in the shaping of the larger imperial event, one without its own strengths and interests, one without agency in the shaping or representation of modern identities. The colonial archive contains many instances of what I consider to be peripheral agency.

Let us briefly examine an example of this agency and its set of interests in the representation of the colonial event. In 1902, Sir Apolo Kagwa, regent of the Kingdom of Buganda, arrived in England to witness the coronation of King Edward VII, one of those events that has been identified, by Terence Ranger, among others, as a defining moment in the invention of colonial traditions.[83] His secretary, Ham Mukasa, kept a diary of the visit, an intriguing account of the colonial subjects' gaze at the imperial center. While Mukasa's book *Uganda's Katikiro in England (Sir Apolo Kagwa Discovers Britain)* provides us with important vistas on the process of inventing tradition—and of the emergence of a native African ethnography—the questions that arise from even a cursory encounter with this book are primarily about location and epistemology: How did Sir Apolo Kagwa locate himself in relation to the imperial center? What was his set of cultural and political affiliations? From what system of knowledge did he read England and Englishness? And what tropes did he and his amanuensis use to figurate the dynastic realm into which they strode with confidence and diffidence?[84]

Sir Apolo's subjectivity, identity, and location were, on the one hand, derived from his function within the British imperial system. He was a committed Christian and a knight of the British empire; as the regent of Buganda, he had been responsible for the incorporation of the kingdom into the imperial sphere and was a strong voice for Christianity and Western education. On the other hand, however, Sir Apolo was a kind of proto-nationalist, a strong advocate for the preservation of Baganda customs and traditions and an ethnographer of cultural practices that seemed to be under threat from Christianity and colonial modernity. His books on Baganda customs have, indeed, come to serve as an important source for our understanding of the precolonial cultures of this East African kingdom.[85] But how could one be a devoted imperial subject and an African nationalist at the same time? Or, to put it another way, how could a discourse be both collaborative and oppositional?

Ham Mukasa's narrative of the discovery of England contains, in several respects, useful lessons on this vexing question. One obvious aspect of this narrative is its concern with questions of authority and representation: Britain is encountered as a strange land of wonders and marvels; the writer's task is to translate this world for a Baganda audience by constantly gesturing to familiar frames of reference. This means that the author must seek techniques that simultaneously reduce the variegated character of Englishness to a coherent narrative and allow British marvels to retain their sense of alienation and distance. Thus, *similitude* (the figure that gestures toward the familiar) goes hand in hand with *thoma* (the figure of the wild and disjunctive).[86] But for Ham Mukasa, as for all colonial travelers, the problem of authority is ultimately one of self-reflexivity and credibility: how and where does he locate himself in relation to England, especially when "if one sees the wonders of England by oneself, and then tells others, one is disbelieved for lack of a second witness?" (74). The writer is a convert to Christianity and the culture of Englishness, but what we detect here, as in almost every passage in the book, is his awareness of the gap between his native land and the English landscape and his awareness too of the strategic distance he must maintain in the face of British alterity. The language of Mukasa's narrative is hence shaped by a double imperative—the desire to be close to Englishness in order to understand its authority and the need to be always vigilant about his difference from its central institutions and categories.

Here I am assuming that, contrary to conventional opinion and, of course, imperial mythologies, one could be a colonial subject and still maintain a strategic distance from the imperial realm. For this reason, the conversion of Mukasa and Sir Apolo—their giving up one cultural value (African animism) for another (Christianity)—must be read as a strategy of cultural translation.[87] Colonial education may want the colonized to trace their ancestry to William the Conqueror, but Ham Mukasa is never in doubt that the ancestors of the English are not his ancestors. Thus, when the two colonial subjects are taken to the Tower of London, what they see are not instruments of their new English culture but "many relics of all kinds from the time of their [the English peoples'] ancestors, old spears and swords, and knives and cannon."[88] And thus, if colonial education aims to turn the colonized into mimic men—as Thomas Macaulay's infamous "Minute on Indian Education" proposes—what I want to underscore here is the colonized subjects' capacity for *dédoublement* from this imposed identity.[89] Mukasa doesn't gaze at England to possess it, he gazes at it to understand its difference; but since the imperial center and the colonial periphery are situated unevenly, his duty is to bring back England to East Africa in a discourse that sustains its alien aura but also domesticates it through analogy.

As the following description of the University of Cambridge Library shows, the prose of cultural translation sustains a sense of wonder but also proposes intelligibility by appealing to the Baganda familiar:

> Of every book that is printed they take one copy, and put it in this building as a remembrance. We saw there a great many books some fourteen to seventeen hundred years of age, and they told us there were about half a million books in the library. Is this not amazing? If you count the number of books in the Bible from Genesis to Malachi, how many would you find? Then, again, how many are there from Matthew to Revelation. Well, this is the way they count their books; one book of every kind is stored up just as Apolo Katikiro wrote *Basekabaka Bebuganda* [Kings of the Buganda], and they took one copy and kept it; in this way the number of five hundred thousand books is made up. (91)

Several conclusions can be drawn from this description: the author is eager to sustain the distinction between England and Buganda; he does this through the use of *thoma* (the insistence on amazement); but he also wants to acknowledge the common referent the two cultures share—biblical books (and worlds) and written texts. As a result, Mukasa represents, perhaps surreptitiously, the relation between the two worlds as equal and mutually affective: the English have given the Baganda the Bible (and literacy); the Baganda have, in turn, given the English ethnographic texts such as Sir Apolo's *Basekabaka Bebuganda.*

I will concede that the colonial library and its cultural texts signify unequal relations of power and knowledge, but this vertical structure conceals a horizontal relationship. In this case, Sir Apolo is subordinated to the symbolic economy of colonialism—his subjectivity depends on his function as an agent of imperialism—but his cultural center is, at the same time, outside the culture of colonialism and its epistemology. And yet, I want to insist that terms such as *center* and *margin* are continuously shifting. Sir Apolo's center is his Baganda culture, but Buganda, in 1902, is part of the British empire; indeed, Baganda culture is already an amalgam of Christian and African beliefs and practices. The writing of this African culture is already an attempt to locate it within the discourse of European modernity that empire promotes with the pen and the sword. As we will see in subsequent chapters, the center can also be the margin and the margin can be the center; this conflation can be the source of both authority and anxiety.

My point, though, is that authority and anxiety cut across the border that separates the colonizer and the colonized, the center and the margin. Indeed, there is perhaps no better illustration of how the conflation of centers and margins leads to authority and anxiety than Raymond Williams's ambiguous cultural location, which I mentioned earlier. Williams is, of course, an important figure in postcolonial cultural discourse not only because he occupies what Radhakrishnan has aptly defined as a subject position that is "both oppositional-marginal and dominant-central"[90] but also because his experiences mirror those of colonized intellectuals in uncanny ways. We thus need to begin by noting some instances of similarity between the border country of Wales and other colonial localities. These similarities should already be familiar to readers of Williams's early novels, where the border country of Wales parallels the colonial geographies represented in numerous fictional works by writers from Africa, India, and the Caribbean. Williams's portrait of a rural landscape in the throes of transformation and of subjects' being reconstituted by the power and pressures of an enchanting metropolitan culture is one of the most persistent in colonial and postcolonial literatures. In addition, the conflicts that Williams reads in Hardy's Wessex novels, which are set in a border country where "the experiences of change and of the difficulty of choice are central and even decisive," echo familiar themes in the literature of the colonized.[91]

In many ways, then, Williams's intellectual journey from the border country of Wales to the metropolitan center mirrors the experiences of postcolonial intellectuals moving from the colonial periphery to the heart of empire. And in spite of his well-known concern with ideals of community and unifying structures of experience, Williams has been one of the most articulate voices for the perennial condition, in both colonial and postcolonial societies, of cultural liminality. Williams's cultural biography thus begins, importantly and inescapably, at the colonial vanishing point, the juncture at which traditional culture and the mother tongue are lost:

> Ours had been an area that had been anglicized in the 1840s—the classic moment usually described as when "the mothers stopped teaching their children Welsh." In fact, there was an intense and conscious pressure through the schools to eliminate the language, which included punishment for children who spoke Welsh.[92]

And yet, even as it seeks to destroy Welsh identities, imperial Britain is the cultural vector that provides the negative consciousness that generates Williams's work. For Williams, as for colonized writers in general, the idea of home is mediated through the symbolic economy of empire:

> From about 1880 there was then this dramatic extension of landscape and social relations. There was also a marked development of the idea of England as "home," in that special sense in which "home" is a memory and an ideal. Some of the images of this "home" are of central London: the powerful, the prestigious and the consuming capital. But many are of an idea of rural England: its green peace contrasted with the tropical or arid places of actual work; its sense of belonging, of community, idealised by contrast with the tensions of failure associated with modernism.[93]

Furthermore, Williams's intellectual project, like that of his postcolonial interlocutors, is intended to read English literature as the instrument for mediating the difficulties that arise when spatial and temporal boundaries are conflated. Reading the tradition of English literature is an attempt to locate oneself in the cognitive maps of Englishness. It is not incidental, then, that at the end of *The Country and the City*, Williams returns to his enunciative position, to the tenuous relation between his Welshness and Englishness dramatized in his fictional works:

> In the late nineteen-forties I knew that I was at last separated from the village in which I had grown up. I began to write what I thought this experience was, in the seven versions that eventually became the novel *Border Country*. . . . I felt a sudden sadness, apparently separate from my theme. I felt, because I think I had been told, that the rural experience, the working country, had gone; that in Britain it was only a marginal thing, and that as time went by this would be so everywhere. I accepted this, at one level, for much longer than now seems possible. It was one of the impulses, I can see now, that kept sending me back to old rural literature and history.[94]

Here, through the act of reading and writing, the author witnesses both the dislocation of the colonized (Welsh) self and its new status in the cultural maps generated by imperial Britain. In both cases, colonial culture provides the totality against which identity is packed and unpacked; to discover Wales and what it meant to him, to indeed become cognizant of the location and power of the periphery, Williams had to pass through the eye of Englishness.

And Williams's experience is not unique in this respect: his story is part of that imaginary political "re-territorialization and re-identification" without which, according to Stuart Hall, "a counter-politics" of Englishness could not have been constructed.[95] Indeed, Hall's own intellectual history exemplifies this process in powerful ways, for after he spent three decades trying to develop a critique of postimperial Britain within its own parameters, both as an editor of the *New Left Review* and as the director of the Center for Contemporary Cultural Studies (cccs) at the University of Birmingham, his work in the 1990s is driven by a desire to understand his location both inside and outside the culture of Englishness. This process has demanded a narrative of retour to the colonial and postcolonial culture of Jamaica, which Hall had tried to escape from when he migrated to England in the 1950s.[96]

For both Williams and Hall, the collapse of the authority and totality of colonial culture has, as we will see in the last two chapters of this study, generated a certain crisis about the relation between centers and margins and about the efficacy of England as a primary referent. For these cultural scholars, whose work is ultimately generated by an unasked question— What does it mean to be Welsh or Jamaican in England?—the collapse of empire (and hence the ensuring crisis of Englishness) make Wales and Jamaica (and Europe) serious cultural alternatives to the old metropolis: "Suddenly England, bourgeois England, wasn't my point of reference any more," asserts Williams. "I was a Welsh European, and both levels felt different."[97]

As we shall see in the last chapter, Williams's new (compounded) identity, which depends on a simultaneous feeling for the local and the global, is crucial to the postimperial reconfiguration of the maps of Englishness. My book is also a study of the cultural and literary forces, movements, and interests that have brought Williams and Hall, my prototype postcolonial intellectuals and writers, to their radical critique of Englishness.

Reading the Maps of Englishness

Each of the texts discussed in the chapters that follow should be read as a calculated response to central questions that emerge in the relation between England and colonial/postcolonial spaces, in a field of identity defined by alterity. These questions are also, too indirectly perhaps, my own responses to some troublesome issues in postcolonial theory and cultural studies: the location of the black subject in British culture, the consolidation of English identity in its spaces of alterity, and the relation between modernism and the crisis of imperialism. Let us consider these issues one by one.

An important concern in the discourse of black British intellectuals since the 1960s is what has come to be known as Powellism—the postimperial evocation of the black body as an ethical threat to "the metaphysics of [English] national belonging."[98] As I will show in the next chapter, Powellism is not an anomaly in the politics of English identity; on the contrary, it draws on tropes and conventions that were consolidated in the "high noon" of empire, especially during the debate on the "condition of England" question in the middle of the nineteenth century. An important difference between black alterity now and then, I will argue, is the strategic position of the black subject within metropolitan culture and the discursive economy of Englishness, the presence of this subject in England itself, as both a producer of English culture and a reader of English texts. Simply put, postimperial (black) British intellectuals have responded to the depiction of blackness as a challenge to Englishness by positing the act of reading as "the mediation by which narrative discourse makes its impact on history" and by showing how a process of cultural mediation affects the central questions of the age—questions about identity, authority, and desire.[99] Situated at once inside and outside the postimperial British nation, these readers are impelled to disclaim the racist discourse of national belonging, a discourse that deploys the figure of race to mediate the political and cultural crisis triggered by industrial decline and imperial decay; but they are also compelled to affirm their own particular modes of affiliation with England, the space that rejects them.

In both cases, however, there is an increasing awareness that interpretative gestures that seek to hallow a space of postimperial black identity confront an inescapable paradox: claims for the significance of blacks in the texts of Englishness do not necessarily subvert or dilate the metaphysical assumptions underwriting English identity. Paul Gilroy is probably right in his assertion that blacks were "an integral means by which England was able to make sense of itself and its destiny,"[100] but as I suggest in chapter 2, a closer consideration of this mode of integration, in the imperial and the postimperial periods, only confronts us with the enigmatic deployment of colonial subjects as inside and outside the parameters established for England and its destiny.

A closely related question is the function of colonial geographies in the generation of English literary texts. In an almost forgotten essay, "The Englishness of English Literature," Peter Conrad has argued that English literature was defined by its retreat from "depleted and defrauded" landscapes, that the English text came to be preoccupied with "the impoverishment of its own locality, the deconsecration of its reality, the departure of divinity from places."[101] English literature, according to Conrad, was generated by a certain awareness of its incompatibility with its spatial structures: since Englishness came to mean "a reduced reality that demeans imagination," it learned to displace its heroic and epic character "to regions of subjunctively wishful geography."[102] Research on this subject has, however, provided us with a different story; it has shown that rather than being a threat to the imagination, such subjunctive geographies were integral to the narrative of Englishness, its identity, structure, and function.[103]

A good portion of my book is concerned with the outward expansion of the English imagination, especially as it is manifested in travel writing in the nineteenth and early twentieth centuries. As I suggest in chapter 3, the narrative of travel is connected to theories of Englishness in a fundamental and inescapable way: it is in the contrastive space afforded to it by its colonies that English identity consolidates itself; if the writers who write the West Indies in the nineteenth century seem obsessed by the epic dimension of England (James Anthony Froude's subtitle for his book *The English in the West Indies* is *The Bow of Ulysses*), it is possibly because they are aware of the extent to which "the phantasm" of the English epic depends on the absent figure of the other.[104]

A lot of work has been produced on the implications of considering colonial alterity as a key ingredient in the constitution of the epistemology of modernity; it is not my intention in this book to take up this debate.[105] The claim that underscores my work here is simple: since we cannot operate outside the colonial episteme and its institutions, our challenge is not to transcend it but to inhabit its central categories, to understand the histories and functions of these categories, to come to terms with their effects, and to deconstruct their authority. But another consideration makes the deconstruction of imperial epistemologies imperative: while the age of empire is considered the high point of the rationalization of the world, the thematization of the Western narrative of history, and the privileging of European cultural traditions, the search for a countervailing tradition within this hegemonic realm is concurrent with its imposition. In other words, even when the culture of colonialism appears to be absolute and its totality unquestionable, its narratives have to contend with the colonized locality as not simply a space of transgression and resistance but one in which metropolitan identities are made and remade. While such spaces of transgression and reconstitution have generally been associated with colonial subjects in the more militant period after World

War II, I will read them (in a slightly earlier period) in the narratives of the women of empire (chapter 4).

Here, my collaborative reading of Mary Seacole's *Wonderful Adventures* and Mary Kingsley's *Travels in West Africa* is not intended to argue for a sisterhood of black and white women united against patriarchal imperialism. On the contrary, what fascinates me in what I call imperial femininity is the female subjects' ambivalent interpellation by the ideologies of empire. These women's narratives are propelled by the belief that empire opens up new opportunities for female subjects in the nineteenth century; women travelers hence seek to consolidate their notions of freedom in the realm of the other—but they also have to contend with the fact that empire is a male affair and they themselves are the other that they seek elsewhere. In addition, while some readers may prefer to read female and black narratives as essentially discourses of resistance and *dédoublement*, I am more interested in the ambivalence of imperial femininity. There are two reasons for this interest. First, such peripheral narratives call attention to some crucial moments of cultural antagonism in the discourse of empire, but they also point to the ways in which alternatives to the *imperium* (even alternative imperialisms) are repressed by the hegemonic. Second, the imperial subject may consolidate itself in its conquest of the other, but it is in the sites of colonial alterity—and in the discourse of its marginal subjects—that the imperial referent is unpacked, sometimes without even noticing it. In these circumstances, writing by women and blacks, even within the hegemonic discourse of empire, must be read as both collaborative and oppositional.[106]

The dialectical relation between collaboration and opposition reaches its apotheosis in the narratives of cognitive failure associated with modernism. Here, the relationship between empire and modernism is defined by a strange configuration of political triumph and cultural failure. For, as Said has noted, "once imperialism . . . had become the settled norm in political ideas about Europe's world-wide destiny, then, ironically, the allure of its opponents, the intransigency of its subjugated classes, the irresistible sway were clarified and heightened."[107] My concern in chapter 5, however, is not with this nascent resistance to empire but with the narrative transformation of some of the tropes and categories discussed in earlier chapters—subjectivity, temporality, alterity, and cognition—under the pressures of a late (and a dying) colonialism. Such transformations, I argue, are engendered by a certain crisis in the epistemology of empire under modernism: because it is no longer seen as the realm in which European modernity thematizes itself, the colonial space is now written as a dangerous project, the source of what David Trotter has aptly described as an "apocalyptic historiography."[108]

But, paradoxically, it is because the imperial locality is conceived as the source of danger and contamination—a state figurated by its primitive other—that it is encountered, in the works by Conrad and Graham Greene that I discuss in this chapter, as a place in which the European subject can come to terms with its repressed or subconscious self. So although the modernist narratives that I discuss set out on fictional and real journeys that seek to break away from the European norm, indeed seem to seek a detour around the supremacist claims of colonial culture by valorizing a certain kind of cultural relativism, they return, in the end, to their domestic scenes of origination. The texts—Conrad's African fictions and Graham Greene's travelogue *Journey Without Maps*—are hence seen as representations of an impasse in the grand narrative of empire. These texts reject the European episteme and turn this rejection into the motor that drives the modernist narrative, but they also recoil from African spaces that are found wanting as alternative locations for cultural identity. Modernist writers are hence caught between the European values they renounce and the alienated colonial spaces they narrativize.

By the time modernism tries to find a way around this impasse, especially in the fiction of the period after World War II, the totality of empire is no more. England is no longer the primary referent for the texts of Englishness nor the cartographic center around which colonial identities revolve. In the aftermath of decolonization, I argue in chapter 6, both colonial and metropolitan subjects scramble to realign their identities and narratives in the absence of empire. My concerns in this chapter revolve around two sets of problems: the writing of identity within the empty spaces once inscribed with the tropes of empire and the representation of the temporal gap between the old forms of colonial culture and the discourse of the decolonized nation. How do colonial subjects respond to the decline of empire? Do they read it as an opportunity, the hallowing of spaces in which they can inscribe themselves, or as the symptom of a crisis—the crisis of modernity and its cultural forms?

While the answers to these questions appeared to be simpler in the early period after decolonization when the new nations of Africa, India, and the Caribbean seemed to offer (national) alternatives to the culture of colonialism, it has become apparent that the dichotomy between empire and nation was not as pronounced as once thought. The age of decolonization has not marked the radical dissociation between England and its colonies, as nationalists on both sides of the divide had expected; on the contrary, the large migration of formerly colonized subjects into the metropolitan center itself has created temporal conjunctures and disjunctures in areas previously marked by the mythology of the island nation.[109] How do you write identities in the space between nation and empire? Where is culture to be located when the parameters that have demarcated it for the last two hundred years have become truncated? My final chapter will discuss several narrative responses to these questions in the works of such postimperial writers as Hanif Kureishi, Joan Riley, and Salman Rushdie. In all cases, my thesis is that it is still within the incomplete colonial project that the postcolonial moment must be located and interrogated.

⊰ 2 ⊱

Through the Prism of Race: Black Subjects and English Identities

In fact racism figures *both* on the side of the universal and the particular. The excess it represents in relation to nationalism, and therefore the supplement it brings to it, tends both to universalize it, to correct its lack of universality, and to particularize it, to correct its lack of specificity.

Etienne Balibar, "Racism and Nationalism"

Nationalism and racism become so closely identified that to speak of the nation is to speak automatically in racially exclusive terms. Blackness and Englishness are constructed as incompatible, mutually exclusive identities. To speak of the British or English people is to speak of the white people.

Paul Gilroy, "One Nation Under a Groove"

If we accept the basic premise of the previous chapter—that questions of Englishness cannot be discussed except in relation to different forms of colonial alterity—then we need to address some of the most perplexing issues in the composition of English identities since the last century. If it seems so evident that the national culture derives its identity, and displays its uniqueness, when it is articulated through moments of crisis staged in the imperial realm, why does this culture strive to assert its authenticity by negating colonial spaces and subjects as constitutive elements in the invention of Englishness? Why does the English nation, which derives its imperial authority from a certain claim to the universality of its values, nevertheless thrive on narratives that celebrate its exclusiveness? Why, in other words, is Englishness written at that strategic juncture in which, to paraphrase Balibar, its universality comes up against its particularity?[1]

The truth is that in the last few centuries, the notion of cultural crisis has come to function simultaneously as a symptom of various problems in modern British culture and as its enabling condition. Indeed, if the notion of crisis has now come to be read as a central category in the cultural discourse on English identities, it is perhaps because it was only through such imperial crises as West Indian emancipation, the Indian Mutiny (1857), and the Morant Bay rebellion (1865)—to cite just a few examples—that the official English mind could reflect on the national character, its economy of representation, and its moral imperative. It was through instances of what Stuart Hall has called "moral panic" about race that mechanisms for mediating domestic problems were developed. In such instances, internal problems came to be mediated through "an excessive preoccupation with the problem of 'race' " as "the English official mind . . . turned the conversation in the direction of 'the blacks.' "[2]

But if the discourse on race has been integral to debates on the "condition of England" question, as I intend to show in this chapter, there has been a remarkable tendency to dissociate blackness from Englishness, a separation that has presented an intellectual and political challenge to the crown's black subjects as they seek their place in the postimperial nation. At its most basic level, this challenge arises when race is abstracted from the discourse on English identity, but blacks and other migrants are deployed as the primary threat to the autochthonous national character. This paradoxical situation in turn raises two sets of problems, which have become central to—and might even have generated—the project of cultural studies in contemporary Britain. First, there is the problem of analyzing alterity in the site of its disavowal: how do you read black subjects and their experiences as important generative agents in the formation of a modern English culture when the most forceful ideas and ideals on English identity insist on the intrinsic and racial purity of Englishness? Second, there is the problem of articulating what appears to be the complex relation between imperial cartographies and domestic symbolic and cultural economies: the emergence of England as a world power in the last few centuries has always been explained in terms of geographical expansion, but by the same token, the spatial chasm between Britain and its domains has made the connection between the two spaces invisible, so that it has become possible, especially since the 1950s, to discuss empire and metropole as if they were two distinct entities.[3]

Thus, while the project of cultural and postcolonial studies has sought to show how imperial spaces have shaped the cognitive map of Englishness, a surreptitious nationalist discourse has tended to sublimate the culture of colonialism to the national interest and to celebrate England's story as what Gillian Beer calls "an island story."[4] By calling attention to this dialectic of imperial affirmation and disavowal, itself a key element in the ongoing struggle over the meaning of a modern British identity, I am assuming that the English official mind was aware of its existence and strategic function. For, as I noted earlier, there are many historical occasions in which crisis in the imperial realm was acknowledged, through official debates and commissions, as intrinsic to fundamental questions about the essential nature of Englishness itself. More often than not, however, such debates functioned primarily as the conduits through which the temporal gap between England and its others could be affirmed. Even writers of discourses that sought to bring colonial problems to the metropolitan space so that the condition of England could be debated somehow seemed to see the colony as a mechanism of discourse rather than a place of indispensable political constitution and cultural invention.

Consider, for example, the Governor Eyre controversy of 1865. There is no doubt, as Bernard Semmel has shown in *Jamaican Blood and Victorian Conscience*, that a relatively minor uprising in a far-off part of the British empire generated opposed commentaries on the narrative of English history and its driving ideas—civilization and progress—and provided the public stage in which essential English values, such as morality and the rule of law, could be debated.[5] What is important about the Morant Bay uprising that triggered this controversy, then, is not that it was the major historical event of the decade; rather, it happened at a strategic moment, a time in which imperialism—and the English domestic scene—were entering a period of transformation and hence uncertainty. As John Stuart Mill was to recall in his *Autobiography*, the Eyre Controversy was a turning point "for good or evil, of the course of human affairs for an indefinite duration" (quoted in Semmel, 60).

In these circumstances, Morant Bay was important for its universality, not its particularity, for its symbolic or discursive position in the construction of an imaginary relationship between England and its colonial other rather than a set of "real" political challenges.[6] Indeed, in looking at both the visual and the discursive representations that emerged from this debate, one could not fail to notice how they foregrounded some central debates on the question of Englishness—such as the notion of freedom and the Whig and Tory versions of national history—rather than the specific problems of emancipation in Jamaica. In this situation, as the illustrators for *Punch* were keenly aware (see figures 2.1 and 2.2), the black subject had been reduced to a figure of public discourse and a universal fetish.

But such a universalism concealed the specific situation in which colonial subjects were to be dragged into a violent debate whose central issues were not the condition of Jamaica after emancipation but a set of questions troubling the English polis in the 1860s—questions of authority abroad and representation at home. Mill's defense of "Negro interests" was, as he himself recognized, a reflection on the character of Englishness itself:

> The taking of human lives without justification, which in this case is an admitted fact, cannot be condoned by anything short of a criminal tribunal. Neither the Government, nor this House, nor the whole English nation combined, can exercise a pardoning power without previous trials and sentence. . . . I do not deny that there is good authority, legal as well as military, for saying that the proclamation of martial law suspends all law so long as it lasts; but I defy any one to produce any respectable authority for the doctrine that persons are not responsible to the laws of their country, both civil and criminal, after martial law has ceased, for acts done under it.
>
> (Quoted in Semmel, 78)

For Mill, Morant Bay was an opportune occasion to comment on some questions about England's destiny that had been troubling him for several years.

And yet although Governor Eyre's activities in Jamaica—Mill's point of reference in this debate—had provided the philosopher with an important platform for reflecting on the state of the nation, events in the West Indies were ultimately subjacent: they provided the facts that illustrated general

THE JAMAICA QUESTION.

WHITE PLANTER. "AM NOT *I* A MAN AND BROTHER, TOO, MR. STIGGINS?"

FIGURE 2.1.

Punch's take on the crisis in Jamaica.

FIGURE 2.2.
Punch's cartoon depicting public debate on the Negro question.

codes about questions of governance and rule, filial responsibility, and the
rule of law. The key terms in Mill's speech to Parliament—terms such as
respectable authority and *the rule of law*—were then, as they are now, subliminal
indices of Englishness, its constitution, and ideals.[7] The latter point was
affirmed by Eyre's conservative supporters, most notably Thomas Carlyle
and John Ruskin, who read the events in Jamaica as a threat to the central
tenets of Englishness and hence depicted the governor as the defender of
order and virtue. "The English nation never loved anarchy," noted Carlyle,
"nor was wont to spend its sympathy on miserable mad seditions, especially of this inhuman and half-brutish type; but always loved order and
the prompt suppression of seditions" (quoted in Semmel, 107). But, again,
the anarchy unleashed by the descendants of slaves in Morant Bay was
important, not in itself but in the way it was easily connected to larger
themes in Carlyle's social lexicon in which Englishness was defined against
a disorder associated previously with the Jacobins, the Irish, and the working class, and now, conveniently, adduced to blackness.

In thinking about what I consider to be the paradox of Englishness—
the need to define the national character against a colonial other that it

must then disown—we need to focus on two points of convergence in the arguments presented by Eyre's liberal opponents and conservative supporters. First, irrespective of their ideological positions, all the participants in this debate assumed that what had taken place in Jamaica constituted a defining moment in English culture. Without much value in real terms, the settlement at Morant Bay was elevated to a symbol of empire and Englishness in crisis. Second, although most of the intellectuals involved in this debate staked their stand from divergent ideological positions (most of which predated the rebellion at Morant Bay), their discourse revolved around a similar set of issues (morality, character, law, representation) that they considered central to the question that troubled them—what kind of nation was England becoming and what was its global destiny? Under the circumstances, as Semmel observes, the encampment at Morant Bay became, in 1865, a symbol of the dissipation that threatened the national character under the stress of empire: "The essential question was whether a nation could long maintain two contradictory policies, democracy at home and repression and terror abroad. Great Britain managed to maintain the distinction between domestic liberty and imperial authority for over a century. She had geography in her favour" (179).

But this conclusion is limited by Semmel's passive acceptance of the illusion of cartographic separation—the belief that empire and nation were conceived as two separate entities. For while such a separation was evident in the state's cultural and political policies, the contradiction between empire and nation was ultimately an imaginary construct, an ideological and rhetorical gesture, a kind of false consciousness that denied the formative nature of the colonial event in the domestic scene. My argument in the rest of this chapter is that the essential question raised by the colonial event and the crisis of representation or interpretation it triggers is, beneath the surface, about the contrapuntal relation between domestic identities and imperial spaces, about external cultural formations and metropolitan notions of self, about the invention of whiteness against the metaphology of blackness. This is the process I read in Carlyle's virulent "Occasional Discourse on the Nigger Question" (1848, 1853), Mill's response on behalf of the black subject, and Enoch Powell's latter-day demonization of blackness (1968).

In examining the ways in which the black subject comes to occupy a central place in English domestic cultural politics in two distinct historical moments, we can begin to understand how race functions as what Stuart Hall calls "the prism through which the British people are called upon to live through, then, to understand, and then to deal with a growing crisis" in the national culture.[8] A primary thesis in this chapter, as it moves from Carlyle and Mill in the nineteenth century to Powell in the 1960s, is that an analysis of the staging of blackness in the invention of Englishness demands a critical strategy that connects temporal moments and performative occasions even when they are denied or derided. This chapter is on the role of alterity in the debates surrounding the idea of an English nation and culture.

Carlyle, Mill, and the Question of Blackness

First, then, a genealogy of the problem of blackness. Everyone knows that Thomas Carlyle and John Stuart Mill are two of the most important icons of English culture in the nineteenth century, but very few people know of the centrality of black subjects in their discourses on the national character. The repression of the black subject in the explication of Carlyle's and Mill's cultural texts is, undoubtedly, a symptom of the problem I have addressed above—blacks have not, until very recently, been considered important agents in the articulation of English subjectivity. The result of this neglect is the unfortunate marginalization of some texts that sought to redefine the politics of English identity through the deployment of blacks but that we now find too embarrassing and frightening because of their overt racist rhetoric.

This is the case of the strange career of Carlyle's "Occasional Discourse on the Nigger Question," first published in *Fraser's Magazine* in 1848 and later collected in the *Latter-Day Pamphlets* in 1853. Because the Carlyle we prefer to read is the cultural icon of the imperial period, the Victorian prophet and sage who gave us *Past and Present* and *Sartor Resartus*, we are not exactly sure where "Occasional Discourse on the Nigger Question" fits in the oeuvre and ideological genealogy of the Victorian man of letters. The critical literature on Carlyle has not been able to provide satisfactory answers, largely because it prefers to see the sage's reflections on race as marginal to his larger enterprise—his diagnosis of the condition of England—or because it sees this document as too ill-tempered for a man of Carlyle's stature. The critical tradition has hence sought to displace this text from the mainstream of Carlyle's thoughts on the condition of England; the consensus, among a cross section of critics, is that Carlyle's temperamental concern with West Indians was an aberration from his primary topic.[9]

But since Carlyle deemed this essay important enough to use it as the signature piece for the *Latter-Day Pamphlets*, we obviously need to pose some troublesome questions: Why did the writer turn his attention to blacks in such faraway places as Jamaica and Demerara to reflect on the threat of revolution and chaos at home? Why would the question of the Negro be considered important to understanding the plight of Irish workers and the crisis of Englishness at a time when the value of the West Indian colonies had diminished considerably? Why, indeed, would Carlyle open his discourse with the claim that the question of the Negro, "as lying at the bottom, was to be first handled, and if possible the first settled"? And to what extent did the hysteria that marked Carlyle's engagement with—and indeed hatred for—blacks represent his own attempt to disavow "the barbaric Celticness" of his native Scotland in his frustrated quest for the authority of Englishness?[10]

Whatever we may think of the general tone of "Occasional Discourse," we have to be honest enough to recognize that beneath its offensive posture, the essay is driven by some of Carlyle's most important religious and political doctrines; that it lies at the very center of his cultural and political project in 1848; and that the style in which he diagnoses the condition of England is not very different from that deployed in his canonical essays such as "Signs of the Times," which Raymond Williams considers to be his "most comprehensive contribution" to English social thought.[11] We now know, thanks to the work of Ian Campbell, that Carlyle's engagement with blacks rested on a set of core ideas that were central to his life and thought: the morality of enslavement, the political necessity of the slave trade, racial superiority, duty and vocation.[12] In addition, as Aileen Christianson has shown, rather than being an isolated response to the debate on emancipation, the "Nigger Question" was part of a larger cultural project whose function was to diagnose the events of 1848.

Writing against the background of revolution in France, Carlyle had begun to focus on a certain set of issues whose resolution was essential if events in Europe could be averted in England. At the top of Carlyle's agenda was the question of labor and governance, regulation and order against democracy and anarchy: "All Carlyle's thought in 1848–49 was, on his own evidence, confused, and, on the evidence of his newspaper articles and letters of this period, interrelated. Consideration of government, democracy, workers, famine, chaos, led from London, to Europe, to Ireland, to the Colonies, and back to London."[13] Even without going into the factors that generated Carlyle's confusion on the philosophical issues of the day and increasing doubts about his authority, coming as he did from the fringe of Englishness, there is no doubt that figures of alterity were important conduits for reflecting on the crisis of the age.

Still, there are some outstanding questions. If Carlyle's racial doctrines as they emerge in "The Nigger Question" are as old as his childhood in Dumfries and originate from his Calvinist background, as does most of his considerable body of social criticism, why did it take an overt engagement with blacks for such ideas to "capture the world's attention?"[14] Why and how did ostensibly remote colonial questions provide Carlyle with a discursive conduit—a mechanism of clarification—out of the confusion of 1848? To answer these questions we need to suspend, as it were, the ideological reasons behind Carlyle's engagement with the blacks and focus instead on the discursive and performative character of his discourse, read it not so much in terms of the rationality it would like to promote, or even the set of ideas that propel it, but its theatricality and affectiveness.

This affectiveness, as Catherine Hall has reminded us, is suggested most latently by Carlyle's decision to change the conventional "Negro" (which he had used when the discourse was first published in *Fraser's Magazine* in 1848) to the derogatory appellation—"Nigger"—when it was published as a pamphlet in 1853. This change in denotation, says Hall, provides us with important evidence of the changes that had taken place in Victorian attitudes toward the black subject in midcentury: the black had moved from being the potential "man and brother" of emancipation discourse to being a demonic figure against which English virtue and civility would be demonstrated. As Catherine Hall observes, the political economy of race had shifted from "the cultural racism of the 1830s with its liberal and progressive attachments" to a "more aggressive biological racism, rooted in the assumption that blacks were not brothers and sisters but a different species, born to be mastered."[15] My concern, however, is not with the conditions that created this economy of representation but with Carlyle's moment of enunciation (a Victorian cultural space subconsciously haunted, in the words of Walter Houghton, "by fear and worry, by guilt and frustration and loneliness") and the place of the black subject as the prism through which these anxieties were experienced and managed.[16]

I want to argue that the black body in Carlyle's discourse is the somatic presence through which the Victorian sage could articulate and embody the unknown, and for him unreasonable, forces that troubled his culture. These problems—the crisis of industrialism, problems of poverty, and the looming threat of Chartism—could best be mediated through the figure of the dark other. The black body could best define and dominate this moment of crisis because it stood as a visual symbol of the invisible forces the Victorian sage was trying to comprehend and control; as the radical figure of alterity, the black could enable the author to map the luminous universe that he thought the Victorians had (foolishly, in his view) foreclosed from their consciousness.

It is important, in this connection, to note that Carlyle did not see a palpable black threat to Englishness comparable to the specter of Jacobinism in France. He wasn't ready to argue that blacks were about to invade England not only because such an argument was laughable but also because the black threat was more symbolic than real—it was a threat to values and moral codes rather than geographical or cultural territory. Thus, if Carlyle's discourse could not stand the test of truth, as his liberal critics were to argue in response, it was because truth was not his concern; his valorization of the black as the radical other was primarily discursive.

In "The Nigger Question," then, the black figure functions as an agent of parataxis, of juxtaposition and comparison: while the West Indian plantations are in ruins, "the Negroes are all very happy and doing well"; while at home "the British whites are rather badly off," our black population in the islands is "doing remarkably well" (3). The use of parataxis is here, as elsewhere in this discourse, underwritten by a transparent ideological intention (we already know where Carlyle stands on the great issues of the day), but its force is primarily performative. The dialectical tension between black bliss and white suffering allows the author to attack the philosophical system that has led to the "reversal" of what he considers to be the hierarchical system established by nature: the ideas of benevolence and Christian philanthropy—products of "a sceptical Eighteenth Century"—have given us "beautiful Blacks sitting there up to the ears in pumpkins and doleful Whites sitting here without potatoes to eat" (5). Since the moment of enunciation here is an imaginary debating hall, the last image, with its powerful visual effect and binarism, makes Carlyle's point better than any philosophical condemnation of Enlightenment liberalism might do.

Moreover, Carlyle's discourse does not appeal to the authority of facts; even when he turns to "real" questions about sugar duties and labor shortages in the West Indies, his rhetoric is always one of insinuation rather than direct reference. In other words, for the writer (or speaker, for this is how Carlyle conceives himself in the discourse), the political economy of sugar duties and labor shortages does not need to be explained to his audience, not only because this audience knows the specific arguments of such debates, but because words such as *duty* and *labor* seem to have a greater emotive force when they are left unexplained. Carlyle's discourse is built on such strategic buzzwords and codes. Indeed, one could well read the West Indies and its black inhabitants as a code word for radical alterity: the forces that threaten the "Norman" order that Carlyle associates with Englishness—the forces of revolutionary terror, working-class anarchy, and even Irish immorality—coalesce in the black body.

When such forces are perceived in their darkest manifestation, then they truly acquire the character of an untamable phantasmagoria. The point, then, is that what is at issue in this discourse is not facts or tangible experiences but imaginary situations and figures with "real life" implications. For if the West Indies has to be represented as the cartographic referent that makes Carlyle's discourse possible, rather than the caricature it has become reduced to in the moment of enunciation, then the author would have to rationalize what appears to be his obsession with absent and outlandish figures and topics. But it is precisely through this kind of irrational rhetoric that Carlyle elevates his discourse from its mundane factual moment to an important level of abstractness: his discourse transcends its ostensible subject—the "Negro"—and becomes a meditation on the values that define modern English society, values that blackness defies by its very somatic presence. Thus, when he deploys the black as a sorry spectacle, Carlyle automatically dissociates it from his British audience; and if the metropolitan subject cannot find a common identity with the former slave, how can the liberal philosophical claim—for the mutual humanity of whites and blacks—be sanctioned?

It is important to recall here that before Carlyle's intervention in "The Negro Question," the most dominant image of the black subject in the English imagination was that of "man and brother," an empathetic figure promoted by the abolitionist movement. What Carlyle sets out to do in his discourse, then, is to undermine the empathy that exists between the black figure and his implied audience. By a masterful use of a negative stereotype—that of the idle and violent black—he demolishes the liberal notion of a universal brotherhood. And just in case anyone has doubts that the claim for a common humanity is against "the order of nature," Carlyle deflates such doubts with a specular image of blackness. He presents us with a sagacious portrait in which "a few black persons rendered extremely 'free' indeed" are shown functioning against the order of nature, "sitting yonder with their beautiful muzzles up to the ears in pumpkins, imbibing sweet pulps and juices; the grinder and incisor teeth ready for ever new work, and the pumpkins cheap as grass in those rich climates" (4). In this scenario, potatoes and pumpkins function as metaphors that inscribe whites and blacks in a situation of "natural" inequality; unlike potatoes, which need cultivation and hence generate the kind of labor that Carlyle considers to be a mark of humanity, pumpkins grow "naturally" and hence reinforce black idleness, a mark of their inferiority. Moreover, idleness has emotive power here not only because it goes against Carlyle's Calvinistic notion of work as the defining characteristic of being but also because it represents the most obvious result of what he considers to be an ill-advised liberal policy—that is, the emancipation of the blacks in the West Indies.

Now, while it is true that Carlyle deploys the foreign other (French, Irish, or West Indian) to confirm his racial and cultural prejudices, blackness affords him an important performative weapon: the black body, because of its specular power, provides the background against which the crisis of Englishness can be read through contrast. The black body hence exists as a trope that provides us with insights into what Carlyle considers to be the territory of subhumanity (a world incapable of the self-genera-tion that is possible only through work), and a warning as to what the English might become if the current crisis (which revolves around ques-tions of labor) is not resolved. Reading the black body allows us to think—contra the Enlightenment—beyond our conceptual systems and, more important for Carlyle, our given moral universe. If the West Indies is to become "a Negro Island," for example, we will be facing a situation that "Imagination cannot fathom"; thus "it will behoove us of this English nation to overhaul our West-Indian from top to bottom and ascertain a little better what it is that Fact and Nature demand of us" (8).

In Carlyle's discourse, then, there is an affinity between the representation of the black as a racialized spectacle and the authority of fact and nature. It is because blacks exist outside the moral system (*fact* and *nature* are always moral terms in Carlyle's thought) that they function as exemplars of the failure of the concepts—political economy, reason, and free trade—that the liberals have been using to describe the condition of England. The "everlasting duty of all men, black or white, who are born into this world," says Carlyle, is to do "competent work" (9); it follows then, within this logic, that "black indolence" is a visible example of how blacks have failed to live up to the standards that define freedom and identity, what he calls "the eternal law of Nature" (11). And thus the black figures who appeared quite peripheral to Carlyle's discourse become indispensable to the intrinsic function of the "Occasional Discourse." Having shown us how blacks have failed to live up to conventional morality (as it is manifested in labor), Carlyle goes on to argue that the only way blacks can do "useful work" is through compulsion; the "idle Black man in the West Indies" cannot realize himself under the conditions of freedom engendered by emancipation; he needs a "better form" of management—"to be *compelled* to work as he was fit, and to *do* the Maker's will who had constructed him with such and such capabilities, and prefigurements of capability" (11).

The key word in this postulation is *prefigurement*, for it suggests that a cultural order of blackness is incomplete without the mastering authority of England. Having asserted that "the Black gentleman is born to be a servant, and, in fact, is useful in God's creation only as a servant," Carlyle concludes that our primary task now is to find ways "to abolish the abuses of slavery, and save the precious thing in it" (22). The essence of blackness, or "the will of the Maker" in the creation of the black subject, cannot be realized except when it is subordinated to whiteness; to claim that blacks and whites can exist in a situation of equality, says Carlyle, is "a palpable falsity, big with hideous ruin for all concerned in it" (25). Blacks are hence indispensable to the reader's understanding of the order of Englishness. They are caricatured and mocked so that we can dissociate them from our normative semantic (and somatic) field: "With a pennyworth of oil, you can make a handsome glossy thing of Quashee, when the soul is not killed in him! A swift, supple fellow; a merry-hearted, grinning, dancing, singing, affectionate kind of creature, with a great deal of melody and amenability in his composition" (12). But this dissociation cannot be complete without some measure of identity; if alterity is to have any value, it must be underscored by the shock of recognition:

> The black African alone, of wild-men, can live among men civilised. While all manner of Caribs and others pine into annihilation in the presence of pale faces, he contrives to continue; does not die of sullen irreconcilable rage, of rum, of brutish laziness and darkness, and fated incompatibility with his new place; but lives and multiplies, and evidently means to abide among us, if we can find the right regulation. (12)

In performative terms, then, the black figures allow Carlyle to reshuffle existing meanings (about the colony and its culture) and to create a new discourse in which the other is both inside and outside Englishness. Aware that blackness evokes the deepest fears in his culture, and confident that whatever happens in the colonies is considered by his audience to be of utmost urgency and importance, Carlyle brings blacks home to England in the form of the fiction he conjures in what he claims is a factual discourse. He invites his readers not only to reflect on what blackness means to them but to see it as the potential double of whiteness in a world in which natural racial and cultural distinctions are being questioned by liberals and revolutionaries. In this situation, Carlyle's moral authority lies in an implicit promise he makes his audience: he will explain the sources of the black threat lucidly and present a plan for countering it; he will also show his listeners that although the colonies are important to the power of England, they are not part of the culture of Englishness. And thus in the field of reference that conjoins metropolis and colony, Carlyle splits the black from the English and excludes the cultural sphere of one from the other; this gesture establishes a semantic disorder (we have to read the two terms as always opposed), but in the process of this splitting and exclusion, he assembles a new space in which English identities, now immune from the sins of blackness (idleness, reckless freedom, anarchy), can be read.

Carlyle's visual image of the black is also one of aesthetic dissemblance: blackness is the mirror image through which Englishness defines itself; it is through the staging of black idleness that "Saxon British" manfulness is affirmed; it is against the backdrop of a black failure to cultivate the land that the white European is declared, "by Nature and Fact," to be "the worthier propriety" (27). "It was not Black Quashee, or those he represents, that made those West Indian Islands what they are, or can, by any hypothesis, be considered to have the right of growing pumpkins there," declares Carlyle (28). The sage goes on to buttress his argument by evoking the romantic image of the West Indies as a land that lies fallow before European cultivation: "Before the West Indies could grow a pumpkin for any Negro, how much European heroism had to spend itself in obscure battle; to sink, in mortal agony, before the jungles, the putrescences and waste savageries could become arable, and the Devils be in some measure chained there" (30).

Carlyle recognizes that black labor is necessary to the continued prosperity of the islands, but his main point, of course, is that this labor must be policed and contained within immutable racial hierarchies. The relation between white and black is not an economical one; on the contrary, the "mutual duties" between the two races are established "under the sight of the Maker": this mutual, but unequal, relationship is "what He has written down with intricate but ineffaceable record, legible to candid human insight, in the respective qualities, strengths, necessities and capabilities of each of the two" (33). In these circumstances, England's natural duty is to police the laws established by the Maker, thus countering the dissolution represented by the "palpable facts" (34), the facts of black idleness and immorality.

But as I have already noted, Carlyle's concern with the "palpable facts" of blackness is a rhetorical ruse, for facts are secondary to the performativeness of his discourse. Indeed, it is precisely in his dismissal of what we understand to be facts, and his contempt for rational argument, that his discourse becomes one of the most important cultural documents of the mid-Victorian period. For as Mill recognizes in his rejoinder to Carlyle ("The Negro Question"), what the author has been able to do, especially under the cover of anonymity, is to appeal to the most emotive force in the canon of Englishness—the idea of the law. But Carlyle's invocation of the idea of the law goes way beyond what Mill considers to be "force and cunning"; within the symbolic economy of English identity, the idea of the law bestows the authority of nature and totality to the nation and its imperial ideology; the law provides the framework in which the ideality of the English nation is affirmed.[17]

As Gilroy has observed, "The subject of law is also the subject of the nation. Law is primarily a national institution, and adherence to its rule symbolizes the imagined community of the nation and expresses the fundamental unity and equality of its citizens."[18] Whether this law is considered to be natural or secular, its concordance depends on the establishment of a binary opposition between the English nation, which is founded on the rule of law and morality, and a foreign other whose very nature either negates law and morality (Carlyle) or subordinates its character to the benign authority of Englishness (Mill). In both cases, however, the black subject functions as the agent of what Homi Bhabha has called "a perpetual performativity," challenging the idea of the law through its real and imagined acts of insurgency and also affirming the necessity of the law and the role of imperial England as the conveyor of this law.[19]

But this performativity has an epistemological dimension: West Indian blacks, who are geographically peripheral to the great questions that have generated mid-Victorian consciousness, and indeed exist outside the cultural norms from which Englishness derives its central meanings, nevertheless inhabit the theoretical centers of such debates. They thus cast what Uday Mehta, writing on the Mills and India, has called "a dark epistemological shadow in which access is uncertain and in any case of apocryphal value."[20] But it is precisely because the other is so inaccessible and apocryphal that it can be deployed with such ease in the demarcation of English culture. For if the colonial other is both malleable (we can shape it to fit whatever philosophical system we espouse) and inscrutable (it is always beyond rational thought), this endows it with tremendous value in a discourse whose power and authority depend—as do most of the discourses on the condition of England—on speech acts.

Thus while Mill attacks Carlyle's discourse as an exemplar of the malevolent forces the liberals have been fighting against in the postreform period, he too sees the treatment of blacks as "a prominent symptom" of the moral condition of England: the nation's revolt against slavery and the slave trade is not merely an affair of sentiment, he insists, but a reflection of the humaneness of English culture. Mill hence posits abolition as an important act of moral rectitude: through the efforts of noble people, "the laws of the English nation" can now fulfill their natural or humane function instead of sustaining injustice (39–40). But because he wants to insist that his deployment of blacks is, unlike what he considers to be Carlyle's mischievous display, driven by an ethical imperative, Mill tries to sublimate the performative aspects of his discourse to its pedagogical function.[21] In other words, he wants to see the question of black slavery not as a pretext to talk about other things but as a subject worthy of the most serious moral and philosophical consideration. Given this moral and philosophical imperative, Mill argues, Carlyle's analytical mistake arises from a reckless appeal to natural law—and its concomitant figures of racial difference—and his "disrespect" for "the analytical examination of human nature . . . from which we have learned whatever we know of the laws of external nature" (46). Without a rational system of analysis to probe the formation of character, says Mill, Carlyle falls into "the vulgar error of imputing every difference which he finds among human beings to an original difference of nature" (46).

As a proponent of the Enlightenment ratio, however, Mill fails to recognize that what was involved in Carlyle's discourse was discursive authority (and the power of persuasion) rather than the rule of evidence. He hence proceeds to establish a rationality that tries, on one hand, to discuss the black subject in its own right but, on the other hand, ends up reading it as an index of the character of Englishness. By appealing to the essential equality of human nature, Mill begins his discourse with the explicit intention of nullifying the categories that sustain alterity: we can never speak authoritatively of "original differences" among human beings, he asserts. As to any notion that blacks are incapable of progress, he says, we do have evidence of "civilized" black cultures in Egypt from which the Greeks "learnt their first lessons in civilization" (46–47).

And yet Mill's ethical imperative is incapable of rescuing the black figure from Carlyle's spurious ontology because in spite of his urgent desire to denounce the Carlylean ideology, he cannot deploy blacks outside a conceptual system—liberalism—whose appeal to a common human identity also presupposes alterity. In this respect, Mill questions any notion of natural differences (which he replaces with the doctrine of environmental variations in character) but finds it difficult to renounce alterity completely: "What the original differences are among human beings, I know no more than your contributor, and no less; it is one of the questions not yet satisfactorily answered in the natural history of the species" (46–47). The quarrel with Carlyle, then, is not about whether blacks and whites are different (they concur on this point) but about (a) the origins of the differences (are they natural or social?) and (b) their function within the moral economy of empire (are blacks naturally degenerate or can they be uplifted and become part of the community represented by the culture of colonialism and the civilizational authority of Englishness?). While it would be reckless to equate Mill's liberalism with Carlyle's nascent fascism, especially as far as matters of race are concerned, it is important to underscore the extent to which both deploy the other as a hermeneutical instrument of understanding Englishness. Mill's basic presupposition here is simple: English identity is defined by a core of immutable values that endow it with what I have already called civilizational authority—the ability and right to change others according to the ideals of Englishness.

Like Carlyle, then, Mill assumes that identities can be defined only in a rhetoric that foregrounds alterity and difference. Unlike Carlyle, however, he accepts the significance of alterity and difference in the hope that they can be overcome through moral and cultural enlightenment. But as Mehta aptly notes, the "expansive range" of difference is limited within the theoretical perimeters of liberalism: "The limiting point of this perimeter is a form of alterity beyond which differences can no longer be accommodated."[22] Neither Carlyle nor Mill can conceptualize empire without its black subjects, but they differ widely on where these subjects are to be positioned: Carlyle accommodates differences by appealing to natural hierarchy, Mill domesticates them by subordinating blackness to the demands of a cultural, moral, and constitutional standard exemplified by England. Alterity remains in both cases because, as we have already noted, it is a precondition for understanding Englishness. As Mill observes, it is in our attitude and treatment of the other that we can gain access to those categories of ourselves foreclosed from rational analysis: "It is precisely *because* we have succeeded in abolishing so much pain, because pain and its infliction are no longer familiar as our daily bread, that we are so much more shocked by what remains of it than our ancestors were, or than in our contributor's opinion we ought to be" (49).

While Carlyle sees emancipation as a degenerative move, a denotation of how England has lost its power and authority, Mill sees it as a humane gesture, a mark of the English people's capacity to sustain the civilization, and the morality that the term *civilization* entails, as pressures of alien barbarism. While Carlyle is concerned with black chy, Mill focuses on the progressive movement, which has changed the black subject's relation to the metropolis. In both cases, however, any sustained contemplation of blackness is also an act of self-reflexivity: it is through the black figure that Englishness acquires the metaphorical structure that enables it to gaze at its self in crisis.[23]

Alterity in the Postimperial Age

One could, of course, argue that far from being the prism through which Englishness gazes at itself, the black subject is nothing more than a social scapegoat—the ritual object onto which the crisis of identity in Victorian England is projected. After all, even a cursory reading of "The Negro Question" or the Governor Eyre controversy reminds one of the extent to which the signs of English identity are perpetually being contested and of the moral gulf that divides the nation every time it contemplates the challenge to its governing paradigms, such as law and morality. At the same time, the black crisis that generates the debates on "the condition of England" question is sidelined as soon as the nation seems to have found its cultural equilibrium. It is tempting to conclude, then, that the deployment of blacks in this discussion is either simply gratuitous or a substitute for prior figures of alterity (the Irish or the French, for example) who no longer seem to carry the force of difference because they have increasingly become more like us. But doesn't the discursive evocation of a black critical mass against which Englishness can be measured stabilize the national culture by establishing a degree of consensus on the parameters of the English character, on the ideal values that define Englishness, and on the necessity of empire? Perhaps. And yet isn't the black mass, because of its geographical distance, easily excluded from the debate on Englishness when it no longer seems useful for discursive purposes? Does the black subject, then, weave its way in and out of Englishness? And what happens when blacks, through migration, become a physical presence in the heart of Englishness?

The truth is, the nature of colonial alterity is bound to change when the black critical mass enters the English physical space. Indeed, if there is any critical distinction between the way blacks and other figures of alterity, such as the Jews and the Irish, were represented in English cultural discourse until the 1950s, it can be explained by the fact that while the last two groups were always conceived as a threat within English culture itself, blacks were seen as radical figures of difference who were, nonetheless, several times removed from the metropolis itself.[24]

But with the collapse of empire in the period after World War II, the parameters of English identity are radically destabilized on two fronts. First, the influx of immigrants from the former colonies ensures that blackness is not simply a semantic or performative category but a real presence and cultural threat to the pastoral image of England as an island. And second, the collapse of empire nullifies the value previously invested in colonial subjects and spaces. The crisis afflicting the English social order as it tries to adjust to identities that are no longer bonded by externalized alterity, a crisis manifested in the works of Enoch Powell, is thus the crisis of reading—and affirming—empire in its absence. For if Carlyle and Mill argue that you cannot conceive of an English identity without its opposite—colonial alterity—Powell's discourse is condemned to articulate Englishness in its condition of impossibility, in what I have already defined as the postcolonial aporia (see chapter 1).[25]

But if Powell has become an important point of reference for the project of postcolonial and cultural studies, it is because he has been aware, more than any other public figure in postimperial Britain, of the ways in which blackness functions as a mediator between an English identity that is split between an imperial positivity (which thrives on nostalgia) and a postimperial negativity projected onto immigrants. And although Powell is better known for his speeches advocating the repatriation of black immigrants from Britain and his denunciation of the idea of the British Commonwealth, which he sees as a threat to national sovereignty, we have to remember that his credentials as an old imperialist are unquestionable. If Powell has become the most impeccable critic of the culture of colonialism and the identities it has spawned, it is because he has traveled to the heart of empire and learned his lesson in the process. After military service in India following World War II, he entered politics to "do something to stop the disintegration of the Empire, which seemed imminent."[26] Powell's crisis, then, is a direct consequence of his historical belatedness: he lives and writes in a moment in which Englishness can draw on neither what Kobena Mercer has called "the strategies of inversion and reversal based on binary opposition" (as in Carlyle) nor the imperial mythology of affiliation (as in Mill).[27]

What is striking in Powell's discourse on the black subject, then, is that the black critical mass has to be rewritten—and demonized—as the primary threat to English national identity without directly associating its presence with England's imperial past. And Powell is not alone in this view of empire as simultaneously desirable (the source of the greatness of Britain) and threatening (the "natural" home of black immigrants). We find a more dramatic example of this schizophrenic representation of past and present in Margaret Thatcher's 1978–1979 campaign rhetoric, in which she vowed to restore the "Great" to Britain even as she raised the specter of the empire's black subjects invading England as an "alien swamp." For Mrs. Thatcher, it was inconceivable that "the alien swamp" was a semiotic sign of the "greatness" of Britain, a reminder of the long reach of empire. What we are dealing with here is not merely historical amnesia or cultural denial but a new strategy for imagining national identity: in the imperial period, as we have already noted, the essence of a British identity was derived from the totality of all the people brought together by empire; in the postimperial period, in contrast, we find a calculated attempt to configure Englishness as exclusionary of its colonial wards.[28]

Powell's case is, however, more complicated. First of all, he has always insisted that his politics of exclusion is based on nationality (what he calls "subjecthood") rather than race or national origin. Second, he has expressed his fondness for the landscape of empire—which he recognizes as the apex of English power—in incredibly sincere terms. As a consequence, *race* and *empire*—very limpid categories in Carlyle and Mill—become very troublesome terms in the politics of postimperial English identity in general and Powell's nationalist discourse in particular. The gist of the problem is this: if Powell is not a racist—and he insists he is not—why does race occupy such a prominent position in his discursive economy? And if his attachment to empire is genuine—and his service to its institutions cannot be doubted—why does he ultimately conclude that the British empire was a "political mythology" and "an invention"?[29]

While many books and essays have been written on the phenomenon of Powellism—hence recognizing its centrality to British cultural discourse since the 1950s—I don't think Powell's critics have quite recognized the extent to which his fear of the other arises from his recognition of his theoretical dependence on the "alien swamp" of immigrants he wants to expunge from the national body. Critics have, in essence, failed to see how Powell's deployment of blacks as a threat to English identity is generated by his—perhaps perverse—acknowledgment of their centrality in his own discourse and of their constitutive power in the ontology of the white subject and English nationalism.[30]

Let us recall that Powell's theory of the nation rests on what appears to be a contradiction: he argues, on the one hand, that true history is "concerned with the life of nations, with their birth, their fortunes, and their death"; on the other hand, however, he believes that there is "no objective definition of what constitutes a nation. It is that which thinks it's a nation"; but if the nation exists only in the imagination, how are we to explain Powell's belief that it is, at the same time, "a cohesive organization of traditions and loyalties" that excludes black immigrants?[31] In *Biography of a Nation*, Powell tries to explain these different presuppositions by arguing that self-consciousness, which he conceives to be "the essence of nationhood," has both internal and external moderators—"one the sense of unity, the other a sense of difference" (7). In the first case, national consciousness implies "the relationship of parts to a whole"; in the second instance, national consciousness "is also a sense of difference from the rest of the world, of having something in common which is not shared beyond the limits of the nation" (7–8). The important point, though, is that this play of identity and difference is only possible within the temporal division embedded in Powell's history of England. In other words, since the dual definition of nationhood discussed above appears in Powell's 1969 introduction to the revised edition of *Biography of a Nation*, an introduction written shortly after the famous "rivers of blood speech" (1968) in which he warned of the dangers that black immigrants posed to Englishness, we can conclude that it carries within it the authors' divided intentions, necessitated by the radical difference between 1955 (the year in which the book was originally published) and 1969, when the racial and cultural character of the English nation was being reconstituted in radical ways by a new generation of immigrants from former British colonies. In 1955 Powell still believed in the imperial mission; in 1968, the idea of the Commonwealth sustained what he saw as the dangerous illusion of imperial possession—dangerous because it rationalized the permanent settlement of black subjects in the mother country.

What I find particularly engaging in Powell's duality, however, is its performative dimension, especially the discursive maneuver that enables the author, in his divided moments of writing, to romanticize a self-generated English identity that can be narrated and theorized only from the standpoint of imperial atrophy. In fact, while Powell disavows chronology in the historiography of the nation, his *Biography of a Nation* is invested heavily in a teleological narrative of Englishness: the history of the nation begins with tribal Celts and reaches its apex with empire; the history of the nation ends with the dissolution of empire, but this is also the moment in which the "true" character of Englishness is revealed. The melancholia that surrounds Powell's representation of this dissolution is a sign of his belief that "real" Englishness can be recovered only when we have torn off the "false masks" of the identity engendered by imperial cartographies:

> Up to 1919 there had, since the loss of the American colonies, been an uninterrupted and dramatic increase not only in the extent of British territory but in the sense of unity and the self-consciousness of the British Empire. In 1919, in extent, in population, and in military power, Britain was the greatest nation on earth. But that climax rapidly passed, and the reaction which followed it was swift and striking. (204)

This passage is a good example of the doubleness of the Powellian performative: it simultaneously affirms the fact of empire and the melancholy generated by its loss; the absolute spirit of Englishness "passes" away in its resolute moment of self-consciousness; the most manifest symbol of Englishness is now only conceivable in its impossibility, in a discourse of national lack. And for Powell, it is in the discovery of lack that the British people's "idea of themselves and their place in the world" undergoes what he calls "severe revision" as the very identity of the nation is called into question by Asian and West Indian immigrants and Welsh and Scottish nationalists (238). But it is in the gap between the dissolution of empire and its long history that Powell seeks to inscribe a "pure" English identity.

The first step in this process, then, is a systematic rewriting and rereading of the past: the history of empire now comes to be seen from a self-consciously revisionist mode as Powell seeks to excavate a space in which the English nation can be conceptualized without external attachments. The second step is for Powell to argue that an autonomous English character thrived beneath the culture of colonialism, untouched by alterity and uncontaminated by the imperial experience. My argument, however, is that a pure narrative of English identity is inconceivable even in the disappearance of empire, for the imperial past—witness the romanticism and melancholy that surround it—shapes even those histories of the nation that would prefer to exorcise empire. For this reason, Nairn's argument that "English nationalism has been travestied by romanticism and confused by imperialism" has to be resisted, and imperialism must be read as the foundation on which the romanticism of English identity is constructed.[32]

Still, one wonders how Powell's deployment of alterity differs from the images and spectacles we have seen in Carlyle's "The Nigger Question." Has the black other been transformed (in relation to the English domestic space) from a transcendental subject to what Sartre would call an "empirical person"?[33] And does this transformation change the discourse on identity and alterity? We can follow Sartre here and argue that so long as the black figure was confined to the distant spaces of empire, it functioned as an absent transcendental subject, "a kind of supplementary category which would allow a world to be constituted"; it had "the pure value of the content of a unifying concept."[34] But as an "empirical person" whom we encounter in our streets and neighborhoods, the black cannot be the object of "empty intentions"; on the contrary, he or she functions as a presence—a subject who claims the authority of sameness—our cultural heritage and noesis. So long as Indians and West Indians remained supplemental categories of Englishness, they endowed England with a romantic notion of its own powers; they also provided the figures of alterity that would reinforce the civilizational authority of Englishness. As we saw earlier in this chapter, the existence of colonial spaces of alterity could indeed provide Englishness with a unifying metaphor—imperialism—in moments of crisis.

Now that the other is in our midst, Powell is saying, we have to read it as an empirical threat. Witness then the careful cultural grammar—Nairn has aptly called it "a scarifying catalogue of the black threat"[35]—that Powell uses to represent the immigrants in "Immigration." First of all, the black other is conceived in primarily demographic and numerical terms: "In 15 or 20 years, on present trends, there will be in this country 3 1/2 million Commonwealth immigrants and their descendants. . . . Whole areas, towns and parts of towns across England will be occupied by different sections of the immigrant and immigrant-descended population" (222). Powell's concern here is the power of numbers, their capacity to transform the character of the domestic space. But the main point, of course, is that that power and capacity depend on their color. This is how the immigrants come to be visualized as one invading black mass occupying the home territory and changing it in ways that would be incomprehensible if the migrants were white settlers from South Africa or Australia. Powell makes this point quite clear when he notes that in Wolverhampton, in the heart of what he calls the "black belt," entire areas have been transformed by "the substitution of a wholly or predominantly coloured population for the previous native inhabitants, as completely as other areas were transformed by the bulldozer"; this "event" has "altered the appearance and life of a town" and has had "shattering effects on the lives of many families and persons" (223).

This representation of the "black threat" is neither original nor particularly specular. What makes it important to the form of Englishness as it emerges in Powell's discourse, though, is the author's constant argument that his conception of the alien other is not racial, his insistence that even when he raises the specter of black criminality, he does not believe—or assert—that black immigrants are more "predisposed to vicious or spiteful behaviour than the indigenous population" (230). The issue, Powell insists, is not racial or cultural difference; it is all a matter of "numbers now and especially in the future"; "the question of numbers, and of the increase in numbers" is "the heart of the matter": immigrants threaten Englishness by threatening to change the ratio between the native and foreign-born inhabitants of the nation (230). If Powell appears indignant when he is accused of racism—as happened in a 1969 interview with David Frost—it is perhaps because he wants the debate to focus on national affiliations rather than the "natural rights" advocated by other members of the anti-immigration movement.

We may assert that in spite of this insistence on numbers, Powell's performance of nationhood is generated by a limpid theory of race. We may even note that his speech acts have struck such a powerful chord in the

English imagination because of their affective appeal to existing racial codes. This is perhaps the case, but it is not the whole story. The power and authority of Powellism, I will argue, are derived from his sublimation of ideologies of race to the objective notion of the nation. In other words, Powell's utterances are authorized not by the science of race but by a notion of "common sense"—what Barker has called the concept of "genuine fear," which acts as "a bridge-concept between an apparently innocent description and a theory of race."[36] Powell's discourse is predicated on "an innocent description" not of the nature of the other or its place in larger designs (nature or providence, for example) but of the "ordinary" English person's response to the visual epistemology of blackness.

Thus in "Immigrants," we have the letter of a constituent—"A middle-aged, quite ordinary working man"—who will not be satisfied until his adult children are settled overseas because "in this country in 15 or 20 years' time the black man will have the whip hand over the white man" (213). And as an example of the fear in which English people live—and of the many voices who feel unwanted in their own country—Powell quotes many instances when "ordinary, decent, sensible people, writing a rational and often well-educated letter" agreeing with his views, have to omit their address for fear of persecution (217). The black threat is already here, not out there in the colonies. Every sensible person knows this; those who deny the reality of the threat have not yet ventured into England's new "black belt" in London or the Midlands.

Powell's staging of "common sense" reaches its crescendo in the now famous letter dramatizing the plight of an old English lady under siege by West Indian immigrants:

> She is becoming afraid to go out. Windows are broken. She finds excreta pushed through her letterbox. When she goes to the shops, she is followed by children, charming, wide-grinning piccaninnies. They cannot speak English, but one word they know. "Racialist," they chant. When the new Race Relations Bill is passed, this woman is convinced she will go to prison. And is she so wrong? I begin to wonder. (218)

Now, even a cursory glance at the semantics of this discourse will show that Powell's descriptions are not racially innocent; his words and images are carefully crafted to appeal to racial stereotypes. But for this discourse to be "sensible," it has to dislodge the vociferous and transparent language of racism by presenting racist representations of the other, not as aspects of a social grammar generated by the speaker himself but as the "genuine" expressions of "ordinary" people responding to a "real" situation. In this discourse, then, the emphasis is shifted from the underlying racial presuppositions to the contingent social condition. The performative power of Powell's representation is, in other words, predicated on the language of everyday life. Nevertheless, Powell's use of quotations and citations (his own and those of others) is intended to confirm his prior utterances on the condition of England; the citation entrenches the rhetoric of prophecy from which this discourse derives most of its authority. What ordinary people are saying now is what Powell has been saying all along.

Thus after presenting us with images of English people under siege from immigrants, the author reminds us of the wide gap between such ordinary people and those without "direct experience [of] the black occupation." By carefully positioning himself as the figure that bridges this gap, the author speaks to us with "experience"—he knows what he is talking about because he lives "within the proverbial stone's throw of streets which 'went black' " (223). In addition, and quite paradoxically, Powell can warn of the dangers that Englishness faces from alien cultural traditions because, unlike his liberal adversaries, he has been "there": he does not merely warn about the dangers of "communalism" in "Indian-dominated" Wolverhampton; he warns with explicit authority ("Communalism has been the curse of India and we need to be able to recognize it when it rears its head here" [221]) because he has seen it in its "natural home."

But there is something more at stake here, something that ultimately links Powell to Carlyle. Implicit in words such as *communalism*, as in the whole discourse surrounding black criminality, Powell's project is only marginally concerned with the other in itself; his primary goal is a systematic diagnosis of the condition of England and, through the plotting of racial and cultural difference, a prophetic evocation of a new theory of the nation. The communalistic Indian family and the black mugger are, as Gilroy and Barker have each argued, counterpoints against which the English family and its laws can be rearticulated.[37] Powell recognizes, as did Carlyle and Mill before him, that the larger question here is not so much about the place of the black in British culture but about the meaning of Englishness under the stress of imperial decline.[38]

The difference between Carlyle and Mill, on the one hand, and Powell, on the other, revolves around the function of colonial culture in the constitution of domestic identities. For the earlier writers it seemed imperative to understand the imperial domain if one was to understand England; in Powellian discourse, as it is presented in *Biography of a Nation*, the essence of Englishness can be discovered only through retreat—"Perhaps after all we know most of England 'who only England know' " (255). This postulation is based on Powell's assumption that, on a deeper level, empire was not a constitutive element of the English character but a passing moment:

> There was this deep, this providential difference between our empire and those others, that the nationhood of the mother country remained unaltered through it all, almost unconscious of the strange fantastic structure built around her—in modern parlance, "uninvolved." . . . So the continuity of her existence was unbroken when the looser connections which had linked her with distant continents and strange races fell away. (254)

The myth that the nationhood of the mother country remained unaltered by the experience of empire, a myth that, as we saw in the last chapter, is rigorously challenged by postcolonial theory, is a powerful one among English nationalists like Powell. This myth is based on the belief that the connections between the metropolitan center and its colonial periphery were loose and ephemeral, that the character of the island nation remained unaltered by its long and extensive contact with colonial spaces, and that when empire collapsed, the relation with the other was dissolved.

Ironically, however, the collapse of empire has foregrounded the inherent relation between England and its colonial spaces, calling attention to the ways in which the idea of an English identity has been transformed by colonial culture and the force of colonial subjects who now inhabit the domestic space. For black subjects born in England, for example, the rupturing of empire is the source of neither nostalgia nor false triumph; on the contrary, it provides an analytic—and performative—moment for redefining themselves in relation to England through a play of difference and identity, negativity and affirmation. As postcolonial subjects whose origins lie elsewhere, as it were, they cannot appeal to the doctrine of the natural home, ideologies of human nature, or the instinctive forces—"traditions and motivations"—that frame English romantic nationalism and even nationality acts passed by the British parliament in the Thatcherite years. This is why a critique of Powellism is so central to the cultural discourse that has been produced by British black writers and intellectuals since the 1970s. For while some commentators might be inclined to dismiss Powell as a minor politician with a flair for excessive posturing on empire and alterity, black cultural discourse begins by recognizing his significance in the rearticulation of the identity of Englishness itself. As Stuart Hall notes, Powellism is more than the "enunciation of a specifically defiant policy about race and the black population by a single person"; on the contrary, it denotes the formation of an "official" racist policy "at the heart of British political culture."[39]

This culture, formed on the cusp that separates the moment of imperial collapse from that of decolonization, is symptomatic of a larger crisis in the British polis—a crisis of authority, of the social order, indeed of the national character and English literature. In countering the imperial discourse of alterity, then, the first tactic adopted by black British intellectuals is to hallow, as it were, a negative dialectic from the tradition represented by Powellism, a dialectic that can be located in what I have already termed Powell's split attitude toward empire. Kobena Mercer has even gone so far as to argue that Powell's discourse is premised on a demystification of empire itself: "By showing that the British Empire was a product of culturally constructed 'myths' invented in the 1880s, he could clear the space for the self-conscious construction of new 'myths' in the 1960s."[40]

Instead of reading race as either an act of bad faith on Powell's part or a mode of false consciousness, postcolonial critics conceive the cultural project of the "New Right" as a sustained attempt to position race as a key ingredient in the imagination of the nation. From a postcolonial perspective (and in the face of Powell's denial that his argument is racist), race is postulated, in Althusserian terms, as an integer of the English nation's imaginary relation to its condition of social and cultural decline after empire.[41] As Paul Gilroy puts it succinctly, racism answers "the social and political turbulence of crisis and crisis management by the recovery of national greatness *in the imagination*. Its dreamlike construction of our sceptred isle as an ethnically purified one provides a special comfort against the ravages of decline."[42] The postcolonial political imperative is to rescue race, culture, and nation from the racists.

The first stage in this process involves, as we have already seen, an acknowledgment of the centrality of the racial other in discussions of nation and identity. It also implies an acknowledgment that a discussion of the imaginary and symbolic deployment of race should be attuned to a paradigmatic shift from the discourse of alterity that was prevalent in the imperial age, to forms of otherness that have evolved in response to the crisis of national culture after empire. Whereas black subjects used to have import primarily in their imaginary presencing in the heart of Englishness (as in Carlyle's discourse), they are now conceptualized through acts of symbolic evacuation from the spaces they now occupy in England itself. This evacuation is, as Gilroy has noted, a key component in the discourse of imperial nostalgia: "The symbolic restoration of greatness has been achieved in part through the actual expulsion of blacks and the fragmentation of their households, which is never far from page three in the tabloids"; blackness and Britishness have thus come to be made "into mutually exclusive categories."[43]

But the modern discourse of alterity cannot be countered by simple acts of deconstruction or *ressentiment*, for however much we may like to dismiss Powell's discourse as socially constructed, in spite of its constant appeal to metaphysical notions of English identity, it is a discourse that derives its power from its claim to common sense and pragmatic considerations. A second discursive tactic adopted by postcolonial subjects, then, is to contest the popular image of a self-enclosed English identity by representing the national culture as a historical experience that is already constituted by empire, already contaminated by the colonial experience. To counter the Powellian pastoral image of England, postcolonial critics of Englishness argue that English culture does not arise from an "internal and intrinsic" dynamic but is generated in what Gilroy calls "a complex pattern of antagonistic relationships with the *external*, supra-national, and imperial world for which the ideas of 'race,' nationality, and national culture are the primary indices."[44]

In discussing this alternative definition of Englishness in "Art of Darkness," Gilroy begins with the basic premise that since the politics of race in postimperial England have changed, it is not enough to counter the discourse of alterity by an appeal to a "narrow anti-racism"; when antiracism defines racism as a moral issue, it fails to understand the cultural dimension of racial politics in the reconstitution of Englishness; above all, antiracism fails to distinguish race and culture as conceptual categories.[45] An analysis of Englishness that fails to differentiate these categories, argues Gilroy, will always define identity in racialized terms and will hence end up falling into the Powellian definition of the national culture as hermetic and pure. In this kind of analysis—in which culture is subsumed by racial markers—the notion of a black British identity is impossible to compound.

Gilroy's tactic, then, is to reject even a positivist appeal to race as a mark of identity; instead, he turns to the idea of culture as an instrument of affiliation. Here, culture has two important functions. First, it is the imaginary process by which black subjects can resolve the contradiction of being diasporic (since they claim origins somewhere else) and British; it is through different forms of cultural formations (notably music and painting) that such subjects can overcome the binarism inherent in the discourse of black alterity. Second, culture functions as a rational instrument, a weapon of reconfiguring "what it means to be English" in the fissures left by postimperial atrophy:

> The desire to make art out of being both black and English has become a major issue in the black art movement and should be seen as part of the long, micro-political task of recoding the cultural core of national life. In this light, the fissures, stress cracks and structural fatigue in the edifices of Englishness become more interesting and acquire their own beauty. (46)

Powell might of course respond to Gilroy by saying that if black subjects can claim their affiliation with Englishness only by recoding a national culture that exists a priori, then their relation to this culture must of necessity be different from that of their white counterparts. But Gilroy would counter this argument by insisting that what is often considered to be the originary moment of the national culture, or rather its key constitutive moments, are already inhabited by black subjects. Indeed, Gilroy makes several related important points in this regard in "Art of Darkness": He argues, first of all, that rather than continue reading black alterity as a threat to English culture, we should consider the ways in which racial difference has been a central issue in the construction of "the idea of universality on which aesthetic judgments depend" (47). And if the modern idea of culture cannot be conceived outside the norms established by aesthetic considerations, then it is imperative that we come to terms with the "other" side of the ideology of the aesthetic, with both the fact that the English idiom rests on principles invented in the discourse on slavery and colonialism and the fact that "the image of the black played an important role in debates over taste, judgement and the role of culturally specific experience in grounding aesthetic principles" (48).

The corollary to this recentering of blackness in the invention of the idea of the aesthetic—and this is Gilroy's second point—is that what black artists and critics are involved in is not merely a reconceptualization of an English culture that antedates them, but a rereading of "that culture's history which places the idea of 'race' at the centre rather than the margin" (48). The third point, then, is how to reread blackness (in English culture) as constitutive of this culture rather than as an unrelenting threat to its essential tenets, as central to its concerns, as inherent in its conceptualization. To this end, Gilroy offers a radical rereading of J. M. W. Turner's famous painting *The Slave Ship*—and John Ruskin's reading of it—as an "illustration of both the extent to which race has been tacitly erased from discussion of English culture and how a 'racial' theme, relocated at the heart of national understanding, can contribute to a new more pluralistic conceptualisation of both England and Britain" (49).

Gilroy's concern here is not simply a reading of race in Turner's picture, but a rereading of Ruskin's tortured interpretation of the painter, a reading that seeks to isolate an English sensibility from the anxieties that were to redefine the forms of the national character in the fateful 1840s. Gilroy's metadiscourse, by returning Turner's painting to its conditions of possibility in the 1840s, challenges the dominant myth of an autochthonous national character driven by a pure artistic sensibility:

It is exciting to discover how the imagery of race and slavery appears centrally in Victorian debates over what England had been and what it was to become. The painting offers one opportunity to appreciate that English art and aesthetics are not simply in place alongside English thinking about race. Thinking about England is being conducted through the "racial" symbolism that artistic images of black suffering provide. These images were not an alien or unnatural presence that had somehow intruded into English life from the outside. They were an integral means with which England was able to make sense of itself and its destiny. (51)

I want, in the next two chapters, to reflect more closely on the relation between what Powell calls the "fantastic" imperial structure and the character of the "mother country" and to examine more closely how in the imperial century, the age in which colonialism and culture became integrated, making sense of England meant encountering the colonial other as both a natural part of imperial Englishness and a potential threat to the idea of the English nation.[46]

ᴈ 3 ᴇ

Englishness and the Culture of Travel: Writing the West Indies in the Nineteenth Century

"Philosophical travel," that is, the concept of travel as science, could leave the problem of time theoretically implicit because travel itself . . . is instituted as a temporalizing practice.

Johannes Fabian, Time and the Other

Theory, insofar as it assumes the rendering present to oneself of a conceptual schema (we say that we "see" something when we understand it), becomes a kind of sightseeing. Both theory and tourism imply a desire to see and totalize what is seen into an all-encompassing vision.

Georges van den Abbeele, Travel as Metaphor

⚲

When he came to provide a moment of closure to *The English in the West Indies or the Bow of Ulysses*, a travelogue haunted by doubts about the moral character of Englishness, James Anthony Froude could not help but affirm what he considered to be the undisputed connections between metropole and colony, links that he believed to be the foundations on which an imperial English identity had historically been constructed:

> The West Indies are a small limb in the great body corporate of the British Empire, but there is no great and no small in the life of nations. The avoidable decay of the smallest member is an injury to the whole. Let it be once known and felt that England regards the West Indies as essentially one with herself, and the English in the islands will resume their natural position, and respect and order will

come back, and those once thriving colonies will advance with the rest on the high road of civilisation and prosperity.[1]

Froude's prose—its incantatory tone and collective posture—assumed both that the West Indies was indisputably part of the organic body of empire and that the interests of English settlers in the West Indies, rather than those of emancipated black slaves, were paramount. After several chapters attacking the culture of the West Indies and its black inhabitants, and after exposing the social and political decline of the islands after emancipation as an example of the crisis faced by Englishness in the troubled 1880s, Froude could not avoid a celebratory moment of closure, one that would reassure his readers at home that the living power of empire would allow them to overcome the crisis they faced both at home and abroad. It is in a tone of imperial authority, then, that Froude could return from the West Indies to assert the moral superiority of Englishness.

But this haughty tone, this confident assumption that the writer and his readers shared a common set of values and one destiny, had not counted on the challenge that it was to face from the colonized subjects it had demonized. These subjects spoke back in the voice of an obscure black schoolmaster and amateur scholar named J. J. Thomas, a man whose self-confidence was such that he could give his book the inflammatory title of *Froudacity*:

> Last year had well advanced towards its middle—in fact it was already April, 1888—before Mr. Froude's book of travels in the West Indies became known and generally accessible to readers in those Colonies.
>
> My perusal of it in Grenada about the period above mentioned disclosed, thinly draped with rhetorical flowers, the dark outlines of a scheme to thwart political aspiration in the Antilles. That project is sought to be realised by deterring the home authorities from granting an elective local legislature, however restricted in character, to any of the Colonies not yet enjoying such an advantage.[2]

Because Froude had deployed the rhetoric of the imperial epic to overcome the sense of crisis that had sent him to the West Indies in the first place (this was imperative if colonial Englishness was to continue to be the grand narrative against which to read the imperial experience), Thomas's task as a minor writer was essentially reconstructive. His goal was to expose imperial rhetorical figures as drapes that covered up the topic that was haunting colonial authority—the fear that, with proper representation, black subjects might come to dissociate themselves from the mythology of paternal empire.

I begin this chapter with the confrontation between Froude and Thomas in order to question two problems that have come to plague studies of colonial culture and discourse. The first concerns what I consider to be one of the more curious limitations of postcolonial theory—its historical amnesia or, rather, its failure to recognize that its attempt to unravel the relation between metropolitan and colonial identities is not an original articulation but a repetition of previous social and temporal entanglements. Indeed, scholars who might be tempted to see the discursive war between Enoch Powell and his postcolonial interrogators, discussed in the previous chapter as evidence of a radical transformation in the terms of colonial discourse, might be well advised to consider the textual encounter between Froude and Thomas as an earlier example of what is now being called postcoloniality.[3]

The second problem is the strategic forgetfulness inherent in most belated attempts to secure an autonomous and immanent English identity. For in the midst of postimperial decline and crisis, Enoch Powell has provided English nationalism with what we may call its working hypothesis: empire gave England power and prestige but left its national character untouched; even at the height of its empire, England remained an island untouched by the landscapes and subjects it dominated; now with postimperial migration, the blacks have come to contaminate the realm. Powell's theory of English exclusiveness begs a simple question: is this dissociation of nation and empire a bad case of rewriting history to confirm comforting ideological positions, or is there a sense in which imperial England managed to develop mechanisms for keeping the culture of the other at bay, as part of metropolitan Englishness but also distanced from it?

The argument I presented in the introductory chapter—that the culture of Englishness derived its values and ideality in relation to figures of alterity—would seem to be a direct rebuttal of Powell's position. But given the depth of England's involvement with the colonies, and the colonial people's involvement with England, there are even more intriguing questions in postimperial revisionist discourse and, indeed, in the whole process by which the relation between empire and nation has been temporalized. How has it been possible to make a compelling case for an "unaltered England" in the face of its deep involvement with the other? What discursive mechanisms are used to represent the colonial space as both "exclusive and expansive" of Englishness?[4]

We can begin to address these questions by examining the relation between English identity, theories of alterity, and imperial travel. This is the kind of relation established, albeit surreptitiously, by Froude at the beginning of *The English in the West Indies*: the author's concern in this narrative is not the nature or the status of the islands per se, but their relation to the imperial center and especially the position of its disillusioned white settlers and their claim to a privileged English identity. Clearly, Froude's desire is for an interpretative position from which he can reflect on an urgent and contentious debate on the condition of England, a debate he sees manifested in Tennyson's "Locksley Hall" and in the continuing argument between the imperial poet and Prime Minister Gladstone.[5] Froude does not embark on his West Indian journey to escape from such debates; on the contrary, by going away he hopes to achieve a better—that is, total—perspective on the domestic condition; he assumes that it is only by traveling to the corners of empire that one can comprehend the "special and peculiar meaning" of Englishness.

Travel is hence posited as a mechanism of totalization: Froude tries to persuade his readers, especially in the incipient moments of his journey, that his tour will serve to affirm the integrity of empire as a *symbolon* that unifies English peoples across diverse geographical spaces and endows them with a privileged identity. Froude is certainly eager to inscribe his journey with the insignias of imperialism and, more important, to promote it as a significant ingredient in the constitution of what he considers to be the totality of Englishness. He thus opens his narrative with ruminations on the Queen's Jubilee and the colonial exhibition, imaginary spectacles in which the imperial center and its periphery are linked together across geographical spaces. The English people he is about to visit, Froude reminds his readers, "have the same blood, the same language, the same habits, the same traditions" as the inhabitants of the metropolis and would "be shattered into dishonourable fragments" (3) if they were denied their inherent Englishness. Like the epic promised in its subtitle,

Froude's narrative is both an inquiry into the condition of Englishness and colonial culture and a confirmation of the already known mythology of empire.

But beneath this affirmation of the unity of English identity, Froude's discourse is generated by a double anxiety, an anxiety that he hopes to overcome with his eyewitness account of the English in the West Indies. The first anxiety is induced by the almost subliminal feeling that the myth of a pure and continuous English tradition and identity in the West Indian colonies is threatened, especially in the post-emancipation period, by the rise of the black subject. Froude worries about a future West Indian Federation in which blacks, having acquired political rights, will be in perpetual conflict with whites. And since he subscribes to the dominant doxa, which decrees that races cannot "blend into one," he is convinced that only an imperial center can secure cultural and racial difference (7). But there is an even greater anxiety in Froude's text, an anxiety about his capacity to secure the all-encompassing vision demanded of him as an imperial historian. Is it possible to develop and valorize an epistemology on the "condition of England" question and the integrity of the English nation and its history? Can travel and distance generate the kind of comprehensive vision that might enhance such an epistemology—an epistemology that will enable us to see empire as part of the realm but also separate from its nativist culture?

Now, if a hermeneutics of Englishness demands temporal circularity, Froude does not believe that we are in a position to understand the historical continuum in its totality: "The past is gone, and nothing but the bones of it can be recalled. We but half understand the present, for each age is a chrysalis, and we are ignorant into what it may develop" (12). Moreover, the "moulting state" in which England finds itself challenges existing interpretative codes: the Victorians are surrounded by a multiplicity of events that make it impossible for them to develop determinate meanings for shifting social vectors. In a situation where the primary complaint is that we live in a condition without a hermeneutics (this is perhaps what the whole "condition of England" question is all about), there is a sense in which imperialized knowledge has its eyes set on some kind of epistemic totality. Can travel provide the evidence that confirms the necessity of empire as part of England's destiny and the symbol that unifies different cultures and traditions, classes and interests at a time when the domestic space seems to be under threat from the forces of historical change? Can empire be read as the singular code that explains the meaning of Englishness at a time when rapid historical and cultural change has undermined the authority of tradition?[6]

I want to argue that Victorian advocates of Englishness can develop a hermeneutics on the condition of England only by going elsewhere: travel functions as a form of metacommentary, allowing the imperial travelers to reflect on, question, demonize, and sometimes assimilate "monuments of other times and places."[7] It is primarily by rewriting the colonial other along the traces and aporias sustained by the trope of travel that the imperial travelers can understand themselves and their condition of possibility; it is in that space linked to England by a dialectic of difference and identity that the Victorian sages can gaze at themselves and hence evolve a system of knowledge through the textualization of alterity and negativity. I will start, then, with two presuppositions. First, there is, in the words of George Stocking, a close experiential and ideological relation "between the domestic and colonial spheres of Otherness."[8] Second, as Johannes Fabian has observed, the deployment of the other is overdetermined not only by temporal, historical, and political acts but by a theoretical or epistemological need: "When modern anthropology began to construct its Other in terms of topoi implying distance, difference, and opposition, its intent was above all, but at least also, to construct ordered space and time—a cosmos—for Western society to inhabit, rather than 'understanding other cultures,' its ostensible vocation."[9] To understand England in the nineteenth century, one must travel to the extremities of empire; to understand what Englishness really means, one must explore how it thrives in the geographies that seem to be most removed from the imperial center.

Travel in the realm of the other is intended to hallow a cosmological or theoretical space that Western society can inhabit; this space is, nevertheless, constructed according to the dictates of a value system that predates touring. Indeed, the topoi of travel already presupposes, and appeals to, the ideologies that define the domestic space itself; the journey elsewhere is, in turn, overdetermined by the paradigmatic values that define the domestic epos and its ethos. As Abbeele has observed, the trope of travel in the Western tradition is the vehicle and tenor of an established ethos: the "dearest notions of the West nearly all appeal to the motif of the voyage," a motif associated with immutable values such as "progress, the quest for knowledge, freedom as freedom to move, self-awareness as an Odyssean enterprise, salvation as a destination to be attained by following a prescribed path."[10] And although I said earlier that touring is necessitated by a theoretical negativity—the need to understand ourselves by appropriating the strangeness and difference of the other—the trope of travel can also be read as a referential gesture that always "brings the unknown back to the known, the strange back to the familiar."[11] Even when the narrative of travel foregrounds its radical departure from established norms (as often appears to be the case in the modern period), it can never release itself from its inherited conceptual schema or doxa.

In the case of the English travelers who write the West Indies so that they can understand the condition of England, there is no doubt that Englishness is always the stable point of reference, even when these authors have grave doubts about the value and identity of the English domestic space. In this sense, Englishness is the equivalent of the *oikos* in earlier narratives of travel: it acts as "a transcendental point of reference that organizes and domesticates a given area of defining all other points in relation to it. Such an act of referral makes of all travel a circular voyage insofar as that privileged point or *oikos* is posited as the absolute origin and absolute end of any movement at all."[12] But this postulation begs a prior question: if the *oikos*—Englishness, in this case—is already a privileged, transcendental, and absolute position, why is it necessary to travel through its opposite—colonial blackness, for instance—to comprehend it? Why is it that "imperial mythmaking" and the construction of the domestic subject have to be reflected by appropriating figures of negation and alterity?[13] Indeed, why do we need to travel at all when the spectacle of alterity has been presented to us as naked and intelligible in Carlyle's "Discourse on the Nigger Question," discussed in the previous chapter?[14]

The Ideologies of Imperial Travel

The obvious response to these questions is that the spectacle of alterity in Carlyle's discourse lacks the authority of personal experience and observation. Whatever the import and affectiveness of this discourse, it is open to the charge of reckless theorization without deference to facts "on the ground" (this is, of course, Mill's critique of Carlyle). Thus, the claim to facticity and the authority of the eyewitness is what makes the narrative of imperial travel different from the Carlylean spectacle. In the middle of his journey through the West Indies, for example, Anthony Trollope strikes at the Achilles' heel of all forms of armchair discourse by noting, in regard to the Anti-Slavery Society, that people who have not lived in the colonies do not have the authority to interfere with their economy: "Gentlemen in the West Indies see at once the Society is discussing matters which it has not studied, and that interests of the utmost importance to them are being played with in the dark."[15] The implication here is that those who have been to the West Indies can discuss its affairs "in light" of their experiences.

Travel, then, is more than a sentimental journey to the reaches of empire; embedded within the new science of natural history, it is driven by an ethnographic mission—what Fabian has called a project "of observation, collection and classification, and description."[16] Thus, a renowned imperial historian such as Anthony Froude, after traveling for a few weeks in a few Caribbean islands, is confident enough about his authority to assert that what distinguishes his work from that of armchair philosophers is the fact that he has concrete knowledge of those things that others talk about in abstract terms: "I have related what I saw and what I heard, with the general impressions which I was led to form" (Preface). There is hence an affinity—in Froude's formulation, at least—between observations made in the field and the general impressions one forms after travel; the purpose of narrating one's journey is to synthesize "objective data" and affect; when observations and impressions have coalesced in the traveler's mind and his or her narrative, a set of *theoretical* assumptions about the relation between nation and empire can be affirmed.[17]

The relation between facts and their effect needs to be stressed for another reason: imperial historians like Froude and Charles Kingsley operate within a historiographic tradition that often wonders whether observed details are compatible "with preconceived principles or interpretations."[18] It is not implausible, under these circumstances, to see travel as an attempt to reconcile details and principles, to bring together theoretical positions held a priori with the field observations that confirm them. But we also need to remember that while such principles appear to be moral, theological, or cultural in origin, they have been valorized and popularized by the discourse of armchair philosophers like Carlyle, Mill, or even the members of the Anti-Slavery Society. Indeed, what one finds so paradoxical about the imperial travelers in the West Indies in the nine-teenth century is that even when they are seeking new evidence to refute the ill-tempered argument about the colonial other in Carlylean discourse, they cannot escape from the rhetorical schema established by this dis-course. As a result these narratives adopt a triadic structure: first, in the tradition of post-Enlightenment travelers, the imperial narrative deploys the West Indian landscape as a source of what Fabian calls "secular knowl-edge";[19] second, in its search for a symbolic economy that can clarify the meaning of the domestic subject, this discourse engages with the other as a visualized object that might embody the unknown;[20] third, the topoi of travel exhibits the colonial landscape as a space of the traveler's displace-ment, thus necessitating the inevitable return to the domestic space.

In all three cases, however, the narrative of the imperial traveler is caught between an almost subliminal commitment to the already given dis-course—Carlyle and Mill on the "Negro question," for example—and the imperative to confer meanings on new experiences encountered, as it were, in the field. In other words, all three movements seem premised on a self-conscious ethnographic structure revolving around the notion of field-work: they deploy the space of the other as a space of interpretation and the vector of what Clifford calls "a shifting series of encounters, percep-tions, and interpretations."[21] These sites are intended to denote the radi-cal difference between metropolitan and colonial subjects but at the same time to affirm the centrality of the other in the cognitive maps of Eng-lishness.[22]

In *The West Indies and the Spanish Main* (1859), for example, Trollope posits the trope of travel as a mechanism of cultural critique and self-reflexivity: the textualization of the West Indian space is seen as a self-conscious attempt to break away from the mid-Victorian doxa on the colonies and their black inhabitants; conceived as a space of writing, the moment of travel comes to represent a discursive and conceptual break with the past. And nothing illustrates this desire for a break from previous discourse bet-ter than Trollope's decision to make the scene of writing contiguous with the voyage itself: "I'm beginning to write this book on board the brig—trading between Kingston, in Jamaica, and Cien Fuegos, on the southern coast of Cuba," he informs us in the first line of the travelogue (1). Thus, rather than open his text with the actual commencement of the voyage seen in retrospect, as the conventions of the travel narrative dictate, Trollope begins by inscribing the circumstances in which "I began the actual work of writing" (5). The implied distinction between the commencement of the journey and its inscription suggests that the latter is not a direct consequence of the former. As Trollope informs us a few moments later, the "proposed business" of his journey is not "to write these pages" but "certain affairs of state" (6).[23] His claim here is that he has not gone to the West Indies to find evidence to confirm certain beliefs he may hold about the islands; the inscription of travel is not a confirmation of the already given discourse on the other but a spontaneous act with the capacity to generate new knowledge about the West Indies.

For Trollope, then, the meaning of the journey lies in its making and narration rather than in any theological meanings that predate travel. The author is hence pleased with his travels in Jamaica, in spite of some unpleasant experiences, because the perils of the tour are compensated by its nonrepeatability—"the tourist always consoles himself by reflecting that he is going to take the expensive journey once, and once only" (20). On the surface of things, then, Trollope differs from his successors (most notably, Kingsley and Froude) in at least two respects: his ostensible rejection of a set of prior ideological or semiotic meanings against which the value of his voyage can be judged; and what appears to be his sublimation of England, as a point of reference, to the islands he visits, which often appear to be his center of focus.

Indeed, it is precisely because he does not foreground England as his primary referent that Trollope is able to use comedy and ironic discourse to burlesque the conventions of travel writing by calling attention to their fabrication: "When men write their travels," he says, "the weather has always been bad, and the ship has always done wonders" (7). This ironic posture also allows the traveler to call into question certain dominant notions about the colonies and their future in the domestic economy. It is, after all, irony that enables Trollope to question the implicit linkage between colonial spaces—as signs on a map—and their purported historical significance:

Kingston, on a map—for there is a map of Kingston—looks admirably well. The Streets all run in parallels. There is a fine large square, plenty of public buildings, and almost a plethora of places of worship. Everything is named with propriety, and there could be no nicer town anywhere. But this word of promise to the ear is strangely broken when performance is brought to the test. More than half the streets are not filled with houses. Those which are so filled, and those which are not, have an equally ragged, disreputable, and bankrupt appearance. (10)

In reading a passage like this, one might be tempted to conclude that Trollope's damnation of the capital of Jamaica follows the demonization of the colonial other that is so prominent in the works of many of his contemporaries (the image of colonial decay and atavism is almost tautological in such narratives). But the self-conscious ironic tone in Trollope's description is different—and important—because by showing that Kingston's "disgrace" is inherent in its foundations (or rather its original planning), he refuses to subscribe to the popular notion that West Indian decay is a consequence of emancipation. Another way of presenting this problem is to suggest that Trollope uses ironic discourse as a substitute for description, the most important technique in the convention of travel writing. For if description appeals to travel writers because it functions simultaneously as a form of interpretation and as a rhetorical construct, it is inherently a camouflaged form of ideological projection and imperial mythmaking; irony, on the other hand, seeks to unmask such myths and ideologies.[24]

As an ironist, then, Trollope does not see his frequent encounters with the Caribbean landscape as an invitation to rhetorically reconstruct the space of the other to confirm dominant ideologies; on the contrary, his telegraphic representations of the landscape seem to call attention to the mundaneness of what other writers have assumed to be erotic localities. Kingston harbor, for example, is described as "a large lagunae, formed by a long bank of sand which runs out into the sea. . . . This is the seat of naval supremacy for Jamaica, and as far as England is concerned, for the surrounding islands and territories" (7). In this kind of description, the author uses a sort of situational irony to undermine the reader's presuppositions about the colonial landscape and its romance; by contrasting the dreariness of the harbor with its symbolic function in the romance of English power in the West Indies, the author seems to call its mythical value into question. Rather than use descriptions to build on the inherited romance of English naval power in the islands, Trollope turns to irony to deflate this romance; in the process, he deliberately rejects the use of what has come to be known as the colonial sublime.[25]

But the most outstanding example of the connection between ironic discourse and the romance of Englishness is to be found in those scenes where Trollope questions the English identity of the colonies, something that most English writers on the West Indies in the nineteenth century seem to take for granted. Writing about the dietary habits of the inhabitants, for example, Trollope is struck by their slavish devotion to English dishes: "They will give you ox-tail soup when turtle soup would be much cheaper. Roast beef and beefsteaks are found at almost every meal. An immense deal of beer is consumed. . . . This is one phase of that love for England which is so predominant a characteristic for the white inhabitants of the West Indies" (16–17). Trollope observes that his hosts in the rural areas of the West Indies live like English country gentlemen, and though "they have every delicacy which the world can give them of native production, all these are nothing, unless they also have something from England" (32). So, where other writers may want to portray white society in the islands as essentially victimized by emancipation, Trollope does not hesitate to direct his caustic tongue at the social practices of white Creoles: "There are spots in the West Indies where men take third bitters, and long bitters, in which the bitter time begins when the soda water and brandy time ends—in which the latter commences when the breakfast beer-bottles disappear" (34–35). The islands and their population present the author with stark binary oppositions, but the purpose of ironic discourse is here and elsewhere intended to undermine the binaries that define the colonial relationship.

What, then, is the value of this kind of ironic discourse, and what does it tell us of the traveler's relation to inherited doctrines on the colonial other? We will see, especially when we deal with the question of the black other more explicitly, that on the epistemological level travel narratives are unified in ways belied by their diverse moral positions. The question I want to pose here, however, is aimed at the presumed oppositionality of Trollope's ironic discourse: Does this irony represent his desire "to undertake a protective self-transcendence"?[26] Does the ironic burlesquing of the English in the West Indies lead to a critical position, a position that places Trollope's discourse outside of "inherited cultural patterns and traditional institutions," and does this positionality, through ironic juxtaposition, bring "a new evaluational perspective into play"?[27]

The truth is, Trollope's travel narrative derives its value from a dialectical irony that simultaneously questions and affirms Englishness. In its evocation of the relation of theory and practice in the ethnography of travel, his discourse valorizes the author's divided ideological intentions. Trollope uses his irony to criticize the culture of different groups in the West Indies, including the English themselves, hoping in the process to develop original insights and perceptions about his objects of observation. Reflecting on Englishness away from England, Trollope is able to establish a critical position that goes against the grain of domestic opinion.

From this critical position, Trollope can argue that, contrary to popular domestic opinion, the future of Jamaica cannot plausibly lie in cane production (36); and although he knows that there are "prejudices" against Demerara in England, he dares to describe the colony as the "Elysium of the tropics—the West Indian happy valley of Rasselas—the one true and actual Utopia of the Caribbean Seas—the Transatlantic Eden" (128). In addition, while everyone in England assumes that the struggle in the West Indies is between blacks and whites, Trollope argues that we cannot understand "the state of the country" without alluding to the position of "coloured men" (73). These examples would hence seem to suggest that travel, as a form of fieldwork, generates new knowledge against the pressures of the inherited doxa, that the journey elsewhere has enabled the traveler to bring back information that was previously foreclosed from his home audience.

But one has to wonder, nevertheless, how original and independent the perceptions developed in the field really are. Do they lead to the articulation of a new theory on the colonial other, or are they surreptitiously founded on inherited paradigms? It is interesting to note that while Trollope sympathizes with the "coloured men" of Jamaica, he can represent their ascendancy only within the racial paradigm that is so central to colonial notions of the other:

My theory—for I acknowledge a theory—is this: that Providence has sent white men and black men to these regions in order that from them may spring a race fitted for civilization; and fitted also by physical organization for tropical labor. The negro in his primitive state is not, I think, fitted for the former; and the European creole is certainly not fitted for the latter. (57)

By affirming the necessity of miscegenation, Trollope has, of course, rejected Victorian social dogma on race; his relation to the dominant racial paradigm has been qualified by what he sees in the "field." My argument, however, is that he can only effect this rejection by appealing to another dogma—evolutionism. For example, while many commentators on the Jamaican racial scene argue that "the mulatto" as "a race" has deteriorated in body and mind (this would seem to confirm the racial paradigm), Trollope's observations lead him to conclude that the ascendancy of this group depends on their mixed racial characteristics; in fact, he is quick to assert that such "deterioration on both sides is necessary to the correctness of my theory" (59). Trollope's narrative simultaneously derives its authority from observations made in the field of empire and from important cultural accounts and doctrines that predate travel.

If colonial culture provides Victorian culture with its dominant social text, it is a text that is, nevertheless, haunted by prior accounts from the imperial archive. Indeed, when we turn to Kingsley's *At Last: A Christmas in the West Indies*, we are immediately struck by the extent to which the narrative of travel derives its authority from its pre-texts as much as from original observations; we immediately recognize how the narrative of travel functions as an elaborate reworking of the colonial library, a rediscovery of the already discovered. The very title of Kingsley's book—and its many lyrical moments—projects the West Indies not simply as a space to be discovered and possessed, but one in which objects already known are to be celebrated and popularized. Kingsley's tour, in other words, is also a retour. His moment of departure for the West Indies is presented as the fulfillment of a long-nurtured desire: "At last we, too, were crossing the Atlantic. At last the dream of forty years, please God, would be fulfilled, and I should see (and happily, not alone) the West Indies and the Spanish Main."[28] Already prescribed by the colonial library, the West Indies that Kingsley is about to encounter predates his journey: "From childhood I had studied their Natural History, their charts, their Romances, and alas! their tragedies," Kingsley says of his prior encounter with the islands (1).

Are we to assume, then, that the "meaning and order" of the West Indies that Kingsley brings on his travel can be represented only according to the terms and images of the colonial library? Can we assume that the only way to represent the Caribbean is to fabricate it in such a way that our discourse on the other can only reiterate what we already know about it?

The answer to both questions is yes and no: Kingsley's discourse is reiterative in the sense that it follows the trace established by prior travel narratives—he informs us that he relishes the opportunity to travel to the West Indies so that he can "compare books with facts, and judge for himself of the reported wonders of the Earthly Paradise" (1). Since boyhood, Kingsley tells us, he has "heard and read much" about the Antilles and he has "pictured them to myself a thousand times" (26); although he tells us that once he encounters the islands "he was altogether unprepared for their beauty and grandeur," they nonetheless confirm his previous views.

So if we accept the premise advocated by Stephen Greenblatt that the aesthetic of wonder, as it functions in the discourse of earlier "discoverers," derives its authority from its claim to historical and legal originality,[29] Kingsley's narrative eschews the authority of the original experience and revels in its secondariness. In other words, since he cannot claim the authority of the marvelous, Kingsley tries to imagine how it must have been for those who saw it "first": "It was easy, in the presence of such scenery, to conceive the exaltation which possessed the souls of the first discoverers of the West Indies. What wonder if they seemed to themselves to have burst into Fairy-land— to be at the gates of the Early Paradise?" (27). The traveler would seem, in such instances, to have undermined his authority by calling attention to his historical belatedness and his displacement from the original experience. His narrative seems to draw attention to the gap that separates him from the true marvel—what Greenblatt calls "a world of objects" that exceeds an "understanding of the probable and the familiar."[30] Kingsley knows that his travelogue cannot match the originality and authenticity of the topological texts of discovery, but he can visualize the original moment and its sublimity:

> They were a dumb generation and an unlettered, those old Conquistadores. They did not, as we do now, analyse and describe their own impressions: but they felt them nevertheless; and felt them, it may be, all the more intensely, because they could not utter them; and so went, half-intoxicate, by day and night, with the beauty and the wonder round them, til the excitement overpowered alike their reason and their conscience. (27)

At the same time, however, the narrative marks the author's temporal separation from the discourse of discovery.

Kingsley's tone is, indeed, one of historical belatedness, and it raises auxiliary questions: What necessitates a historically belated narrative of travel if it cannot match the power of the original? On what authority is such a narrative constructed? In reading the above passage, we cannot fail to see how the conquistadores' ability to experience nature spontaneously is achieved at the expense of their *reason* and *conscience*, two terms that lie at the very center of Kingsley's discourse. To put it another way, Kingsley belongs to an age in which travel—as a horizon of cultural meanings and self-reflection—functions as a vehicle of reason and morality rather than simple sentiment or raw adventure; in the nineteenth century, travel has become part of a new science of human culture (ethnography), which does not derive its authority solely from a sensory economy; rather, the ethnographic text falls back on a claim to scientific authority, derived, as Fabian has noted, from natural history.[31]

In these circumstances, Kingsley recites previous (sentimental) discourse but also claims scientific advances beyond it, advances that are inherent in his capacity to subject landscape to both the rules of taxonomy and analysis. Thus, the colonial landscape becomes a discursive space in which sensory experiences can be subjected to the rules of reason and morality. This convergence of scientific analysis and moralizing is manifested most clearly in Kingsley's elaborate use of descriptions—and the representation of topography in general—as a source of scientific and ethical meanings. Simply put, Kingsley operates from the natural historian's premise that the study of animals and plants, rather than the observation of human life, provides us with deeper meanings about the order of nature and things. Without a sustained probing of natural life, argues Kingsley, we see in travel "but the outside of people, and as we know nothing of their inner history, and little, usually, of their antecedents, the pictures which we might sketch of them would be probably as untruthfully as rashly drawn" (3).

The natural landscape—and as we will see later, black subjects—are a better source of knowledge because they provide the traveler and ethnographer with what Arjun Appadurai has called "gatekeeping concepts" or "theoretical metonyms."[32] In addition, the natural landscape provides Kingsley with the most profound exemplification of God's original intentions: nature "hides with a kind of eagerness every scar which man in his clumsiness leaves on the earth's surface" (16). Because the work of nature marks the ideals against which human shortcomings have to be constantly measured, it is a better showcase of the innate values of the colonial landscape and the moral conscience of its custodians—the colonizer (figure 3.1).

On encountering the streets of Port of Spain, for example, what strikes the travelers' eyes with "most pleasurable surprise" and makes them realize "into what a new world [they have] been suddenly translated—even more than the Negroes, and the black vultures sitting on roof-ridges, or stalking about in mid-street—are the flowers which show over the walls on each side of the street" (91). In the face of such examples, it may appear tautological to argue that the localities of travel are fabricated to "become showcases for specific issues over time"[33] or that the representation of topography in the narrative of travel seeks to "educate the moral sense by way of the physical sense."[34] Within the imperial project, however, the more important question concerns the hermeneutical codes provided by the spaces of alterity, spaces in which, as I noted in earlier chapters, ideas of culture, of biology, and human nature are being reconstituted. The questions to be posed here concern the exact nature and import of the hermeneutics developed within colonial culture: what kind of instruction does the showcasing of the colonial space provide and how is a hermeneutics of the colonized landscape connected to the crisis of the domestic subject?

We can best approach this question by recalling that in *Alton Locke* Kingsley had attempted what Raymond Williams has called "an informed, angry, and sustained" account of industrialization at home while trying, at the same time, to provide moral lessons for the domestic crisis associated with Chartism.[35] In view of Alton Locke's decision to immigrate to America, and his subsequent death in transit, we can conclude that Kingsley could not imagine or invent a community outside the "prison-house of brick and iron" exposed in his novel.[36] While it is not my intention to speculate on the reasons for Kingsley's inability to transcend the objective conditions of the industrial north to imagine an alternative—albeit utopian community—outside industrialism, I want to reflect on how and why his engagement with the West Indian landscape gives him the freedom to imagine ideal communities outside the "prison-house" of Englishness.

First of all, given the density and elaborateness with which Kingsley describes the Trinidadian landscape, we can easily conclude that he reads the space of the other as nothing less than the stage on which the history

FIGURE 3.1.
Charles Kingsley's version of the tropical landscape.

of imperial possession is dramatically displayed: to travel to the West Indies is to encounter the semiotic signs of Englishness on display; it is to commemorate the unerasable historical presence of empire. In essence, if Kingsley's attempts to represent the domestic situation in *Alton Locke* had become stranded in pessimism about the future of England, the representation of the colonial space provides a countering sense of pride in being English. If industrial England had come to be defined by the realistic novel, the colony continued to be the space that generated romance and utopia. And so we enter the space of the other not to discover its unique history (does it have a history?) but to restage our unique national identity—to witness the triumph of the English spirit unencumbered by the disease of industrialism.

In this regard, Kingsley rarely fails to comment on the transformative power of Englishness in the colonies; by becoming English, for example, Trinidad had gained "more than mere numbers": "Had it continued Spanish, it would probably now be, like Cuba, a slave-holding and slave-trading island, wealthy, luxurious, profligate; and Port of Spain would be such another wen upon the face of God's earth as that magnificent abomina-

tion, the city of Havana"; alternatively, it could have become a free republic, like Venezuela, "combining every vice of civilization with every vice of
savagery" (85). Compared to Spanish possession or Creole nationalism,
the same Englishness that Kingsley attacked at home now becomes a
preferable alternative.

Furthermore, for Kingsley, as for Froude before him, a reflection on
the overseas landscape is tantamount to reading the central texts of imperial history. As he looks into the darkness of the Atlantic at the beginning of his West Indian journey, to quote one of many examples, the historian finds that he cannot interpret this new landscape except in terms
familiarized by what I have already called the pre-text of empire and the
romance it valorizes: "And as we looked out into the darkness, we could
not but recollect with a flush of pride, that yonder on the starboard beam
lay Flores, and the scene of that great fight off the Azores, on August 30,
1591, made ever memorable by the pen of Walter Raleigh—and of late by
Mr. Froude" (5). The key phrase in this sentence is "we could not but recollect," for it suggests a certain compulsion toward the romance of English history, the history that motivates and authorizes the journey
through the other's landscape. From the sinking of the Spanish armada
to the exploits of Drake and Hawkins, Kingsley projects himself "on the
track of the old sea-heroes" (5). Through the evocation of this imperial
romance, the author affiliates himself with an *ethos* and a *theoria*, two pre-
conditions for even the most fundamental form of self-representation
and ethnography.

Now, such an *ethos* and *theoria* might present ideological problems for
Kingsley—the wars that have created the imperial space go against his
pacifist grain—but he is cognizant of the fact that Englishness, confronted by crisis and challenge at home, can be reclaimed only in its glorious past, however unpalatable that past might be:

However we may deplore those old wars as unnecessary; however
much we may hate war in itself, as perhaps the worst of all the super-
fluous curses with which man continues to deface himself and this
fair earth of God, yet one must be less than Englishman, less, it may
be, than man, if one does not feel a thrill of pride at entering waters
where one says to oneself,—Here Rodney, on the glorious 12th of
April, 1792, broke Count de Grasse's line . . . thus saving Jamaica and

the whole West Indies, and brought about by that single tremendous blow the honourable peace of 1783. (44)

The essence of Englishness—and, alas, masculinity—is predicated on a certain affiliation with the romantic history of empire. But the romance of empire, like the masculine identities that it valorizes, is driven by anxieties about its own efficacy. Indeed, one could argue that imperial history must always be conceived as romantic as a compensation for its tragic acts and consequences; as Kingsley knows only too well, the colonized space is also the depository of collective anxieties about the past. He knows that "a dark shadow hangs over all this beauty; and the air—even in the clearest blaze of sunshine—is full of ghosts" (43); he also knows that in the current situation, in which the islands are misused and neglected, there is no romance to counter the social and cultural decay (43). Kingsley's evocation of history is hence an attempt to counter present weariness with past valor (43–44), to compensate what many commentators see as post-emancipation decline with the nostalgia of older narratives of conquest and possession.

But there is another way of discussing the evocation of history and historicity in the narrative of travel: it is in the act of temporizing the imperial landscape—and of allegorizing its romantic history—that the traveler can address, in the words of Lisa Lowe, "national anxieties about maintaining hegemony in an age of rapidly changing boundaries and territories."[37] For if, as we saw at the beginning of this chapter, Anthony Froude opens *The English in the West Indies* by drawing our attention to the crisis of culture that has gripped the imperial center, he is eager to counter the resulting angst with the romance of English naval history, carefully recast in the Odysseus myth: "If ever the naval exploits of this country are done in an epic poem—and since the Iliad there has not been a subject better fitted for such treatment or deserving it—the West Indies will be the scene of the most brilliant cantos" (10). The restaging of the epic history of empire serves two functions in the colonial narrative of travel: it is a performative celebration of imperial history that is clearly intended to counter the crisis of culture and society that has gripped mid-Victorian England; at the same time, it enables the authors to support their claim that the value of the West Indies, and of empire in general, cannot be adjudicated in market terms because these possessions are, above everything else, spiritual and historical markers, bearers of what Froude calls "the feelings with which great nations always treasure the heroic traditions of their father" (10).

In this context, Froude's allegorization of the sea—"the sea which is eternally young, and gives one back one's own youth and buoyancy" (19)— is an attempt to recover a past beyond utilitarianism and use-value. Against the present state of what he calls "lamentations," Froude commemorates "the brilliant period of past West Indian history" (26), which is by his calculations nothing less than the history of the English in the West Indies, a white and male history in which the islands function as the designated depositories of national memory and romance. When he reflects on the West Indian landscape, then, what Froude sees is not the native Arawak or Carib cultures, or the social formations instituted by African slaves or Indian indentured laborers, but the historical spaces in which the triumphant moments of Englishness were played out; his gaze is directed at "a shadowy procession of great figures who have printed their names in history" (27). Within the parameters established by the romance of imperial history, the West Indian islands have value primarily in relation to the great drama of empire. Writing about the West Indies is, first and foremost, a restaging of the imperial spectacle: "Adventurers, buccaneers, pirates pass across the stage—the curtain falls on them, and rises on a more glorious scene. Jamaica had become the depot of the trade of England with the Western world, and golden streams had poured into Port Royal" (30).

It is in the author's staging of the imperial spectacle that the character of Englishness emerges in its most defining and refined moments. In recounting Rodney's monumental struggle with the French, for example, he enthralls his readers with both a famous naval battle and a world historical character—an Englishman—who seizes the times because "his country's fate is in his hands" (33). The value of the place to be visited is, consequently, determined by its role as the staging of the imperial romance: Froude is eager to visit Dominica, he tells us, because "it was the scene of Rodney's great fight on April 12. It was the most beautiful of the Antilles and the least known" (129). For Froude, the beauty of Dominica—and indeed its historical significance—cannot be dissociated from Rodney's victories against the French. In other words, the value of the island depends not on what it really is—a minor player in the imperial economy—but on its positionality in the semiotics of English patriotism and what it tells us about the present state of England: "I was anxious to learn what we had made of a place which we had fought so hard for," Froude confesses (130).

Because Froude presents Dominica as a stage on which Englishmen have played out the destiny of their country and, through their words and acts, valorized the essential character of Englishness, his visit to the island is both a return to the romance of the past and a confirmation of contemporary incapacity: "England has done nothing, absolutely nothing, to introduce her own civilization; and thus Dominica is English in name only," he laments (145). Thus the narrative of travel assumes a temporal disjunction between England, as a site of crisis, and the West Indies, as a monument to the glories of empire. Located in this disjunctive moment, the traveler can measure the character of the English nation in crisis against the romance of "pure" imperialism.

The Racial Economy of Travel

But it is when we turn to the representation of black subjects in the imperial narrative of travel that we begin to understand the ways in which the emplacement of the domestic subject in the space of the other is ultimately a showcase for Englishness itself.[38] For it is in the representation of this subject that travel narratives affirm the metaphors and metonyms that inform English identity. In other words, the valorization of the black other—as either a savage or a utopian figure—provides the mirror in which Englishness reflects on its own identity and the potential threat to the givenness of its social and cultural construct. The ideals that define nineteenth-century Englishness—a patriarchal domestic space, a harmonious social order, and psychological restraint—cannot be conceived except in what Michel-Rolph Trouillot has called the "savage slot" against which order at home and utopian impulses sought abroad are measured and contrasted but always linked as dyads in the same paradigm.[39]

But to retain its pure character, the domestic space must, nevertheless, be conceived as ontologically different from its colonial possessions. It is not by accident, then, that writers like Trollope, though English to the core, decry the transplantation of English culture to the colonies: Jamaican planters are ridiculed for leading the lives of country gentlemen while cane and sugar, their "ugly and by no means savory appurtenances," are located "somewhere out of sight" (31); in the midst of the delicacy provided by "native production," their lives seem incomplete "unless they have something from England," Trollope notes with scorn (32). As we have already observed, ironic discourse allows Trollope to promote what appears to be a divided or contradictory perspective on the relation between self and other: the representation of the West Indies is, on the one hand, intended to provide a mirror in which we can understand the state of the empire as the union of center and margin; on the other hand, however, the authority and desirability of Englishness depends on a systematic differentiation of domestic and colonial spaces.

We need, in fact, to stress that while touring the West Indies might provide respite to the crisis at home, the colonial locality is never considered to be a cultural supplement for the domestic realm. The spectacular—and specular—representation of black figures is here, as in Carlyle's discourse, intended to underscore the "natural" differences that separate the two realms of empire. These representations must be read as specular because, as I noted earlier, their primary function is performative and their desired result is affective—blackness is, even in simple metaphological terms, the mark of radical difference. A case in point: Trollope is barely two hours in Jamaica when he is struck by "a negro of exceeding blackness"—"I do not know that I ever saw skin so purely black," he says (16). A little later, writing on the place of black men in colonial society, he cannot help but comment on the visual presence of blackness: "To an Englishman who has never lived in a slave country, or in a country in which slavery once prevailed, the negro population is of course the most striking feature of the West Indies" (42). To his credit, Trollope goes on to note that one soon gets used to "the black skin and the thick lip" and that within a week "the novelty is gone," but still his commentary on the somatic force of alterity is apt because it points to the important ways in which a certain epistemology of blackness generates the imperial aesthetic.

Simply put, blacks can be processed and controlled when they are turned into ethnoerotic objects.[40] They are visualized as objects that are simultaneously attractive and repulsive, different from established cultural norms but at the same time belonging to the human family. Jamaican Creoles, notes Trollope, are a strange race because they lack the norms that define a community: "They have not hitherto any country of their adoption. . . . They have no language of their own, nor have they as yet any language of their adoption. . . . They have no idea of country, and no pride of race; for even among themselves, the word 'nigger' conveys their worst term of reproach" (42). But this gesture of sociological distanciation is not unequivocal, for although the colonial subject is deprived of the key ingredients of civil society, it cannot be banished completely from the human community; to do so would deny this subject its ethnographic function in imperial discourse. Thus, when Trollope says of black Creoles in Jamaica, "There is no race which has more strongly developed its own physical aptitudes and inaptitudes, its own habits, its own tastes, and its own faults" (42), he is conceding the colonial subject some form of civility, albeit in its more primitive state.

Is the doubleness implicit in the discourse of the other a calculated strategy or an arbitrary form of representation? Trollope balances his sense of the Creoles' aptitude and civility with a stern rendering of their faults; and, significantly, the stress here is not on the Africans' ability to evolve a new culture in exile but on their failure to master "white civilization," which they now imitate "as a monkey does a man" (43). And thus we read the Creole as a subject that exists simultaneously outside the norms defined by Englishness (which they can only imitate) and outside the savage spaces of their African ancestry. In their liminality, these subjects are close to white civilization, but not close enough.[41]

Compared to Carlyle, of course, Trollope's representation of the West Indies is a model of restraint: he deliberately avoids figures of demonization, and rarely do his observations and experiences fail to focus on some of the positive qualities of the blacks he encounters. But when it comes to fundamental matters of doctrine, or when he turns to volatile questions on the black ontology, Trollope's experiences in the field do not seem to prompt him to question or revert inherited theories; on the contrary, going elsewhere seems to reinforce these theories. Consider, for example, the relation of blacks to Victorian doctrines of labor and vocation: Trollope describes blacks as "capable of the hardest bodily work" but also as "idle, unambitious as to worldly position, sensual, and content with little" (43). As for the blacks' intellectual capacities, Trollope is sure they cannot reason; although he will not subscribe to the common belief that the black is "without mental power," he is certain that "he seldom understands the purpose of industry, the object of truth, or the result of honesty" (43).

Why is it that even when observed experiences provide an imperative for the author to reject inherited doctrines, he always seems to retreat from such experiences and fall back on the theoretical discourse he has inherited from Victorian anthropology?

The most obvious answer is that Trollope is a product of his times, that while the thrust of his travel narrative, especially the dialectic of irony that informs it, might suggest that going elsewhere is the epistemological quest for a position outside the given, he cannot escape from a hegemonic discourse that assumes the superiority of English culture and civilization. And thus the grammar he uses to represent black figures reeks of most of the "gatekeeping concepts" of evolutionism; his basic assumption is that whatever its strivings might be, the black subject is already delimited by its position in the great chain of being (42–47). This assumption leads to a second explanation for Trollope's inability to abandon inherited beliefs when observed experiences seem to militate against them: the representation of blacks as visual objects is here determined, as in the case of Carlyle and Mill, by the debate on the condition of England rather than by any desire to develop new knowledge about West Indians. Thus, while Trollope's observations and experience of blacks—and indeed his relations with them—are apparently sympathetic, his conceptual encounter with them is limited by what Fabian calls "intellectual and social prejudice":[42] the representation and categorization of colonial alterity is dictated by the topos of difference, which entails, in turn, a hierarchical relation in which white intellect and authority are mirrored through black deficiency.

For this reason, though Trollope's blacks are not overtly demonized, they are clearly pigeonholed in a familiar schema: they can be taught to "observe" and "often read," but they can "seldom reason"; they embrace religion fervently, but we have to doubt "whether religion does often reach their minds" (44); and, ultimately, we have to be convinced that in "many respects the negro's phase of humanity differs much from that which is common to us, and which has been produced by our admixture of blood and our present extent of civilization. They are more passionate than the white men, but rarely vindicative, as we are" (45). From such examples, we can conclude that Trollope deploys a familiar racial topography and the rhetoric of difference that defines it. But we need to go beyond this habitual discursive mode and focus attention on the ways in which Trollope, like many imperial travelers, represents black difference in order to secure "whiteness" as a category that unifies different European nationalities, cultures, and classes. If we take Trollope's case to be exemplary here, we could argue that it is in their conceptual encounter with the other that the imperial travelers reinforce evolutionary thinking, the emergent paradigm in English social science.

But there is a second way in which domestic imperatives determine the economy of the narrative of travel: Trollope's keen sense of black life in the West Indies is secondary to his need to recognize—but also (conceptually) reorganize—the other as a political object in a domestic debate that is both about the condition of England in a time of crisis and about her dominant position on the evolutionary tree of human life. Trollope satirizes the "friend of the negro" who has embarked on the task of rescuing "his black brother from the degradation of an inferior species"; he mocks those who, by attempting to raise blacks "up at once with the glories of civilization round [their heads]," work against God's purpose, which "has created men of inferior and superior race" (46–47). In such moments, Trollope's travels and observations in the West Indies have inevitably returned him to the dominant (theoretical) position back home. As he notes,

> my theory—for I acknowledge a theory—is this: that Providence has sent white men and black men to these regions in order that from them may spring a race fitted by intellect for civilization; and fitted also by physical organization for tropical labour. The negro in his primitive state is not, I think, fitted for the former; and the European white Creole is certainly not fitted for the latter. (57)

Another important example of the way in which domestic imperatives come to provide the prism through which the colonial subject is represented is the constant image of the black as a subject alienated from labor and the cognitive value of work. This problem is remarkable for the way it moves from narrative to narrative without any obvious revision. Consider then, that for Trollope—as for Carlyle—there is an explicit connection between labor and the idea of progress, property, and even propriety: "Without a desire for property, man could make no progress. But the negro has no such desire; no desire strong enough to induce him to labour for that which he wants. In order that he may eat today and be clothed tomorrow, he will work a little; as for anything beyond that, he is content to lie in the sun" (47). The black's inferiority is marked by his or her inability to desire property and master surplus value. A similar assumption underlies Kingsley's belief that the black can only "exert himself when he really needs to do so" (142). Not unexpectedly, the figure of black subjects without concepts of work and property finds its most Carlylean articulation in Froude's portrait of free blacks in Grenada, men and women who have regressed to living off the natural environment, reproducing "as near as possible the life in Paradise of our first parents, without the consciousness of a want which they are unable to gratify, not compelled to work, for the earth of her own self bears for them all that they need, and ignorant that there is any difference between moral good and evil" (73). In spite of the contentious debates that surround the place of the West Indies in the domestic moral economy, travel to the islands does not seem to change substantially the debate initiated by Carlyle; in spite of the authority endowed by field observations, Trollope, Froude, and Kingsley seem unable to rise beyond the a priori theories that define colonial subjects, especially when it comes to matters of race.

We can understand the conformist character of imperial discourse much better by examining two discursive strategies in Froude's narrative: his tendency to theorize rather than merely represent the West Indies and his fabrication of field observations to fit into an imperial totality. Consider, for example, his much-vaunted "authentic particulars" of West Indians entrapped in atavism:

> The curse is taken off nature, and like Adam again they are under the covenant of innocence. Morals in the technical sense they have none, but they cannot be said to sin, because they have no knowledge of a law, and therefore they can commit no breach of the law. They are naked and not ashamed. (49)

Two rhetorical strategies are obvious in this representative description: first, there is the inevitable association of the black body and nature—the other exists in a world before sin or the law, beyond self-consciousness and morality; second, the author takes it for granted that the theory that animates his description—the theory of black alterity—is universally shared by his audience. So, though Trollope and Kingsley at least pretend that their theories might be amenable to change in the face of their experiences in the West Indies, Froude's narrative is already delimited by an authoritarian moral—and hence theoretical—premise that cannot countenance any challenge to its established mode of knowledge.

But whatever the tone each author adopts in the representation of a colonial other at variance with the governing codes of English civility, what we have are narratives in which the ethnographic act—the gesture of travel, learning, and discovery—is sublimated to imperial fantasies, desires, and anxieties. The black woman is a particularly revealing site for such desires and anxieties: her body is the standard conceptualization of the strangeness of the other, the doubleness of its attraction and revulsion; as the most radical figure of alterity, the black woman is the space in which theories of blackness are constituted and reformulated. It is not by accident, then, that Trollope's narrative encounters the West Indies first and foremost in the figure of a woman, which is also a form of specularized blackness: "I landed at St. Thomas, where we lay for some hours; and as I put my foot on the tropical soil for the first time, a lady handed me a rose, saying, 'That's for love, dear. . . . Yes, it shall be for love; for thee and thine, if I can find that thou deservest it.' What was it to me that she was as black as my boot, or that she had come back to look after the ship's washing?" (6).

Trollope's narrative is replete with such scenes of flirtation and possible seduction (24–26), even eroticism (53); his only gripping descriptions are those in which an island is represented as a figure of latent male desire:

To my mind, Dominica, as seen from the sea, is by far the most picturesque of all these islands. Indeed, it would be difficult to beat it either in colour or grouping. It fills one with an ardent desire to be off and ramble among those green mountains—as if one could through such wild, bush country, or ramble at all with the thermometer at 85. But when one has only to think of such things without any idea of doing them, neither the bushes nor the thermometer are considered. (121)

What we have here is a surrogated representation of the field of (sexual) fantasy, the field in which Trollope engages with black women. For while

Trollope often associates the black woman with what he considers to be extreme forms of blackness ("I shall never forget that big black chamber-maid"[132]), he also represents her as the clandestine figure of a certain white male desire for the feminized black other. But the representation of the relation between the white male traveler and the black native woman has to be surrogated in the landscape because his desire for her cannot be consummated. It can only be projected onto the natural landscape, which, as we have already noted, is feminized.

Alternatively, the black woman's body provides the travelers with a metaphor through which they can concretize their conjectures about the other. For writers like Kingsley, for example, the "average Negro women in Port of Spain" is a shocking figuration of black difference even in a Westernized metropolis: "Their masculine figures, their ungainly gestures, their loud and sudden laughter, even when walking alone, and their general coarseness, shocks, and must shock" (88). But such images of black women are not merely intended to embody the radical alterity of colonial subjects; they are important strategies in the discourse of Englishness and the condition of England, for what makes black women so striking to these authors is that—even as stereotypes and fetishes—they are "naturally" posited against the Victorian doxology on women.

Thus, when we read the travelers' representation of black women as powerful and independent, and when we try to sort out where their disdain ends and their desire begins, we are also encountering their own ambivalence toward the politics of gender in Victorian England. Thus, even as he mocks the freedom of West Indian women—"young ladies flirt, as they dance and play, or eat and drink, quite as a matter of course" (126)—Trollope cannot help comparing their freedom to the imprisonment of "some of our starched people at home"; in this contrastive mode (and mood) he cannot condemn this flirtation as immoral, nor can he conceal his enjoyment of its manifestations (127). Kingsley might be troubled by the power and influence of black women—and their "masculinity"—but their presence always forces him to reflect on the condition of the imprisoned Victorian woman: "The Negro women are, without doubt, on a more thorough footing of equality with the men than the women of any white race," he notes (32).

Such contrastive moments are excellent examples of a critique of Victorian society that the travelers never realize. In other words, while my argument in this chapter has been that the colonial space provides the imperial traveler with a mirror for visualizing Englishness, there are many instances in which this same space provides opportunities for a sustained critique of the domestic space. Indeed, the examples I have cited would seem to confirm Bhabha's assertion that the colonial subject is "constructed within an apparatus of power which contains, in both senses of the word, an 'other' knowledge—a knowledge that is arrested and fetishistic and circulates through colonial discourse as that limited form of Otherness, that fixed form of difference, that I have called the stereotype."[43]

As one sees in J. J. Thomas's *Froudacity* and its counter-discursive strategies contra Froude—to cite just one common example—an alternative articulation of the colonial subject arises from the slippages inherent in what would appear to be the totalized apparatus of imperial discourse.[44] The questions I want to pose here, though, relate to the retardation of this "other knowledge" in the colonial text itself. Why is the oppositional perspective always silenced in these texts, even as it is hinted at? Why is it that narratives of travel that start with different motives for touring—and hence divergent ideological intentions—seem to converge in their systematization of alterity and their management of the other?[45]

I can best respond to these questions by restating my basic premise in this chapter: underneath most imperial narratives of travel is the epistemological desire to articulate a point of counter-distinction against which English identity can be measured; in its many manifestations, then, the West Indies functions as an alter ego for Englishness. Nothing dramatizes the travelers' desire for a counteractive savage space better than our travelers' engagement with Haiti—a place that English travelers feel impelled to visit (in reality or in their imagination) even though the black republic is not on their itinerary or within the orbit of Englishness. For if the West Indies as a whole functions as a heterotopia—it makes the cultural spaces of Englishness real and attractive through contrast—Haiti is "the savage slot" that enhances the utopian possibilities of the domestic epos.[46] As a radical site of alterity, Haiti is the spectral metaphor of blackness—an imminent threat to the idea of Englishness; against the metropole's idea of order and civilization, the black republic stands as the embodiment of chaos and disorder (figure 3.2).

When Trollope encounters Soulouque, the exiled Haitian monarch in Jamaica, for example, he is quick to note that the king is "a black man. One

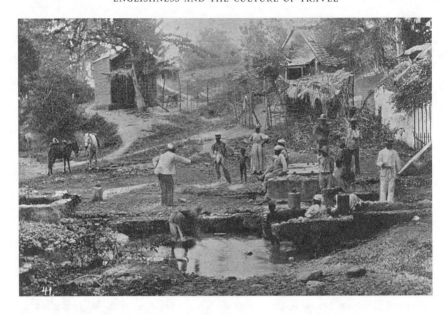

FIGURE 3.2.
Reading Haiti, a scene from Hesketh Prichard's *Where Black Rules White* (1900).

blacker never endured the meridian heat of a tropical sun" (86). The metaphology of blackness attracts Trollope because, as we have already seen, it embodies the dark and unknown forces evoked by Haiti. Such forces can either be represented through a farce that might militate against the threat Haiti poses to Englishness, as in Trollope (90), or it might (in Kingsley) be left simply unspoken. Indeed, Kingsley's strategy, as he reflects on the magical practices that threaten Christianity in Haiti, is to refuse to name such forces in public lest they excite disgust in the "civilized world": "But of Haiti I shall be silent; having heard more of the state of society in that unhappy place than it is prudent, for the sake of the few white residents, to tell at present" (291).

The mediation of the radical other through an iterative discourse that replays its figures of savagery and difference is ultimately connected to questions of power and representation. For as Froude constantly reminds his readers, what is at stake in the whole debate on the West Indian question, both at home and abroad, is whether the islands can function as a space in which (a) "the influence of the English race in their special capac-

ity of leaders and governors of men" can be extended or (b) black subjects will be allowed to govern, and thus represent themselves. Froude's
response to these questions is already apparent in his presuppositions: governance cannot be effected outside the assumption of racial superiority
and the civilizational authority of Englishness—"The English have
proved in India that they can play a great and useful part as rulers over recognized inferiors" (97). As to the idea of black governance, "the state of
Hayti stands as a ghastly example of the condition into which they will
then inevitably fall" (81). As for the future, we need only to look at Haiti
to see what the West Indies will become without the moral authority and
governance represented by Englishness: "The African Obeah, the worship
of serpents and trees and stone, after smouldering in all the West Indies
in the form of witchcraft and poisoning, had broken out in Hayti in all
its old hideousness" (126). For all three travelers, then, the civilizational
authority of Englishness is secured by the horrific backdrop of the Haitian dystopia.

But I am not calling attention to these moments of ideological conjuncture to support the claim that imperial discourse is either uniform or
hopelessly imprisoned in its intellectual tradition; I'm not even trying to
support the claim that this discourse, since it is a mechanism of European
power over the other, cannot fulfill an insurgent function or proffer spaces
of resistance. While there is a lot to be said, one way or the other, for the
controversies surrounding Edward Said's notion of a totalized or essentialized Orientalism, I want to argue that it is not enough to label colonial
discourses as purely instruments of power or, conversely, as discursive formations informed by some measure of colonial insurgency.[47] My primary
focus is how this discourse tries to fulfill different functions at the same
time; how it functions as a critique of its conditions of possibility but
affirms those conditions in the process; how it valorizes the field of observation as a source of reexamining the relations that govern the colonizer
and the colonized but ends up affirming the Carlylean dogma and its
desire to manage blacks as what Fabian calls political and scientific
objects.[48]

For however much we may want to individualize the diverse narratives
of imperial travel that we have inherited from the nineteenth century, we
have to concede their theoretical unanimity: they are already animated by
existing themes and delimited by discursive regulations that precede travel.

It is certainly important to note that Trollope goes to the West Indies without any prior intentions of writing down his "purposeless wanderings" (6), but he does end up writing a narrative that confirms existing conventions of travel and important theories about the relation between metropole and colony.

And when we look closely at Kingsley's ideological modulations, we read a startling example of what I consider to be the inherent circularity of imperial discourse: the writer goes to the West Indies as a man of largely liberal and Christian sympathies and, as we saw earlier, reads the Caribbean landscape for evidence of a benevolent nature; but he finds it difficult to reconcile his theological perspective, his observations in the field, and his intellectual inheritance. On the question of labor, for example, Kingsley is a strong advocate of emancipation and the establishment of "a moral bond" between employers and employees (118–19); but he also supports the strict control and regulation of indentured Indians because such surveillance "has been found necessary, in order to protect the Coolies both from themselves and from each other" (118).

But the necessity of such regulation in Kingsley's discourse does not arise from his field observation of Indian laborers, or the slightest attention to their views or perspective; rather, the traveler reaches his conclusions from three mutually informing sources—official reports (both oral and written), intellectual Orientalism, and evolutionary doctrines. Kingsley's reliance on official sources is evident in that he is a guest of the governor of Trinidad (to whom his travelogue will be dedicated) and that we rarely hear him listening to any "subaltern" voices. When he comes to represent such voices, then, he relies on an Orientalist discourse that precedes his tour, a discourse in which the romance of the East is carefully balanced by its vices: the Indians have brought thrift and industry to the West Indies, and they are the "surplus of one of the oldest civilizations of the old world" (121–22), but they are also prone to usury and "over-early marriage" which is "a serious evil" (233). Evolutionism may be the silent paradigm in Kingsley's discourse, but it is manifested in the racial hierarchy that underlies his globalized racial tropes: for even as he observes the ways in which the peoples of the West Indies are brought together by "organized nature" and the will of Providence, Kingsley assumes that the white Creoles sit on top of the evolutionary ladder, well above the Indians who, in turn, sit above the blacks whose primary property is their physical form (173).

As for Froude, the end of the journey becomes a metacritical moment. While he had promised us that the purpose of his tour was to acquaint himself with the real condition of the islands, Froude's pronouncements at the moment of return, like most of the views enunciated in the course of the journey, are generated not by field experiences or observation but by "a loyal pride in the greatness of my own country, and a conviction, which I will not believe to be a dream, that the destinies have still in store for her a yet grander future" (365). So the ethnographic imperative in the narrative of travel is eventually subsumed by the need to conserve the discursive field and to affirm the essential and organic nature of Englishness. An excellent example of this circularity can be found in Froude's relation to the Governor Eyre affair: before he left England for the West Indies, the historian thought that "Mr. Eyre had been unworthily sacrificed to public clamour"; the view he brings back from Jamaica is "the same in essentials, though qualified by clearer perceptions of the real nature of the situation" (257). And thus touring becomes a form of retour: opinions formed before the commencement of the voyage are not dissipated by experience; on the contrary, they are authorized by the weight of personal observations.

But if everything out there is already known and taxonomized, why bother to travel at all? If the moment of closure confirms opinions, concepts, and categories held by the traveler before he set out on his voyage, the journey itself would appear to be gratuitous. But it is important to remember that journeys that began with anxieties about the metropole—and Froude's narrative is exemplary here—end with a sublime affirmation of the sites of Englishness. The journey to the reaches of empire confers a certain enunciative authority on the traveler, an authority that is important because these narratives are ultimately addressed to the domestic audience, which is reminded, in the midst of doubts about English identity and destiny, that the alternatives to civilization and progress are barbarism abroad and decay at home.

While Froude may claim that he writes as "an outside observer unconnected with practical politics, with no motive except a loyal pride in the greatness of my own country" (364), his narrative is a self-willed intervention into the debates on the future of England and empire. It is precisely this disclaimer of political affiliation that enhances Froude's authority on the moment of return: the discourse of travel is now shown to be a discourse generated by the writer's unconditional love for the domestic space. Contrasted with what lies out there—what we have already seen of the black apparitional—we have to agree with the narrator that there is no alternative to the domestic epos. But as I have observed, the unanimity assumed by the imperial voice is achieved through the containment of what we may call colonial dissent.

⊰ 4 ⊱

Imperial Femininity: Reading Gender in the Culture of Colonialism

> When the other speaks, he or she becomes another subject, which must be consciously registered as a problem by the imperial or metropolitan subject.
>
> Fredric Jameson, "Modernism and Imperialism"

> We are deeply interested in the topological deconstruction of masculinist universalism. But when questions of the inscription of feminine subjectivity arise, we do not want to be caught within the institutional performance of the imperialist lie.
>
> Gayatri Chakravorty Spivak, "Imperialism and Sexual Difference"

I cannot read Mary Seacole's *Wonderful Adventures of Mrs. Seacole in Many Lands*, an autobiographical account of a black woman's journey through the landscape of empire, without recalling Raymond Williams's memorable introduction to *The English Novel: From Dickens to Lawrence*:

I keep thinking about those twenty months, in 1847 and 1848, in which these novels were published: *Dombey and Son*, *Wuthering Heights*, *Vanity Fair*, *Jane Eyre*, *Mary Burton*, *Trancred*, *Town and Country*, *The Tenant of Wildfell Hall*.

What was it just then that emerged in England? It was of course no sudden process of just a few months. But we can see, looking back, those months as decisive. The English novel before then had its major achievements; it had Defoe and Fielding, Richardson and Jane Austen and Walter Scott. But now in the 1840s it had a new and major *generation*. For the next eighty years the novel was to be the major form in English literature. And this was unprecedented. What these months seem to make above all is a new kind of consciousness, and we have to learn to see what this is, and some ways of relating it to the new and unprecedented civilisation in which it took shape.[1]

It would perhaps have been too much to ask Williams to have included Seacole's work in this gallery of major English narratives produced in mid-century; after all, *Wonderful Adventures*, though located in the 1840s, was not published until 1857. And even if the book had been published during the great decade of the English novel, it most likely could not have entered the literary canon, not so much because this kind of narrative would have been considered as lacking in value or merit but simply because colonial subjects like Mary Seacole were not considered to be English. The connection between Williams's magisterial reading of the genealogy of the English novel and Seacole's narrative lies elsewhere—in the culture of colonialism. For the most distinguishing event in the unprecedented civilization that produced the great English novel was the colonial culture that would connect, let's say, Charlotte Brontë's *Jane Eyre* and *Wonderful Adventures*. The Thornton Hall of Jane Eyre is connected, through the figure of Bertha Mason, to Mary Seacole's West Indies.

This is not the place to raise the question of Williams's blindness to such colonial moments. This topic has been dealt with exhaustively by such post-colonial scholars as Gauri Viswanathan.[2] What interests me in the above passage is the uncanny way in which Seacole's text, like the great novels of the 1840s, was produced on the cusp that both joined and separated metropole and colony (discussed in my introductory chapter) and under the pressures of a new kind of consciousness, which demanded a different type of narrative of English identity. For what was ultimately responsible for the production of both metropolitan and colonial texts in the eventful 1840s was, as Williams recognized, the crisis of community. And while Williams has explained this crisis purely in terms of domestic events—most notably a "powerful and transforming urban and industrial civilisation"—we now know that colonialism was the one major event that called prior relationships into question and generated the split that took place between "knowable relationships and an unknown, unknowable, overwhelming society."[3]

In the great novels of the 1840s, as numerous critical studies have shown, figures associated one way or the other with colonial alterity had come to represent the unknown, unknowable—and hence overwhelming—force that called into question what Terry Eagleton has termed the "seamless evolutionary continuum" that was supposed to endow English social institutions with the "stolid inevitability of a boulder" and turn society into "a marvellous aesthetic organism, self-generating and self-contained."[4] It is not an accident, however, that the great novels of this period were produced by women, or that gender was to function as the dyad through which the crisis of the knowable community was mediated. For if colonialism was the key paradigm for representing and understanding the new community, and if the crisis of identity in this period arose from the displacement of the myth of Englishness as an organic continuum, then women were ideally placed to understand the ways in which alterity was constitutive of identity, of how the narrative of order and civility was predicated on the disorder and excess excluded from the big houses of Englishness such as Mansfield Park or Thornfield.[5] It was because of their liminality in the culture of empire that women writers came to read colonialism as both threat and possibility: it was a threat because it was a patriarchal affair in which women were excluded in the name of a stifling domestic ideology; it was an opportunity because it destabilized the very categories in which this ideology was formulated.[6] And thus the central questions here are how modes of alterity serve as gateways to identity and how inherited cultural formations become forms of alienation.

In considering how the other speaks within the perimeters established by the culture of colonialism, however, the more immediate problem is not simply how to deconstruct imperial masculinity but how to read the oppositional moment already implicit in the discourse of imperial power and expansion. Yet how does one read an oppositional discourse that derives its authority and identity from the institution of empire and imperial practices? How, for example, does one read colonial subjects and white women in the service of empire but outside its hegemonic field? The truth is, students of colonial discourse and postcolonial theory do not know what to do with the women of empire—whether these women are European or native. They don't know how to read them within the project of the Enlightenment and colonial modernity, nor do they know how to explain or rationalize female subjectivity and institutional function beyond the existence of women as objects of male discourse or desire.

Often seeking to align themselves with poststructuralism and postmodern theory, postcolonial theorists find it easier to talk about women in the colonial project as intercessors of a homosocial relation—a process of male exchange or struggle in which both black and white women are deployed as the mediators of racial anxieties or objects of fantasies and desires—rather than subjects in their own right.[7]

Reading the feminine in the culture of colonialism, then, is a project driven by a paradox. We want to read woman as the absolute other in the colonial relation so that we can unpack the universalism of the imperial narrative and its masculine ideologies, but the result (positing white women as figures of colonial alterity, for example) can be achieved only through the repression of their cultural agency and the important role they play in the institutionalization of the dominant discourse of empire and the authority of colonial culture. In addition, when we try to discuss women as constitutive elements of the high imperial norm, we encounter a set of ideological and interpretative problems that are the effect of both the inscription of feminine subjectivities in the culture of colonialism and our own reading preferences. How, for example, do we read the colonial experiences of such women as Mary Seacole or the English ethnographer Mary Kingsley, who seem to write their narratives—and their identities—in the service of empire even when they exist at its margins? Do we praise them for rising beyond domestic confinement and finding new opportunities in the colonial frontier, or do we condemn them for failing to transcend (male) ideologies of empire, including those of racial and caste superiority?

There is, of course, ample evidence to show that English women were actively involved in the project of colonialism and saw the imperial enterprise as constitutive of their own agency and identity; but we also know that most of the women involved in the politics and culture of colonialism related to it in different ways than their male counterparts did. After all, if empire seemed to be overly masculinized, it was to provide a point of contradistinction between men's work and female domesticity. Indeed, the Manichaean division between masculinity on the colonial frontier and demure femininity at home was crucial to the sustenance of the fiction of Englishness in the Victorian period. Women who found themselves in the field of empire were traveling in a forbidden space; but precisely because it was exclusionary, the colonial frontier promised female subjects new modes of subjectivity.

In any case, the ambivalent location of women in the colonial economy of representation has created what has come to be known as the "complicity/resistance" dialectic, a schema whose primary goal is to show how women saw empire as an opportunity for freedom and advancement but found it impossible, given their own subordinate positions in the domestic economy, to unconditionally valorize the imperial voice.[8] Much of the critical writing that seems to grow out of this dialectic is, however, constrained by its own anxieties: the desire to reclaim imperial women as subjects who had managed to challenge Victorian gender norms, and to break away from national ideologies that imprisoned women in domesticity, is haunted by the fear that by valorizing the positive function of empire in the constitution of female subjectivity, we might mitigate the ideologies of white supremacy embedded in the theory and practice of imperialism. For how does one argue that such a terrible undertaking as imperialism could also function as the avenue for new subjectivities or that it could lead to a reconfiguration of gender relations in the nineteenth century? Mainstream feminism, as Gayatri Chakravorty Spivak has complained, has not found a way out of this dilemma.[9] But is there a way out—or is the dilemma a theoretical cauldron whose meaning lies in its intractability?

We can respond to this problem in either of two ways: We can argue, for example, that the women of empire did not conceive the colonial mission as a terrible undertaking—the source of modern guilt—but instead viewed it as the only real alternative to domestic imprisonment. We can then conclude, with Spivak, that the "active ideology of imperialism" provided the "discursive field" in which feminist individualism was produced; and that what Mary Poovey calls the "individualizing elaboration of subjectivity" in the 1840s and after was facilitated by the colonial mission.[10] If we accept this premise, however, we must insist on reading women's narratives, within the culture of colonialism, as instrumental in the changing discourse on colonial spaces and, by extension, the role of women in the domestic realm. And while this feminine intervention into the imperial discursive economy cannot be read as uniformly oppositional, it must, nevertheless, be seen as reconstitutive of its objects of reflection—the European woman in the colonial space and the natives she represents.

In addition, as Sara Mills has noted, the limitation imposed on imperial women writers by colonialism should be read not as a barrier to their self-inscription but as "discursively productive, in that these constraints enable a form of writing whose contours both disclose the nature of the dominant discourses and constitute a critique from its margins."[11] As I suggested at the beginning of this chapter, the great women novelists of the 1840s were the products of such constraints, which were, however, also the source of the transgressiveness that Williams confused for passion.

A second way around the "complicity/resistance" dialectic is to argue that the location of imperial women, both inside and outside the parameters established by colonialism, parallels the identities of those colonial subjects who had been constituted by the culture of empire and often identified with its goals even when they criticized its discriminatory practices. We have to remember, in this regard, that when we talk about the women of empire—or colonial subjects in general—our subject is both the colonizer and the colonized, different groups of people written into the European narrative in asymmetrical—but sometimes identical—ways. Reading woman in the culture of colonialism and in the service of empire demands, then, that we renounce the binary opposition—between self and other—promoted by the dominant (masculinist) narrative and see imperial femininity as an invitation to us to read colonialism's culture in its contradictions and complicities, as a chiasmus in which the polarities that define domination and subordination shift with localities, genders, cultures, and even periods. We will be returning to this chiasmus often in this chapter.

My first concern here, however, is the inscription of the colonial female subject in the imperial economy of representation and the question that this subject raises: Is the female colonial subject the absolute figure of alterity encountered in masculinist discourses, a stereotype (defined by Bhabha as the fetishized and fixed "form of difference"), or a free agent staging its consciousness of freedom within the limits imposed by imperialism?[12] Are we to read these women, as they are represented in colonial discourse, as fixed or as constantly shifting?

Consider, for example, the following juxtaposition of Mary Seacole and black servants in Trollope's travelogue, discussed in the previous chapter:

I took up my abode at Blundle Hall, and found that the landlady in whose custody I had placed myself was a sister of the good Mrs. Seacole. "My sister wanted to go to India," said my landlady, "with the army, you know. But Queen Victoria would not let her; her life was too precious." So that Mrs. Seacole is a prophet, even in her own country.[13]

And a few moments later we hear:

> At the inns, as at private houses, the household servants are almost
> always black. The manners of these people are to a stranger very
> strange. They are not absolutely uncivil, except on occasions; but
> they have an easy, free, patronizing air.[14]

Here, the presence of Mary Seacole, an important figure in the map of
colonial Englishness, is valorized (through the voice of her sister), only to
be undermined by the uncivil black bodies that haunt Trollope wherever
he goes in the West Indies. The black woman, in the persons of Seacole
and her sister, has a unique identity and agency; but she is also part of an
undifferentiated mass described as strange and uncivil. Thus, if the black
woman is the radical figure of difference in dominant imperial discourse,
as I argued in the last chapter, we need to add that she is a figure that oscil-
lates between agency and identity, between stereotype and fetishism.

The second question, though, concerns how women write themselves as
colonial subjects: do they rise beyond the fixed mode of the fetish to claim
a large measure of agency, and to what extent is their identity shaped by the
integers that define colonial culture itself? To answer this question, I want,
in the rest of this chapter, to bring together the texts of two women of
empire—Mary Seacole's *Wonderful Adventures* and Mary Kingsley's *Travels in
West Africa*—not only to investigate how women were interpellated by imperialism but also to explore some issues that continue to plague many
attempts to psychoanalyze empire and its narratives. What does it mean to
be a colonial subject in the nineteenth century? If my general thesis that the
complicitous relationship between colonial centers and margins is indispensable to understanding Englishness holds, then we have to understand
the nature of this complicity, its points of resistance, and its attempt—and
ultimate failure—to transform its opposition into critique.[15]

Mary Seacole: In and Out of Englishness

Mary Seacole is a "colored Creole" from Jamaica, a product of the culture
of colonialism and a subject of the British empire. These are basic facts.
But they cannot be taken for granted, for the terms that describe her—*colored* and *Creole*—are also appellations that mark her as a particular kind of

colonial subject, a subject constituted within the margins of the imperial system but also privileged within it by circumstances of birth (a Scottish father) and the laws of caste ("colored" Jamaicans occupy an intermediary position between the formerly enslaved African and the white Creole). In these circumstances, Seacole is neither the classical subaltern of colonial discourse nor an insurgent figure of anticolonial resistance.[16] At the same time, however, a colonial subject, even one who seems to celebrate the dominant codes of Englishness, doesn't have the same status or authority as those persons who, because of their race and genealogy, are construed as English to the backbone. There is indeed a sense in which Seacole's life—and the narrative that celebrates this life—is a calculated attempt to affirm her subjectivity and status as an English subject against the dominant culture, which seeks to marginalize or to mock—as Trollope seems to do—her claim to the right of property and propriety within the culture of colonialism.

Between her desire to be accorded the full rights of a British subject and the autochthonous definition of the category of the English nation as exclusive of colonial peoples and cultures, Seacole lives in and out of Englishness, attracted by its culture and civilizational authority but haunted by its exclusive racialism. Indeed, I propose to read her "wonderful adventures" as a discourse generated—and haunted—by the gap that separates her desire for Englishness from the realities of imperial power, the ideologies of a British community overseas, and the claim—or insistence—that the colonized are always marginal to the imperial center. Throughout her narrative, Seacole desires identification with a geographic space—England—that she cannot call home. And if home—the *oikos*—is the travel narrative's point of departure and closure, as we saw in the previous chapter, its difference in Seacole's narrative haunts her subjectivity, and this, in turn, triggers many unacknowledged instances of melancholy in her book.[17]

Simply put, although Seacole comes from an influential—and sometimes powerful—Jamaican Creole culture, she cannot write this natal space as a source of identity because it does not have the same authority as Englishness:

I was born in the town of Kingston, in the island of Jamaica, some time in the present century. As a female and a widow, I may be well excused giving the precise date of this important event. . . . I am a Creole, and have good Scotch blood coursing in my veins. My father was a soldier, of an old Scotch family; and to him I often trace my affection for a camp life; and my sympathy with what I have heard my friends call "the pomp, pride, and circumstance of glorious war." Many people have also traced to my Scotch blood that energy and activity which are not always found in the Creole race, and which have carried me to so many varied scenes; and perhaps they are right. I have often heard the term "lazy Creole" applied to my country people; but I am sure I do not know what it is to be indolent.[18]

While Seacole is certainly proud to be a Creole; she is also aware of the liminal nature of this identity, an identity that seeks to emplace itself between the Manichaean allegory that separates the black and the white in the colonial landscape, the figure that enabled the discourses that I examined in the previous chapter. In spite of this instability, however, Creolity is an important conduit into Englishness, precisely because, as a cultural term that derives from both the African and the British parts of the colonial equation in Jamaica, it can be narrativized as contingent and malleable; it is not fixed by the fetishism of blackness and whiteness inscribed in colonialism's racial taxonomy.

Indeed, Seacole begins with the premise that as a Creole she can turn herself into whatever she wants to be; in fact, I want to argue that writing *Wonderful Adventures* is her ultimate attempt to claim her Englishness: she invites us to read her narrative—and self-portrait—as a form of self-willed entry into the social codes that define the proper Englishwoman (figure 4.1). In addition, because writing is Seacole's strategy for establishing affiliation with her English audience, her narrative tends to emphasize—even overemphasize—her British cultural and genealogical connections. Thus, although many of the skills she deploys as a nurse are learned from her mother and the Creole medicinal tradition, her self-portrait tends to leave the source of her expertise amorphous. This vagueness is matched by a certain kind of brevity when it comes to representing scenes of the author's colonial childhood in Jamaica. Under these circumstances, narration becomes an act of disinvesture, in which maternity and nativity are sublimated to the ideals of an imperial identity—an identity derived, significantly, from the father. At the same time, however, the narrative carries—subconsciously, perhaps—the conflict between Seacole's Jamaican maternity and her desire for the lost Englishness represented by her Scottish father. (As we saw in the introduction, British colonial culture does not allow for the distinctiveness of the Celtic fringe; every Briton is, as a colonizer, also English.) Seacole's desire for Englishness, like all desire, is marked by an absence: for while she turns out to be a strong advocate of Victorian domesticity and femininity, her travels are constantly haunted by the absence of the cultural values that sustain the ideals of the English home.

The most incongruous moments in her narrative, as we will see below, are those in which she celebrates domesticity as the ideal value for a woman in the middle of places, such as the Central American jungle or the Crimean battleground, where women are not supposed to be. This incongruity, however, is crucial to Seacole's project: as a colonial subject, she cannot take values such as home and woman for granted, so she has to continuously reinvent them. As a discourse of identity, then, Seacole's adventures seem to be driven by her desire for England as both the imagined site of colonial fulfillment and her heritage; but the gesture of writing the adventures is ultimately motivated by the author's awareness that colonial subjects cannot take their English home for granted; Englishness is an identity they must claim through gestures of writing and reinvention.

The trope of travel is thus an avenue for exploring the implications of this ambiguous identity and a means of postponing the problems raised by the author's ambivalent location in and out of Englishness:

> As I grew into womanhood, I began to indulge that longing to travel which will never leave me while I have health and vigour. I was never weary of tracing upon an old map the route to England; and never followed with my gaze the stately ships homeward bound without longing to be in them, and see the blue hills of Jamaica fade into the distance. At that time it seemed most improbable that these girlish wishes should be gratified; but circumstances, which I need not explain, enabled me to accompany some relatives to England while I was a very young woman. (4)

England enters Seacole's childhood imagination—and her adult memories—as a longing, an image without a substance, but also as a figure of

FIGURE 4.1.

Mary Seacole before the Crimean War.

Courtesy of National Library of Jamaica.

desire. For this image to be realized, Jamaica must fade into the distance, be reduced to a phantom, so that England can be rewritten as the real place of identity. But this scenario—this gesture of reversing the real and the imaginary—becomes more complicated when Seacole, like a sleeper waking out of a dream, realizes that the metropolis is merely a symbolic or imagined figure while the island of Jamaica is the only real space of emplacement, that reversals are possible only in the imagination.

And so the questions persist: Where is Seacole's real home? How does one write oneself in the chasm between desire and reality? In the discourses of Seacole's Anglo-African predecessors, most notably Olaudah Equiano, home is simultaneously in Africa (a pastoral ideal that cannot be recovered but must serve as a counterpoint to dystopic slavery) and in England, whose ideals, if not realities, could very well secure new Anglo-African identities in the future. Equiano, as is well known, writes his narrative from what appears to be the security of his new English home.[19] In Seacole's narrative, in contrast, home is located in a desired elsewhere that is preceded by its *grapheme* (the map) and *symbolon* (the ships) but that, as we shall see later, remains distant and perhaps unattainable; England is claimed as the colonized subject's space of emplacement even when her identity is clearly marked as outside the historical and cultural referents that define Englishness; in this case, the metropole is a catachresis—a "concept metaphor without an adequate referent."[20]

Some readers might object to this comparison of Equiano and Seacole by drawing attention to their different contingent circumstances: Equiano is born a slave and writes in the name of the abolitionist cause; his narrative must, out of rhetorical necessity, underscore enslavement as a moment of radical loss and the inherent freedom of Englishness as a consolation prize; his imagined Africa provides a unified ontological moment that slavery tears away but that Englishness restores. In contrast, Seacole is born a freewoman and comes of age in the period after emancipation; the goal of her narrative is not release from bondage but the affirmation of the "free colored's" entitlement to an English identity. Her contingent situation is hence important not only because it overdetermines her relation to the imperial center but also because it adjudicates authorial intentions and audience expectations. Like Equiano before her, Seacole is a product of her time, of its dominant writing conventions and moral codes.

But one should also add that what makes the project of identity so complicated after emancipation—which must also be located in Williams's generational project (the 1840s)—is the fact that the binaries of slavery and freedom—and the moral economy they denote—have collapsed. In West Indian slavery, as elsewhere in the Americas, blacks have hitherto been defined as objects and have thus implicitly belonged to England because they are owned by English people. With emancipation, however, blacks are no longer defined as objects; they are legal subjects, but they are subjects whose relation to England (as most political debates in the West Indies in the nineteenth century indicate) is tenuous if not confused.[21] The cusp between slavery and freedom, reification and agency, explains many moments of silence in Seacole's text—her silence about race, about her family history, and indeed, about the problematic Jamaican identity that shadows her book. Such instances of silence are paramount because, as we have learned from poststructural theory, they are important indices of what the subject is allowed to say within the culture of colonialism and the reality of imperial rule.

In discussing Seacole's utterances and silences, we have to begin by identifying what Raymond Williams calls (again with specific reference to the 1840s), the interlock of "dominant and residual forms, and the even more complex process, in relation to that interlock, of specific and still-forming modes of emergence."[22] Williams's argument is that much of the working-class literature of this period reproduces dominant bourgeois forms but, nevertheless, carries elements of its repressed culture. Colonialism complicates the notion of residual forms, however, in ways that class does not, by posing some elementary questions: What is the colonial subject's "mode of emergence"? Indeed, how does the colonial subject write itself in a discourse of imperial power especially when the priority of that discourse is the negation of the other as a speaking subject? Can autonomy and subjectivity be written within a discourse whose overwhelming priority—and reality—is domination, a discourse that seeks to reduce the colonized to a silent object?

These questions are particularly difficult to answer in relation to Mary Seacole's narrative because, unlike later colonized subjects, she does not read Englishness and colonialism as negative elements; on the contrary, she assumes that it is only within the dominant codes of Victorian England that she can inscribe herself as a subject. What makes Seacole's narrative melancholic, then, is that the forms of Englishness she desires resist absolute appropriation by the colonial subject and evade her strenuous striving to get the English reading public to identify with her in the same way she has identified with them (i.e., by putting her life on the line to serve England in the Crimean War).

I want to explore, in some detail, Seacole's strategies of identifying with Englishness and the resulting slippage of identity. Let us begin by noting that her narration of Englishness is predicated on an archetypal mid-nineteenth-century trope—what Williams calls "the new bourgeois ethic of self-making and self-help."[23] The act of writing the self is configured as the establishment, by the colonial subject, of its own discursive space within the master narrative of mid-Victorian Englishness. Seacole clearly emplaces herself in this narrative by valorizing its defining codes—individualism, moral restraint, and public duty. Thus while the title of Seacole's narrative might seem to celebrate the romance of adventure, the meaning of her travel is secured by its larger moral purpose—the self-advancement of the subject and her (public) sense of moral good. At the beginning of her narrative, for example, Seacole is faced with personal grief (the death of her husband and her mother [6]), but rather than function as an obstacle to self-engenderment, her private grief becomes, in the retrospective and contemplative moment of writing, the condition that enables her to enter the public sphere defined by colonialism:

> I was left alone to battle with the world as best I might. . . . Although it was no easy thing for a widow to make ends meet, I never allowed myself to know what repining or depression was, and so succeeded in gaining not only my daily bread, but many comforts besides, from the beginning. Indeed, my experience of the world—it is not finished yet, but I do not think it will give me reason to change my opinion—leads me to the conclusion that it is by no means the hard bad world which some selfish people would have us believe it. (6–7)

Here, the narrator's agency cannot be considered outside the moral grammar denoted by self-will and hard work: Seacole defines her identity and success in terms of her ability to overcome the obstacles nature throws in her way (10). In the process of overcoming such obstacles, she masters—and affirms—the bourgeois success ethic and its attendant moral codes, including female domesticity. But unlike the characters of mid-Victorian novels such as Charlotte Brontë's *Jane Eyre* and Elizabeth Gaskell's *North and South*, the colonial subject cannot be authorized solely by this middle-class ethic; on the contrary, as Seacole knows only too well, subjects at the margins of the colonial system also need to justify their inclusion in the English or European sphere in which the bourgeois ethic has greater authority and resonance.[24]

The common tactic here is for the author to elevate her subjectivity to another level, to transform her individual self-making into a collective romance that she and her English audience can share. In this regard, Seacole narrates her adventures not merely as the individual striving of a colonial woman against the forces of nature but also as the collective struggle of the forces of civilization—which she represents—against barbarism. Thus, the Isthmus of Panama, where Seacole "self-makes" herself in preparation for her later service in the Crimea, is described as a dystopic space, a lawless state, a "luckless, dreary spot" (10) of human refuse and disease. And as the narrator focuses on "this unhealthy and wretched" country, the reader recognizes the familiar language of the imperialized gaze and the common drama in which civilization encounters barbarism.

The important point, though, is that for Seacole (casting herself as the representative of Englishness in Panama), barbarism, which is often characterized by what she constantly refers to as "excess of license" (20), can be countered only by Victorian moral restraint. And thus the reader is often invited to identify with the narrator, who, in the face of such excess, stands out as the embodiment of feminine conduct; femininity, in turn, becomes the moral code that links her to her bourgeois audience in England. Struggling to make her way through the incomplete Darien highway in Panama, to cite just one example, Seacole flounders about terribly, and what stands out is not her eventual triumph over the wilderness but her ability to maintain her femininity in conditions that seek to negate it:

> And as with that due regard to personal appearance, which I have always deemed a duty as well as a pleasure to study, I had, before leaving Navy Bay, attired myself in a delicate light blue dress, a white bonnet prettily trimmed, and an equally chaste shawl, the reader can sympathise with my distress. (13)

Let us provide a context for this portrait of demure femininity. Nine-teenth-century women travelers have been criticized for portraying themselves in such conventional "feminine" terms even when their adventures seem to defy the domestic definition of femininity. What has been forgotten in such a critique, however, is the travelers' deployment of feminine conduct as an affective device: for it is by contrasting the conventional figure of the woman traveler as delicate and prim and the alien wilderness and barbaric culture in which she travels that the writer can foreground her success over nature and convention. The prim dress, like the legendary long skirt, is a reminder of the odds women travelers have to overcome to get where they are going; but it is also a reminder to the dominant culture that in spite of their travels in the colonial frontier, they still maintain their femininity (figure 4.2).[25] When the implied readers imagine Seacole climbing the Darien escarpment in her delicate dress (or Mary Kingsley sailing up the Ogowe in her long skirt), we are figuratively reminded of how far the woman traveler has moved from the scene of domestic imprisonment signified by her accoutrements without losing her "moral" character. In essence, it is precisely because of the femininity of women travelers that their achievements stand out in a (masculine) field—the colonial sphere—where they were supposed to be absent.

Another way of putting this is to argue that if women travelers were to travel like men, they would lose the empathy that is so crucial to the success of their projects. Seacole makes this point more limpidly when she comments on the status of the woman traveler in a terrain often dominated by masochism: "My present life was not agreeable for a woman with the least delicacy of refinement; and of female society I had none. Indeed, the females who crossed my path were about as unpleasant specimens of the fair sex as one could well wish to avoid" (50). The measure of Seacole's success in this world is her ability to overcome adversity without losing her femininity or, as we shall see later, her feminine authority. Regrounded against masochism, this femininity makes Seacole worthy of the Victorian reader's sympathy.

One may argue, in response to my postulation here, that in the end Seacole affirms feminine conduct as it has been defined by the dominant male culture, that her portrait of the ideal woman comes directly from hegemonic Victorian gender norms and functions. My reply to this concern is that her whole narrative is an appeal to the dominant moral and social

FIGURE 4.2.
Mary Kingsley at the age of 34.
Courtesy of Liverpool City Libraries.

codes of Englishness—bravery, decorum, morality, and feminine conduct. Seacole's self-portrait, as it emerges in the narrative and even in her official portrait, is that of a woman—in the Victorian middle-class sense of the word. Paradoxically, this Victorian feminine norm is one that the dominant culture denies colonial women.[26] By stressing her femininity in the field of empire, Seacole is able to do two things at the same time: (a) counter the masculinized image of black women that dominates traditional imperial discourses and (b) establish empathy with the implied reader, clearly defined as someone who shares (with Seacole?) the dominant moral and social codes of the period.

But if Seacole's goal is to be accepted as a feminine subject in the traditional Victorian sense, then we may wonder why she seeks to assert her femininity in spaces (of adventure and war) that are supposed to endanger such an identity. The most obvious response to this issue is to argue that, as far as Seacole is concerned, the adventure or journey has no value in itself, but is a preparation for the fulfillment of what she sees as her patriotic duty—maternal service to England in the nation's hour of need. As we will see in a moment, however, we cannot talk about Seacole's maternal service outside the economy of travel and the bourgeois ethic. Indeed, the narrator begins her adventures in the Crimean War by insisting that her reasons for going to the battlefield were altruistic, that she was motivated by a sense of patriotic duty and honor. When war breaks out, Seacole tells us, it triggers a mood of national enthusiasm that she shares wholeheartedly; she longs to go to the battlefield and be useful "to my own 'sons,' " ready to suffer "for a cause it was so glorious to fight and bleed for!" (75–76). War presents Seacole with a kind of sublime moment of identification with England—she longs to serve "with all the ardour of my nature" (76).

Seacole's struggle to serve—or to become what she calls "a Crimea heroine" (76)—also demands a narrative in which patriotic duty can be fused with the romance of bourgeois self-making. In other words, her identification with England is predicated on her ability to overcome the forces—sexism and racism, in particular—that seek to suppress the sublimity that emerges out of her love of country and queen. When she decides to go to the Crimea "upon my own responsibility and at my own cost" (80), she is in effect casting herself—because of her unique individuality—as capable of expressing her love for England in spite of hindrance and danger. To be in a position to serve England, to be one with the nation of her dreams, is to give that dream, the dream of being English, tangible (symbolic) value.

But Seacole also goes to the Crimea to do something else—to sell goods and make money. Indeed, given the amount of effort she puts into her firm, and the primariness of her function as a trader as opposed to her role as a nurse, there is always a lurking suspicion that her patriotism is not as altruistic as she would like her readers to believe. Seacole preempts such suspicions by conflating patriotic duty and monetary exchange: although she will be known in the Crimea as the owner of the "firm of Seacole and Day," she tells us, her business arrangements "were not allowed to interfere in any way with the main object of my journey. A great portion of my limited capital was, with the kind aid of a medical friend, invested in medicines which I believe would be useful; with the remainder I purchased those home comforts which I thought would be most difficult to obtain away from England" (81–82). And thus in one stroke she appropriates two important ingredients of the bourgeois myth—duty and self-advancement. Such myths function, in turn, as important gateways into the culture of Englishness.

Now, if I seem to spend a disproportionate amount of time discussing Seacole's appropriation of mid-Victorian ideologies and her attempts to identify with the imperial center, it is because, as I have already noted, she cannot take her Englishness—or even her subjectivity—for granted. Even as she looks back on her life and fame, Seacole is aware that her English identity is not a given entity but something that her narrative has to construct and justify; she knows that the line between her given identity and her desired identity is thin. Even her wish to serve England is a reminder of her marginality within metropolitan culture:

> Now, no sooner had I heard of war somewhere, than I longed to witness it; and when I was told that many of the regiments I had known so well in Jamaica had left England for the scene of action, the desire to join them became stronger than ever. I used to stand for hours in silent thought before an old map of the world, in a little corner of which someone had chalked a red cross, to enable me to distinguish where the Crimea was; and as I traced the route thither, all difficulties would vanish. (73)

Since Seacole does succeed in going to England and serving her "imagined community" in the Crimean War, we could read her narrative as a process of turning her desire for an English identity (previously represented by a map) from an existential situation into an experiential one. This explains why *Wonderful Adventures* is about not colonial life in Jamaica but the transformation of a West Indian Creole into an Englishwoman. But even if we read this text as an optimistic narrative of Englishness, we cannot forget the conditions under which it is produced, conditions that call into question not only the moral codes Seacole valorizes but also the identity she celebrates. In other words, while many narratives of identity derive their meaning from an evocation of "raw experience"—and hence repress the mechanisms by which such identities are invented through narration—Seacole's appropriation of Englishness depends on a calculated appeal and valorization of literary conventions. As a writer, she seems aware of the extent to which her subjectivity and reputation depend on existing conventions of writing and established strategies of representation. The most obvious example of Seacole's sense of convention is her constant appeal to her implied reader, an appeal that often borders on flattery and seduction: "Would you like, gentle reader, to know what other things suggestive of home and its comforts your relatives and friends in the Crimea could obtain from the hostess of Spring Hill?" (138).

Seacole's narrative goes out of its way to transport its reader to a point of identification with its heroine; the text insists on close contact—and intercourse—between the colonial writer and the metropolitan reader. Indeed, it is by invoking what Peter de Bolla has called (in a different context) "the codes of polite social intercourse" that Seacole seeks to insert herself, the speaking voice, into the intersection where the colonial body becomes a metropolitan subject.[27] Her constant regrounding of the values she shares with her implied readers is an essential strategy of inscribing herself into their moral and social universe; like her Anglo-African precursors, she is aware of the centrality of the "talking book" in the construction of a new (post-emancipation) identity.[28]

Talking through writing is also an attempt to resolve a larger problem: if an English identity cannot be realized except through the evocation of figures of alterity, as I have argued in the previous chapters, how can the colonial subject—as the other in this equation—appropriate and narrate an identity that has located her outside normative subjectivity? A superficial reading of Seacole's adventures might lead us to conclude that she is not aware of her location as the other within the parameters of empire. After all, doesn't her constant deployment of the trope of the other—the Hispanic, the Greek, the Turk, the Jew—already presuppose a nonproblematic embrace of English selfhood? The most obvious response to this question is that the only way Seacole, a "colored" woman, can claim her Englishness is to find and demonize alternative figures of alterity, the barbarians against whom her civility is measured. Some readers might even conclude, especially when they consider her evasion of the problem of race, that Seacole lives in total denial of her blackness and would hence never locate herself as the other of Englishness.

There is something to be said for both perspectives, but I find them unsatisfactory because they rest on the erroneous premise that Seacole assumes that her English identity is nonproblematic. This premise is actually countered by the narrative in at least two ways. First, Seacole makes a clear distinction between her desire for Englishness—the motor of narration in the *Wonderful Adventures*—and her location as a colonial subject. There is, as it were, a clear distinction between Jamaican Creoles (of which she is one) and English people: "I think all who are familiar with the West Indies will acknowledge that Nature has been favourable to strangers in a few respects, and that one of these has been in instilling in the hearts of the Creoles an affection for English people and an anxiety for their welfare, which shows itself warmest when they are sick and suffering" (60). Creole and English are separate entities conjoined by an imperial identity.

Second, unlike blackness—the radical figure of difference—a Creole identity is liminal; it is a mark of the space between colonial blackness and "real" Englishness. Because of its cultural instability, Creolity denotes the possibility of a shift from the status of a colonial subject to that of metropolitan Englishness. This explains Seacole's cautious differentiation of herself, as a "yellow" Creole, from other black subjects ("I am only a little brown—a few shades duskier than the brunettes whom you admire so much" [4]). Within the imperial matrix (and this begs some comparison with postimperial racial discourse), Englishness is a cultural rather than a racial category; for colonial subjects like Seacole, it is a privilege that must be earned by a topology that transcends simple chromaticism.[29] For Mary Seacole, this topology is provided by autobiographical or travel writing: it is through writing that the colonized self exhibits its mastery of the codes and conventions of Englishness; the travel narrative functions as a scene of differentiation providing the temporality that separates the natal space (in this case Jamaica) and the scene of colonial desire (England). In the act of writing, Seacole stages her English identity.

But the moment we read identity as staged, then, we have to acknowledge the ways in which it simultaneously calls into question essentialist notions of the natural home and the "interdictory" alterity assigned to it by colonialism.[30] My assumption here is that although the discourse of colonial alterity cannot allow Seacole to narrate her life story as the reconciliation of the writing self to its "natural" identity rather than its given identity, she nevertheless displaces her otherness in what Bhabha would call "the nineteenth-century European desire for an authentic historical consciousness."[31] But this conclusion only complicates the problem of reading identity in zones of alterity.

For in spite of her constant staging of Englishness, and her desire for bourgeois consciousness, Seacole's life is often conditioned by the reality of imperial ideologies and is thus surrounded by the insignias of the very difference she seeks to overcome. She cannot escape from the realities of color and race, of a marginalized femininity, and of spatial displacement. Throughout her stay in the Crimea, for example, Seacole portrays herself as the embodiment of female domesticity—and the private sphere—in the public domain of war and male adventure. Her public image and reputation in the Crimea rest on her capacity to provide English soldiers with the "comforts of home"; for these lonely soldiers, she is "Mami"—the surrogate mother (138). And yet, her performance of this family romance ultimately depends on a repression of the experiences that make it possible: the subject's point of origination in Jamaica is carefully elided in the text; she advocates the values of the private sphere, but we know very little about her own private life, which she seems to consider insignificant to her narrative.

In this situation, the reader may conclude that Seacole's identity ultimately depends on her function as a colonial agent, that she has no subjectivity outside the imperial infrastructure. If this is the case, then we must consider another critical problem: can the colonial subject represent herself in a structure that negates her autonomy and constantly frustrates her desire for agency? One could argue, for example, that subjectivity and agency are not dependent on each other—that Seacole can be an agent of empire only on her own terms, that her subjectivity is a form of self-engenderment. The culture of colonialism provides the colonial subject with the narrative conventions, discursive field, and ideological codes for its self-representation. Alternatively, one could argue that Seacole has autonomous agency but no subjectivity, that she uses her experiences and her narration of them (her agency) to inhabit the culture of Englishness. But one might object to this sense of agency—or subjectivity—within the discursive field of empire by claiming that what Seacole ultimately considers to be her autonomous identity is already an impossibility, that it is constantly blocked by the dominant codes that have positioned her as a fetish, as a figure of alterity. If this is the case, imperial agency can secure her identity only if it finds detours around inescapable questions of race and color, the most obvious symptoms of her marginality and alterity.

Let us reflect on this problem further: Seacole's narrative counters the colonial fetish by regrounding the subject's identification with the ideals of civilization and her adoption of the imperial gaze. Although ordinary English people who encounter her might assume that she is different from them, Seacole assumes that because of her moral and cultural values she is English in everything but her slight touch of color. But this mode of identification with the colonial center becomes quite problematic when Seacole goes to England and realizes that the question of her color and race will not go away, no matter how much she identifies with Englishness. Seacole recognizes the reality of color and race (this needs to be emphasized), but she writes around it in a rhetoric that simultaneously registers the value of her Creole culture and valorizes the desire for Englishness as an alternative identity. If in Panama she sublimated her race to her status as an English subject, in England she promotes her Creolity as the source of her authority: "Now, I am not for a single instant going to blame the authorities who would not listen to the offer of a motherly yellow woman to go to the Crimea and nurse her 'sons' there, suffering from cholera, diarrhea, and a host of lesser ills. In my country, where people know us, it would have been different" (78). As she tries (without success) to be sent to the Crimea as part of the English delegation, Seacole wonders whether what she had previously termed "American prejudices against colour" have taken root in England (79).

Clearly, Seacole is aware of the tenuousness of her English identity. Indeed, my central argument here is that it is by writing her adventures in the service of England that this colonial subject tries to deal with that tenuousness. Furthermore, when we consider Seacole's use of citations—mostly from official and military sources—to publicize and justify her role in the Crimea, we realize that it is only through writing that a colonial subject can claim a place in the drama of imperial culture. Seacole, unlike Miss Florence Nightingale, cannot take her English identity, or her role as a Crimean heroine, for granted: she has to etch it in the public consciousness by writing a narrative. But even her narration of a personal experience—usually the source of the authority of the eyewitness—is not evidential enough. It cannot have the resonance we saw in the travel narratives of men like Trollope, Kingsley, and Froude, where what is seen is assumed to be accurate, truthful, and real. Aware that she is twice deauthorized (as a colonial subject and as a writer), Seacole can only hope that she can appeal to her reader's sympathy while confirming her story by using citations from such authoritative organs of the established culture as *Punch* and *The Times*.

My argument, then, is that beneath Seacole's optimistic portrait of the colonial subject in the service of empire (and the tone of *Wonderful Adventures* is clearly celebratory) lies the author's barely suppressed sense of crisis, a crisis about her own identity and authority. Seacole ostensibly writes her narrative to call attention to the role she had played in England's imperial drama in Central Europe, but she also writes, against the background of her post-Crimea obscurity and destitution, to demand recognition as an Englishwoman. *Wonderful Adventures* provides numerous instances of the author's devotion to England, but the fact that she had been forgotten until she published the book stands as clear evidence of the unstable nature of her acquired reputation and identity. In addition, she writes a narrative in which her own unique status as a colonial subject depends on a certain valorization of the colonial mission, its cultural project, and its hegemonic aspirations.

In short, Seacole can be recognized as an English national only by unconditionally espousing the imperial cause. To be a colonial subject in the nineteenth century, then, is to exist in a cultural cul-de-sac: you cannot speak or exist except in the terms established by the *imperium*; you have to speak to exist, but you can utter only what the dominant allows you to utter; even when you speak against the culture of colonialism, you speak its language because it is what constitutes what you are.[32] The question of oppositionality in colonial discourse is certainly more vexing than we are made to believe. The point, though, is that oppositionality is not a discursive category that is inherent in any subject simply because of its race, gender, or location in the colonial matrix.[33] We need to keep this truism in mind to understand the enigma of Mary Kingsley.

Locating Mary Kingsley

Now, Mary Kingsley has become a canonical figure in the study of colonial discourse—but where does she stand when it comes to the great issues of late imperialism and how are we to read her against the polarities of race, culture, and gender that are the subject of this chapter? We can learn much about the location of European women in the culture of colonialism from the following encounter between Kingsley and the Scottish missionary Mary Slessor, as it is reported in *Travels in West Africa*:

> I made a point on this visit to Calabar of going up river to see Miss Slessor at Okÿon district. . . This very wonderful lady has been eighteen years in Calabar . . . ruling as a veritable white chief over the entire Okÿon district. Her great abilities, both physical and intellectual, have given her among the savage tribe an unique position, and won her, from white and black who know her, a profound esteem. Her knowledge of the native, his language, his way of thought, his diseases, his difficulties, and all that is his, is extraordinary, and the amount of good she has done, no man can fully estimate. Okÿon, when she went there alone—living in the native houses while she built, with the assistance of the natives, her present house—was a district regarded with fear by the Duke and Creek Town natives, and practically unknown to Europeans. It was given, as most of the surrounding districts are, to killing at funerals, ordeal by poison, and perpetual internecine wars. Many of these evil customs she has stamped out, and Okÿon rarely gives trouble to its nominal rulers, the Consuls in Old Calabar, and trade passes through it down to the sea-ports. . . . This instance of what one white can do would give many important lessons in West Coast administration and development. Only the sort of man Miss Slessor represents is rare.[34]

We can read, in this passage alone, the archetypal tropes of imperial conquest and control: Kingsley's prose may sometimes seem to maintain some ironic distance from her subject (is "veritable white chief" to be read as an example of her well-known irony?), but she represents Slessor as the symbol of civilization poised against the dangers of the savage African space; the hierarchical relations between self and other are clearly maintained, as is the missionary's function in the service of empire and trade. Slessor's domination over Okÿon is, in addition, coded in the central terms we identified in male imperial discourse in the previous chapter: her weapons are white authority, knowledge, and racial superiority. Even her famous house is a mark of the colonial reorganization of African spaces (see figure 4.3). Here, the binarism between white colonizer and black native remains intact. Most important, Kingsley can place Slessor in the imperial economy of meaning only by sublimating her femininity to male authority: in the colonial sphere, Slessor's authority is exclusively male, and her femininity is secondary.

At the same time, however, this discourse contains important ideological fissures, some of which I will discuss in greater detail later in this chapter. What is offered for admiration is not a colonial system—Kingsley is admonishing the failure of the colonial administration in this passage—but a unique individual within the economy of empire. Kingsley is writing for an audience that already knows that Slessor's uniqueness lies not only in her single-handed mastery of the savage space but also in her ability to have risen from a mill girl in Dundee to become the virtual governor of Cross Rivers. The distance between Dundee and Okÿon, then, is a mark of what women can achieve, without restraints, in the open field of empire. Because it seems free of the gender ideologies that constrain white women in the metropolis, the imperial field is construed as a social space for freedom and fulfillment. And as to the question of the binary opposition between black and white, let us note that in the African scene described by Kingsley above, there are subtle divisions of class and caste in which the natives of Creek Town are aligned with the Europeans against the dangers of the Okÿon bush; and Slessor (and European traders) are pitted against the nominal consul in Calabar. In the midst of it all is an authorial posture that doesn't offer us much guidance. And so the question persists: where does Kingsley stand in all this?

Well, it has always been difficult to associate Kingsley with the hegemonic—and yet ambivalent—culture of late colonialism when some of

FIGURE 4.3.
The house Mary Slessor built in the African bush.
Courtesy of Dundee Museum and Art Galleries.

the certainties of English dominion overseas seem to be undermined even as Britannia rules the waves. But we have to keep in mind that when Kingsley writes her travels, the experience of empire—and the ideologies driving imperialism—are facing important revisions and challenges: for the first time the colonial enterprise is facing opposition at home. There no longer appears to be one hegemonic imperial ideology. At the same time, however, it would be a mistake to align Kingsley with the emerging anticolonial movement; after all, she was an imperialist who "believed that England . . . had every right to extend her trade across the globe and to protect the English flag, emblem of the highest form of justice."[35] And yet her *Travels in West Africa*, as the sample above illustrates, seems to resist this categorical identification with the imperial cause; her rhetoric seems to go against the grain of official discourse and even to call its central claims into question.

Clearly, Kingsley doesn't speak the aggressive language of imperialism, nor does she adopt the panoramic vision of colonial adventures in Africa like Stanley, Speke, or Burton. Kingsley's narrative is a different kind of imperial discourse, one underwritten by irony, parody, and reversal. It is, nevertheless, a discourse underwritten also by a certain investment in imperialism and its mission. Given the paradoxical nature of *Travels in West Africa*, we have to develop an analytical schema for reading it as a discourse that exists both inside and outside colonialism; only in these terms can we begin to understand its moral and ethnographic authority. Under these circumstances, Kingsley's experiences parallel those of colonial subjects such as Seacole.

Locating Kingsley within the imperial tradition invites further reflections on the relation between gender, the cartography of empire, and the form of the travel narrative. Some of the attendant theoretical questions here have been posed by Billie Melman in *Women's Orients*: Were metropolitan women, in their encounter with the colonial locality, still heirs to "a hegemonic and homogeneously patriarchal tradition," or did gender generate a separate vision of empire? Were travel—and travel writing—a cultural practice that constituted "a break away from the precepts and aesthetics of the very notion of separate, masculine and feminine spaces," a form in which the feminine interest was channeled?[36] I will take several issues as axiomatic here. For one, I will assume that women travelers have a distinct vision of the imperial space and that the discourse on empire is transformed when it is informed by issues of gender, class, and sexuality; I will also assume that since Kingsley subscribes to central imperial doctrines, she secures, in her writing, a female voice "that asserts its own kind of mastery even as it denies domination and parodies power."[37]

But I want to go beyond these formulations and call attention to several contextual issues: First, we must locate Kingsley not simply within the imperial project as a generalized category but within a specific historical juncture (late colonialism) in which Englishness is defined by triumph and crisis. Here, we are better placed to read both Kingsley's own cognizance of the crisis in colonial practices and her attempt to rescue imperial ideologies by appealing to their ideality. Second, Kingsley's narrative needs to be read not as the continuation of the Victorian tradition I discussed in the last chapter but as one of the key founding documents of modernism. By locating her discourse within the ideologies of modernism, we will be able to foreground its sense of disenchantment with imperial ideologies, its instrumental promotion of an African ethnography, and its ambivalent deployment of African spaces and cultures.

The first question to consider, though, is the nature of Kingsley's discursive authority in relation to that of her male precursors. How does her travel narrative differ from texts by Du Chaillu or Burton, the male explorers who preceded her in West and Central Africa? Does gender make any difference to the rhetoric of imperial authority? Because Kingsley believes in the ideals of imperialism—culture, education, civilization, and free trade—rather than some of its vulgar forms of administrative mastery and control promoted by these men, her focus in *Travels in West Africa* is not on the dominant image of Africa as a blank darkness that awaits possession through exploration, or an irrational object that defies traditional modes of knowledge and nullifies the relation between a subject and its object of representation. Rather, Kingsley's concern is with the continent as an object of knowledge in its own right, as a valuable cultural and natural treasure, and, ultimately, the site of her own engenderment. So while other travelers in this period may read Africa as an enchanting and yet corrupted—and corrupting—place of darkness (Conrad's "Outpost of Progress" and *Heart of Darkness*, discussed in the next chapter, exemplify this tendency), Kingsley's Africa is seen as a discursive object that can fill "the vast cavity" in the observer's mind (1). Indeed, Kingsley begins the narration of her journey by defying conventional wisdom about the imperial space: Africa can be a source of information and knowledge, she asserts, but for us to deploy this knowledge in the service of the colonial project, we have to learn to go beyond the discourse of rumor, hearsay, and atavism that thrives in European Africanist circles (2–6).

But to situate herself in Africa—to prove that "there was any amount of work for me worth doing there" (11)—Kingsley must also assert her cultural authority within the patriarchal traditions of imperialism and imperial travel, for colonialism is, after all, conceived as a male enterprise. What this means, among other things, is that she must prove why Africa is worthy of study and what qualifies her—as a woman—to be its student. Kingsley's relentless use of irony and parody is hence intended to distance her from contemporary Africanist discourse and, at the same time, to bring her closer to what she considers to be the object of knowledge itself—the real Africa. Irony, in other words, allows Kingsley to negate dominant discourse on Africa in the colonial library; by calling attention to the disjunction between what is said about Africa and what Africa really is as it is witnessed by her, she also manages to turn the oppositionality of irony into a source of authority.[38] While others go to Africa to confirm what is already known, Kingsley promises to come back with original knowledge.

An important aspect of Kingsley's style, especially as it seeks to deflate the hyperbole of previous travel narratives, is her use of mundane prose, a prose that seems to go against the tradition of aesthetization that has come to be associated with imperial travel. Consider, for example, the following description of the accoutrements of West African Muslims:

> Quite "rational dress" hats in fact, for their broad brims hang down and shade the neck, and they also shelter the eyes to such an extent that the wearer can't see without bending up the front brim pretty frequently;—but then I notice there always is something wrong with a rational article of dress. Then the bulbous dome top keeps off the sun from the head, rain runs off the whole affair easily, and bush does not catch in it. If I had sufficient strength of mind I would wear one myself, but even if I decorated it with cat-tails, or antelope hair, as is usually done, I do not feel I could face Piccadilly in one; and you have no right to go about Africa in things you would be ashamed to be seen in at home. (18–19)

This description easily moves from a nondescript representation of observed data to a note of comic play, a combination that is crucial to Kingsley's ambivalent position, for it allows her to show simultaneously that African cultures can be known and represented but always have to be read distinctly from their metropolitan counterparts because they have a different rationale.

Read against the works of her precursors in West and Central Africa, Kingsley's prose is an exercise in affirmation and negation; her sentences are constructed to simultaneously affirm and deconstruct accepted views on Africa: "My experience of Cape Coast on this occasion was one of the hottest, but one of the pleasantest I have ever been through on the Gold Coast" (26); "The view was exceedingly lovely and extensive. Beneath and between us and the sea, lay the town in the blazing sun" (27). In addition, Kingsley's descriptions are, as many critics have noted, designed to deflate the assumptions of novelty, originality, and wonder circulating in late-nineteenth-century writings on Africa.[39] The author's operative dictum seems to be that what you see on the surface conceals deeper and rational meanings.

The opposition between the visible African landscape and its hidden meanings is an important source of the writer's authority for another reason: by contrasting the superficial image of Africa with the continent's "deeper" meanings, Kingsley is also engaged in a subtle subversion of contemporary versions of Africa—and African affairs—that have ossified the land and its people into an undifferentiated mass, the source of casual conversation and gossip. Topics such as the Ashanti campaign of 1874 generate casual conversation around European tables, notes Kingsley, but such small talk deprives them of the "sound previous education" because "superficial dealings with them are quite impossible, for the names of places and people in Ashanti are strange and choppy, and you will get mixed as to which is which if you don't take care" (35).

But if Kingsley strikes the posture of an educated observer of African affairs, her narrative goes out of its way to repress the authority of a unique female voice. For while her own female subjectivity is as much an issue in the narrative as is Africa itself, Kingsley's discourse eschews the heroic as it seeks to make the reader part of the African landscape.[40] In short, Kingsley's narrative does not ask the reader to be a passive receptacle of an exotic event beyond his or her reach; on the contrary, the act of writing is designed to involve the reader in the writer's encounter with Africa; the implied reader (the second person) is often asked to participate in the reconstruction of the adventures encountered during the travel: "Still, even if your peculiar tastes and avocation do not take you in small dug-out canoes into the heart of the swamps, you can observe the difference in the local scenery made by the flowing of the tide when you are on a vessel stuck on a sand-bank, in the Rio del Roy for example" (90). In her representation of Africa, and in relation to her readers, Kingsley seeks no special privileges.

In a situation in which the traveler refuses to claim the uniqueness and privilege of the bourgeois subject, we have to look for her authority outside the circuit of voice and location. In other words, while Pratt is right when she argues that Kingsley creates value "by decisively and rather fiercely rejecting the textual mechanisms that created value in the discourse of her male predecessors,"[41] it is equally true that her feminine authority cannot stand without a strategic appeal to the discursive apparatus of patriarchal imperialism. Another way of putting this problem is to argue that Kingsley's utopian desire—her conception of a humane colonialism—depends on her ability to see empire as a project that can be reformulated through discourse. My concern here is not so much Kingsley's well-known advocacy of a new imperialism driven by fair trade policies rather than administrative avarice, but the ways in which her narrative— unlike Conrad's, for example—represents Africa as a place that does not horrify her English readers, at least not in the way it horrifies them in Conrad's Africanist texts.

But does Kingsley, by humanizing Africa at a time when it has become more fashionable to demonize it, rationalize the imperial project in ways that her contemporary Conrad cannot? True, Kingsley's narrative is a powerful critique of the destructive forces of imperialism, but her appeal to the better side of the colonizing mission invites greater European participation in the conquest of Africa. In other words, if Conrad's Africa horrifies the reader by insisting on the radical alterity of the "heart of darkness," Kingsley's portrait of the continent makes it more desirable and worthy of consumption. The last claim may appear startling since, as I have already argued, Kingsley's mission is to represent African peoples— and their cultures—as autonomous entities rather than mere projections of European fantasies; in the end, though, her portrait of Africa—and her representation of Africans—are ambivalent in ways that are as comforting as they are troublesome. Her discourse is truly radical in its adoption of cultural relativism as its organizing (ethnographic) principle: she is respectful of native modes of knowledge and cognition and always considers Africans to be important informants, especially of the effects of colonialism on indigenous institutions (49, 85).

Kingsley's work is hence important because of its radical break with the imperial monism we discerned in our discussion of imperial historians such as Froude and Kingsley (chapter 3). Instead of positing the narrative of empire as a singular and rational process that subsumes colonial culture under the banner of enlightened and paternal Englishness, she adopts what S. P. Mohanty would call a methodological relativism, which pursues "the possibilities of change, variety and difference, and began thereby to pose the question of otherness."[42] As a cultural relativist,

Kingsley assumes that African cultures are not uniform and unchanging but are marked by regional and ethnic differences; her Africa is also defined by temporal transformations and a sense of historicity (60). But such accession to local knowledge, to the efficacy of native institutions and temporality, is subordinated to the larger goal of the imperial project itself. Africa's relation to Europe is still secondary: its peoples and cultures are changing and evolving, but they occupy a lower rung on the evolutionary ladder. The fear here is that if African cultures were shown to be as good as European ones, there would be no need for a civilizing mission and the ideology of progress. And since Kingsley is ultimately on the side of civilization and progress, her authority cannot be secured outside inherited theories on the Africans' "mechanical deficiency" and lack of reason (28).

Kingsley spends a lot of time studying native institutions and their normativity, but she is also keen to affix African cultures on the existing evolutionary grid; she has a good sense of what cultural difference means for human culture, but such differences only make sense when they have been represented in the inherited taxonomy on race and class. Thus, cultural differences, even among Africans themselves, are conceptualized in strict hierarchies: "Physically the Bubis are a fairly well-formed race of medium height; they are decidedly inferior to the Benga or the Krus, but quite on a level with the Effiks" (63). Even with the wealth of evidence before her, Kingsley's Africans fall into two basic categories—"Negroes" and "Bantus" (64)—categories that European science has developed to explain the nature of the African.

As it emerges in *Travels in West Africa*, Kingsley's ethnography is driven by a series of other ambivalences worth mentioning: She believes that the colonizer is in Africa for the good of the Africans—for the cause of progress and civilization—but she is also a strong critic of the imposition of Western institutions on African peoples. European civilization is the source of degeneracy in native cultures: "Nothing strikes one so much, in studying the degeneration of these native tribes, as the direct effect that civilisation and reformation has in hastening it" (403). She believes in the inferiority of Africans, and yet she recognizes and respects the intrinsic value of their cultures; she loathes to see these cultures give in to Western institutions. If her harshest tone seems reserved for half-civilized Africans, it is because Kingsley—and this is an important mark of her modernism—is also in search of the primitive. Like Graham Greene after her (see chapter 5), she finds the African wilderness around the Ogowe River preferable to the pseudo-Western cultures of Sierra Leone. Indeed, when Kingsley looks at Freetown, the self-styled Liverpool of West Africa, what she sees is not a thriving metropolis but a culture in a state of dilapidation (15), defined by inauthenticity and sham (21).

In contrast, the African forest, that great symbol of hermeneutical delirium in her contemporary Conrad, is represented as a source of knowledge and insight. In Conrad's novels, as we will see in the next chapter, the forest cuts us off from understanding; in Kingsley's travels, in contrast, one encounters the ecology of the forest, a "twilight region" that eventually becomes intelligible: "As you get trained to your surroundings, you see more and more, and a whole world grows up gradually out of the gloom before your eyes" (102). Such intelligibility, however, also depends on the subject's interest in the ecology of the forest and her ability to decode it: "Unless you are interested in it and fall under its charm, it is the most awful life in death imaginable. It is like being shut in a library whose books you cannot read, all the while tormented, terrified, and bored" (102). For Kingsley, then, the figuration of Africa depends not on self-projection but on critical reflection. There is, however, an obvious paradox in Kingsley's writing of Africa within the imperial project: she wants to preserve native institutions and to protect them against European institutions, but she also waves the banner of progress and trade that leads to the decimation of the very cultures that she wants preserved.

Now, there have been several attempts to explain this paradox, but the most intriguing one is provided by Pratt in *Imperial Eyes*. Kingsley's Africa, according to Pratt, functions as a utopian space—a place in which "European innocence" is performed—and a maternal site of engenderment that is, nevertheless, contained within the structures of domination and control associated with imperialism.[43] In this context, Kingsley's modernized imperial discourse seeks to clear a cultural space for the engenderment of the domestic female subject but to sustain as well the larger ideologies that enable its engagement with Africa. Engendered in the space of the other, the imprisoned European woman cannot but have some affinity with the natives whose lives she chronicles; but she can be in this space only because it is under European control. How can Kingsley's humanism be reconciled to the practical effects of

imperial rule and of trade that inevitably destroy African lives and institutions?

We can arrive at an answer, I believe, by locating Kingsley in the emerging discourse of functional anthropology, a discourse that seeks to
describe native institutions in their intrinsic form while accounting for
the ways in which they were transformed by the forces of European
progress.[44] Three aspects of this new way of looking at colonized cultures need to be explored: the author's conception of the ethnographic
stance as a discursive practice distinct from the writings of adventurers
and travelers; her reformulation of the gatekeeping theories and accepted
practices of ethnography; and her retooling of knowledge to serve the
desires and interests of the new imperialism. In regard to the first point,
we need to note that Kingsley's adoption of a self-conscious ethnographic stance does not in itself guarantee the authority of her discourse.
As James Clifford has noted in a different context, "At the close of the
nineteenth century, nothing guaranteed, *a priori*, the ethnographer's status
as the best interpreter of native life—as opposed to the traveler, and
especially to the missionary and administrator, some of whom had been
in the field far longer and had better research contacts and linguistic
skills."[45]

An important metacritical function of Kingsley's narrative is to secure
the authority of ethnography so that it can carry more weight than the
adventure narratives of her precursors. Her tactic here is not to deny the
authority of missionaries, such as Mary Slessor, or colonial administrators, such as Harry Johnston, nor even to renounce the works of adventurers, such as Du Chaillu, but to credentialize herself by mapping out a
new mode of scientific knowledge in which presuppositions are married
to field observations. Thus, while the work of adventurers is a display of
presuppositions and that of missionaries and administrators is a collection of field data without interpretation, Kingsley seeks to produce a
report that conjoins fieldwork and explanation.

It is important, then, that Kingsley casts her presence in Africa as a nat-
uralist and ethnographer rather than a traveler or explorer. She defines herself as a "collector" in a constant state of confusion and without the
authority to make sense of the material she collects in the field; she does
not have presuppositions, only hypothesis. She describes the Oil Rivers,
for example, as

too big a subject to compress for one thing; for another I do not feel that I yet know enough to have the right to speak regarding them, unless I were going to do so along accepted well-trodden lines, and what I have seen and personally know of the region does not make me feel at all inclined to do so. So I will wait until I have had further opportunities of observing them. (72)

Unlike the imperial travelers discussed in the previous chapter, Kingsley does not assume that what she sees is a given nor does she present the authority of the eyewitness as incontestable. Her authority is postponed until enough data can be gathered, or until a proper perspective can be achieved. The right perspective, we are made to understand, is one in which the culture under observation is seen as a totality; it is also a perspective in which observed data are organized around a set of theoretical principles. The relation between fieldwork (the source of data) and theory (the set of principles) is hence circular: one cannot develop a theory without enough data, but data do not yield meaning until they can fit into an explanatory schema. Whether collected in notes or memory, data are an assortment of unconnected facts—"a rag-bag"—that needs theory to "tidy" it over (73).

It is only after she has been through her designated regions of West Africa that Kingsley feels she has acquired enough knowledge to provide a sustained analysis of her primary interest—the African fetish. At the end of her journey, in the copious chapters dealing with fetishism, Kingsley overcomes her earlier doubts about her authority as an ethnographer; her work has now acquired the professional authority of her discipline; it can now be judged according to the standards of fieldwork set by early anthropology—"a new fusion of general theory and empirical research, of cultural analysis with ethnographic description" (121). This standard, however, is not one she is content with, and she often uses her fieldwork to reformulate existing ethnographic theory and practice and even to cast doubt on its efficacy:

I went out with my mind full of the deduction of every book on Ethnology, German or English, that I had read during fifteen years—and being a good Cambridge person, I was particularly confident that from Mr. Frazer's book, *The Golden Bough*, I had got a semiuniversal key to the underlying idea of native custom and belief. But I soon found this was very far from being the case. His idea is a true key to a certain quantity of facts, but in West Africa only to a limited quantity. (435)

Now, Kingsley does not urge her readers to jettison such canonical anthropological texts as Fraser's *The Golden Bough* or E. B. Taylor's *Primitive Culture*; the purpose of her fieldwork, she asserts, is to point to the limits of universal deductions on human culture. Kingsley's ethnography is simultaneously authorized by the foundation documents of English ethnography and by her tenuous relation to this tradition. Her work, however, tries to establish a method in which facts are read beyond their "raw state" (as universalisms) by being examined in "the conditions that surround them" (436). In this respect, she is a precursor of the functional school that follows her—the school associated with Malinowski. Simply put, Kingsley meets most of the criteria that Clifford and others have established for the scientific discourse of ethnography, which, it has been assumed, developed in the 1920s: she validates her persona as a fieldworker by displaying her vision of ethnographic practice as both "scientifically demanding and heroic"; she is one of the few travelers of the period to insist on the importance of native languages in the anthropological project; she considers herself to be a participant observer representing these cultures from within, as it were; she is self-conscious about her method; she focuses on a particular institution (the fetish), which she considers to be the key to understanding the ensemble of cultures that she confronts; and she desires a synchronic rather than a diachronic vision of these cultures.[46]

Ultimately, however, the kind of reconfiguration of ethnographic theory and practice that we see in Kingsley's work is also a belated attempt to recover and promote the ideals of empire at a time when they are either being challenged at home or discredited by a new generation of ruthless imperialists. In other words, Kingsley, like Malinowski after her, credits colonial authorities with good intentions while deploring the degeneration of native institutions under modernization.[47] Herein also lies her modernism: she cannot detach herself from the instrumental reason of empire (progress and industrialization), but neither can she embrace its ethical and cultural values.[48] As the place in which the painful division between instrumentality and the ethical is played out, Africa is that space in which European civilization might be able to grasp its originating values—"It is always interesting to observe the germ of our own institutions existing in the culture of a lower race," she notes (285). This vision of Africa as the germ of "our civilized" institutions, or the childhood of mankind, is an important idea in the discourse of high modernism, which will be discussed in chapter 5.

ᛝ 5 ᛞ

Belated Englishness: Modernism, Narrative, and Colonialism

When you can no longer assume that Britannia will rule the
waves forever, you have to reconceive reality as something that can
be held together by you the artist, in history rather than in geography. Spatiality becomes, ironically, the characteristic of an aesthetic rather than of political domination, as more and more
regions—from India to Africa to the Caribbean—challenge the
classical empires and their cultures.

Edward Said, *Culture and Imperialism*

There is perhaps no greater visual representation of the canonical moment of
modernism than Patrick Heron's oil painting of T. S. Eliot at the National
Portrait Gallery in London (figure 5.1). What this cubist portrait represents, among other things, is the moment of arrival of avant-garde art, as
it were: for rather than alienate the viewer from the object of reflection, or
even call into question traditional modes of representation, as early modern art was supposed to do, this portrait reinforces the authority of the
modernist movement and aesthetic. Indeed, compared to the masked figures of alterity that make early cubist paintings such as Picasso's *Les Demoi-
selles d'Avignon* signs of what William Rubin calls "primordial horror," signs
that "conjure something that transcends our sense of civilized experience,"[1] the portrait of Eliot is quite comforting. The solemnity and the
steady gaze speak of "high church" tastes; the posture is that of the master of an Oxbridge college. Clearly, this portrait seems so abstracted from
the primitivism that was such a major influence on Eliot's poetry—and the
cubist tradition to which the painting belongs—that few visitors to the
National Portrait Gallery would be inclined to make any association

between Heron's painting and Fang masks such as Mary Kingsley's famous *Mavungu* (figure 5.2).

But then who would associate T. S. Eliot's work with the popular culture of his native St. Louis and the Creolity represented by the jazz and blues traditions of this midwestern American city? And yet this is what postcolonial writers have done—returned modernism in general, and T. S. Eliot in particular, to his Creole roots in the New World, dislocated him from the normativity of high modernism that he helped institute and called attention to the repressed context of his texts. If T. S. Eliot's high Anglicanism was an attempt to escape his New World roots, his lasting influence in the postcolonial world comes not from the refined aesthetic he championed, or the primitivism he borrowed from the native cultures of the colonized space, but the most quotidian aspects of his aesthetic.

For example, in their search for a poetics outside the inherited imperial ("standard") language, Caribbean writers in the 1930s and 1940s could hear in Eliot's "speaking voice" the possibilities of what Kamau Brathwaite was later to call "national language":

> For those of us who really made the breakthrough, it was Eliot's actual voice—or rather his recorded voice, property of the British Council (Barbados)—reading "preludes," "The Love Song of J. Alfred Prufrock," *The Wasteland*, and later the *Four Quartets*—not the texts—that turned us on. In that dry deadpan delivery, the "riddims" of St. Louis (though we did not know the source then) were stark and clear for those of us who at the same time were listening to the dislocations of Bird, Dizzy, and Klook. And it is interesting that, on the whole, the establishment could not stand Eliot's voice— and far less jazz.[2]

In Brathwaite's reading of Eliot's modernism as a form of dislocation— one rooted in cultural practices that the colonial establishment had sought to repress—we have an important glimpse of the way in which the aesthetic crisis denoted by modernism, which was also the crisis of late colonialism, offered incredible opportunities for both metropolitan and colonized writers.

We now know—thanks to postcolonial theory—that some of the greatest revolutions in European systems of cognition, modes of repre-

FIGURE 5.2.

Mavungu, Mary Kingsley's nail fetish.

Courtesy of Pitt Rivers Museum, Oxford University.

sentation, and narrative structures were overdetermined by the presence and force of imperial spaces. We know, for example, that the relatively stable subject-object relationships we encounter in nineteenth-century theories of representation, the widespread confidence in history and teleology, and what Said has called "narrative progression and triumphalism" were all generated by unshakable confidence in the imperial enterprise.[3] We also know that the emergence of a deep anxiety about the imperial enterprise and the culture of colonialism, an anxiety that is both historical and philosophical, was to lead to a radical reconceptualization of narrative forms and indeed of the idea of the aesthetic itself. The moment of English modernism, in spite of a certain canonical insistence on its ahistorical and hermetical character, was generated by a crisis of belief in the efficacy of colonialism, its culture, and its dominant terms—a progressive temporality, a linear cartography, and a unified European subject.

But if modernism was generated by the questioning of such imperializing categories as teleology and cartography, we also need to acknowledge the ways in which the modernist aesthetic came to function as the staging ground for the structures and precepts it sought to deny. How, for example, did the rhetoric of failure, an important signature of modernism, emerge from the modern writer's disillusionment with the imperial mission and his or her nostalgia for older forms of social organization?[4] How did the modernist aesthetics' concern with apocalypse and atrophy, fragmented cognition, and disjunctive subjectivities, emerge from the material conditions that this aesthetic sought to transcend?

The truth is, we have become so accustomed to reading the modernist text as an attempt to keep out the contaminants of the world outside the aesthetic sphere that we have forgotten how often modernist art forms derive their energy from their diagnosis of the failure of the imperial enterprise, and how modernism produces its narrative authority by becoming enmeshed—against its overt intentions, perhaps—in the politics of empire and in the conflict between colonial culture and a changing global economic and cultural system. More specifically, modernist narratives are about failure—the failure of traditional authority, inherited modes of representation, and the European subject—but they also derive their authority from the staging of this failure in the colonial space. There is, therefore, no better place to read this failure than in that unstable cognitary zone in which modernism seeks aesthetic solutions to historical problems and ends up displaying its style as the most blatant symptom of the very problems—the crisis in capitalism, fragmented subjectivity, and imperial atrophy—that its aesthetizing strategy sought to keep out of the text.[5]

We can take it for granted, then, to paraphrase Fredric Jameson, that modernism is "an ideological expression of capitalism" (and hence imperialism) and that the texts of nascent modernists (such as Conrad) are to be found "in the increasing fragmentation both of the rationalized external world and of the colonized psyche alike."[6] Our critical problem, however, is how to read the triad relationship between a rationalized European experience, colonized (African) spaces, and the cultural forms of modernism. Several questions come immediately to mind here: How and why does Africa come to occupy such an important role in the discourse of modernism? Indeed, why is the continent one of the important places in which European anxieties are staged or projected in the era of late colonialism, which is also the nascent moment of modernism? How and why does the triumphant narrative of empire discussed in previous chapters become transformed into that discourse of melancholy and death whose apogee is T. S. Eliot's *The Wasteland*? And—once again—why is the death of the European subject by necessity staged in the colonial space?

Let us address the first question by taking a step back from what has now come to be considered the normative moment of modernism—the period after World War I. Let us begin by recalling that one of the striking features of Mary Kingsley's encounter with Africa, discussed at the end of chapter 4, was her deep involvement and fascination with the Fang people of Gabon and their art forms. Now I have described Kingsley's concern with indigenous African cultures, and especially their forms of knowledge, as a mark of her relativism and hence her modernism. For Kingsley, Africa is not merely a place onto which European anxieties can be projected but also a cultural system with its own grids and norms; she considers Fang objects and subjects worthy of study and understanding in their own right. Her political argument is that understanding the other is imperative if the decline of empire is to be halted and the totality of the cultural systems created by colonialism understood and appreciated. And yet, in the end, it is difficult to say whether Kingsley is fascinated with the Fang's reputation as vicious cannibals or their ability to produce remarkable works of art—what she calls fetishes. There is a sense in which Kingsley's fascination with the Fang as cannibals is inseparable from her admiration of their art; indeed, one crucial sign of her modernism is the way in which her image of Africa is sometimes underwritten by an admixture of revulsion and attraction and—quite often—is mediated by the paradox of purity and danger, which has been discussed so effectively by Mary Douglas.[7]

Indeed, when one pays closer attention to Kingsley's discourse on the African fetish—or scrutinizes her collection of Fang artifacts, such as the *Mavungu* figure—what one detects is the insignias of what will soon come to be called modernism. For one, African masks produced by none other than the so-called Fang cannibals will soon make their way into the salons of Europe, where, in the hands of painters such as Matisse and Picasso, they will forever change the European discourse on representation, on mimesis and subjectivity. On another level, however, Africa enters the cognitive structures of modernism precisely as a fetish, a figure that, like Kingsley's *Mavungu*, attracts us both because of its radical alterity and its sense of danger. And if we accept Jameson's premise that "modernism can at one and the same time be read as a Utopian compensation for everything reification brings with it," the African fetish is both a staging of reification in its most radical manifestation and the form in which it is negated.[8] In other words, the African fetish represents alterity in its most extreme form; it represents the forces that reason and civility cannot contain. But it is in such figures of excess that the deepest human forces, the forces from which the ideals of culture spring, are represented. Later in this chapter we will see how such modern writers as Joseph Conrad and Graham Greene deploy Africa as a fetish in their efforts to reconcile their negation of modern civilization with the utopianism inherent in even the most frightening sites of cultural difference.

The answer to the second question—how does the triumphant narrative of empire degenerate into stories of death and melancholy associated with late colonialism?—can be sought in sites of representation that predate high modernism and the historical decline of empire at the end of the nineteenth century. For one, the existence of colonial subjects who write about themselves even as they accept their imperial identity is symptomatic of a crisis beneath the synchronic vision of empire. The existence of native voices that challenge the unitary force of the *imperium*—and hence its dominant tropes—would seem to suggest that the forms of diachronic representation that, in Said's view, radicalize imperial discourse can be read even before imperialism enters its terminal phase in the period after World War I. Said's argument, as it emerges at a crucial juncture in *Orientalism*, is that the old imperial project was governed by a set of binomial oppositions, a panoramic perspective, and synchronic essentialism, all resulting in a comprehensive vision in which the realm of the other was always assumed to be instinctively intelligible and the center and margin were bound by what were often presented as the laws of nature and history.[9]

But as early as the 1850s, as we saw in Mary Seacole's adventures, there is a sustained attempt by the colonized subjects themselves to resist the "consolidated vision" of colonialisms and to rewrite themselves otherwise, or at least to gaze at the empire from the margins of its cartography. And while such gestures of self-representation and counter-discourse often seem to be limited by the colonial subjects' acquiescence in an imposed imperial identity and their appeal to the ideals sanctioned by the culture of colonialism and the colonizing mission, their existence already destabilizes the imperial narrative in subtle ways. In other words, the discourse of colonialism, which the imperial travelers who have been discussed in previous chapters represented as flowing in only one direction (from the center to the margin), is reversed in defiance of the imperial teleology itself.[10] The fundamentally totalizing image of empire—and thus the unitary trope of the dominion or commonwealth that secures the cartography of the imperial center by linking it to the colonial periphery—is challenged, even in its dominant moment, by a diachronic, but stillborn, discourse of alterity.

In addition, as Mary Douglas would say, the disorder that threatens the pattern of the colonial narrative cannot simply be condemned as an aberration, because even in its destruction of existing patterns, it is the condition of possibility of colonial order and civility. Disorder hence comes to "symbolise both danger and power."[11] It is important to remember, in these circumstances, that the notion of a totalizing colonial culture depends, as numerous writers in the nineteenth and early twentieth century recognized, on an ambivalent epistemology: the structures and cartographies of empire are always unstable (the imperial economy and system of governance are often plagued by crisis and potential disaster), but the image of empire, both at home and abroad, is one of a totalized object of knowledge and a spectacle to be celebrated in endless exhibitions.

Toward the end of the nineteenth century, however, the synchronic image of empire begins to collapse under its internal strains. By the time of the Berlin Conference of 1884, when European powers meet to partition Africa, the imperial ideology seems to have reached its apex, but the structures and referents of empire have entered a state of terminal decline. If for most of the nineteenth century imperial ideologies had been sustained by an inherent belief in European cultural superiority and the efficacy of the civilizing mission, the emergence of modernism forced such gatekeeping concepts as civilization, progress, and even science to lose much of their earlier authority. The great irony of what Hobson was to call the "new imperialism" lies in the dialectical divide between its ideological manifestation and its instrumental instability. The division of Africa, for example, was to be interpreted as the performative moment of European triumph, but beneath the well-orchestrated events in Berlin there lurked the memories of disasters at Fashoda and Khartoum, to mention just two examples.[12]

English modernism is thus the product of a fascinating paradox in the culture of colonialism: it emerges at a time when imperialism seems to have institutionalized a rationalized global community, but it mediates a situation in which the central categories in this institutionalization—temporality, reason, subjectivity—have lost their traditional authority. This ambivalent context needs to be emphasized for two reasons. First, while I agree with Said's claim that late imperialism is characterized, as in the works of T. E. Lawrence, by the emergence of a diachronic narrative, what we are dealing with here is not simply a shift in semiotic signs or a new instrumental attitude. In other words, we cannot attribute the changes we see in the works of Lawrence—or, for my purposes in this section, in the African writings of Conrad and Greene—to a change in these writers' attitudes toward imperialism and its economy of representation.[13] The shift from a synchronic to a diachronic narrative must be attributed, above everything else, to a basic transformation in the nature of the colonial object itself and the writers' mode of cogniting it.[14] While it is true that the ideal of empire dominates cultural discourse in England as much in the 1890s as it had fifty or so years earlier, the imperial spaces can no longer be conceived—or represented—as spaces that secure English identity. A new imperial spirit may circulate in official circles in England in the 1890s, but as David Trotter has succinctly observed, it is an imperialism driven by a sense of decay and decline rather than one of achievement and success.[15]

My concern here is the implication of this decline—and the resulting crisis of cognition—on the representation of the colonial space in imperial narratives. My argument is that while Africa is a valuable prize for every major European power (hence the scramble and partition), it cannot function as a stable referent: either it is perceived as a great unknown space, to be discovered and managed through writing, or it is seen as an object of horror, a threat to European identity. And yet this space that threatens European subjectivity is, as many canonical readings of *Heart of Darkness* have argued for years, one of the few places in which this subject can recode its world or even hallow a space in which it can contemplate itself.

In the cultural discourse of a nascent modernism, this ambivalent attitude has important consequences: implicit in this image of Africa as the last frontier of subjectivity and self-reflection is also the belief that the coding of the world (and thus of the empire) has changed in radical ways; we have entered a period in which, as Conrad's novels exemplify so well, older models and codes of representation have become worn out and can no longer provide stable referents or function as the objects of what Jameson has called "semiotic purification."[16] In the economy of modernism, then, the representation of colonial spaces is no longer subsumed under an imperial normativity or authority; on the contrary, the modernist representation of the culture of late colonialism, at home or abroad, functions under an aesthetic program that simultaneously affirms the imperative of colonization but also questions imperial ideologies.

In addition, an important characteristic of what will come to be known as modernism is the existence of "a personal private style, as unmistakable as your fingerprint, as incomparable as your own body."[17] This notion of a private style leads to a crucial transformation in the representation of the colonial space in the 1890s: the set of uniform tropes and styles we saw in the representation of the West Indies and Africa in the previous chapter—tropes that survive for more than half a century and cross racial and ethnic lines—are nowhere to be found in modernist discourse. For example, writers like Conrad and Kingsley can travel in the same general area of Africa at about the same time and return with radically different narratives, different in terms of both their ideologies and their styles.

For Mary Kingsley, as we have already seen, the African landscape is worthy of ethnographic reflection; the continent is the source of a material culture that needs to be understood if the imperial mission is to live up to its idealist goals of civilization and cultural upliftment. For Conrad, on the other hand, the African forest is the symbol of hermeneutical failure, of the European subject's incapacity to deploy the cognitive systems inherited from the Enlightenment. Under these circumstances, Kingsley narrates Africa in order to enhance the potential of its landscape, even to harness its disorder and excess to the patterns of modernization. But for Conrad, what is most attractive about the African landscape is its capacity to proffer modes of cognitive disorder that nullify the possibility of understanding itself; his African narratives perform the impossibility of cognition. Conrad's performance of cognitive failure is both a reflection of the political crisis that has come to afflict late colonialism and a metacommentary on the status of the aesthetic in the social sphere. In Conrad and Greene, as I will show, the cultural spaces of late colonialism are transformed into objects of aesthetic reflection.

The Colonial Aesthetic

The issue of a colonial aesthetic associated with modernism is generated by questions about empire as a cultural formation in crisis. How do you represent the colonial system when its value has become the source of doubt and its ideals no longer carry what was previously assumed to be a universal authority? What kind of narrative emerges when the colonial space, once read as the source of national power and individual engenderment, is now perceived as a spent and corrupting force, the agent of death and abnegation? We can glimpse some answers to these questions by reading Conrad's African tale "An Outpost of Progress" (1897), a haunting parody of the ideal of progress and trade and a powerful representation of late-colonial neurosis.[18]

In this story, in which Africa functions as both the last frontier for the engenderment of the European subject and the place of its ultimate death, we read, first and foremost, the emergence of representative strategies that revise the narratives of travel and alterity discussed in the previous chapters: the space of the other is no longer conceived as the terrain in which we can develop new knowledge about the self by reading it in a binomial relation with the colonial other. Indeed, if Victorian travelers like Froude go to the colonies to affirm the necessity of the imperial mission and its ideals, as I argued earlier, Conrad's story is cautionary in this regard—it is a calculated dramatization of the inefficacy of such ideals and their inevitable doom. And if revisionary imperialists like Mary Kingsley see trade as the only remaining justification for colonization, then "An Outpost of Progress" has to be read as the debunking of the last major justification of the imperial ideology.

In Conrad's story, the trading station—the sign of Europe in the heart of darkness—is both the beacon of civilization and the symbol of the barbarism that lurks beneath the ideality of the colonial mission in Africa. Moreover, if we accept the philosophical argument that global imperialism is the ultimate play of the Weberian dictum on the rationalization of the world, then we have to read Conrad's trading post as an illustration of the ultimate consequence of this process—absolute reification, degeneration, and decay. And as is often the case in Conrad, the shift from rationalization to reification is achieved through a simple recoding of traditional modes of representation:

> There were two white men in charge of the trading station. Kayerts, the chief, was short and fat; Carlier, the assistant, was tall, with a large head and a very broad trunk perched upon a long pair of thin legs. The third man on the staff was a Sierra Leone nigger, who maintained that his name was Henry Price. (214)

Represented in truncated terms, the white men in the outpost are deprived of the traditional primacy that dominant subjects are supposed to have over the objects they dominate; reduced to the appellation and aspersion that have come to be read as the symbol of unnaming itself, the black man is, nevertheless, given a full name, which might not be his real name.[19] In this equivocal act of naming and unnaming—and this is the significant point—both colonial and colonized subjects are reduced to the same level, conflated with each other, similarly objectified, and hence collapsed into the world they claim to dominate.

This point becomes more apparent when we realize that Conrad's concern with reification as a code of representation is driven by his need to
question the claim that imperialism has succeeded in systematizing the
world by instituting certain social and cultural totalities based on the principle of reason. The agent of systematization in Conrad's story, the man
who had "planned and had watched the construction of this outpost of
progress" lies "under a tall cross much out of the perpendicular," a symbol of the impossibilities of the ideals he had set out to promote. The
agent of civilization has died, yet the consequences of his actions and discredited ideals remain, both as insignias of his failure and as evidence of
the inevitable corruption of the African landscape.

The outpost is hence a symbol of the failure of the idea of progress
but it also represents the persistence of this ideology; it is a monument to
a social system in which rationalization is negated by reification. In affirming the power of reification over rationalization, Conrad's goal is to
unpack the idealism that underlies both the colonial project and the claim
that imperial spaces engender new subjects. This point is obvious in his
deployment of fetishism as a supplement for trade; in this short story, as
in the whole of Conrad's oeuvre, commerce and colonization are, as David
Simpson has noted, the most visible signs of the displacement of the self
and its social grounding.[20] Reduced to mechanical functions, disembod-
ied and disempowered by the forces that were supposed to engender them,
the agents of commerce have become fetishes: "Society, not from any tenderness, but because of its strange needs, had taken care of those two men,
forbidding them all independent thought, all initiative, all departure from
routine; and forbidding it under pain of death. They could only live on
condition of being machines" (217).

Indeed, what makes Africa, as a colonial space, different from Asia is its
innate capacity to reduce society to the same level as violent nature, one
without tenderness or feelings, and thus one that displays the same character and performs the same function as industrial capitalism. It is not by
accident, then, that whereas India's capacity for alienation is represented
by such modernist writers as Kipling and Forster in terms of its cultural
institutions (the Museum, Temple, and Mosque), the most prominent
insignia of Africanness in modernism is the forest. The African forest
would hence appear to negate the ideals of culture and civilization.

And yet, if Jameson is right in his claim that the characteristic form of rationalization is "the reorganization of operations in terms of the binary system of means and ends,"[21] Conrad's story is about the failure of the means/ends opposition. For without a clear sense of the binary between subject and object, human and mechanical functions, colonizer and colonized, the cognitive systems constructed by the colonial cultural system no longer seem useful to the subjects themselves or the cultures they represent. But what does Africa have to do with the collapse of the old cognitive system? Africa is important for Conrad and his fellow modernists for two reasons. On the one hand, an amorphous African presence evokes a world that, in the popular European imagination, is linked with death and danger—Africa threatens the *cogito*, the most privileged term in European modes of thought since the Enlightenment (or at least since Descartes). On the other hand, an engagement with Africa generates a new discourse on the relation between the self and what Conrad calls society, for it is in the empty spaces of the continent that preexisting codes and systems of cognition will be shown to be null and void.

Clearly, if the aesthetic of modernism is to provide a critique of modernization, it must be able to exhibit cognitive failure in the process of narration. And of course, Conrad's African stories are some of the most powerful examples of how, in the "dark continent," the project of colonial modernity is called into question by the irrational and charismatic forces of residual primitivism. In "An Outpost of Progress," then, the imperial ideals of trade and progress are ironized through their linkage with "the Evil Spirit that rules the lands under the equator" (215); the European subject, which in imperial ideologies claims superiority and transcendence over the colonial landscape, is now subjected to "the subtle influences of surroundings" (216). Conrad makes quite clear that the story of progress is not one of colonial mastery but one of degeneration and atavism. In the second instance, Africa sustains the epistemology of modernism by creating circumstances in which fetishism challenges traditional modes of self-cognition and even realistic representation: if you cannot sustain clear distinctions between European subjects and African surroundings, between rational systems and evil spirits, then representation must be reduced to an impressionistic flirting with figures and images, unexpected reversals and transformation.[22]

The result of this mode of cognition is the centrality of fetishism and narcissism as what Simpson calls "the central tropes in Conrad's analysis of the colonial experience": "The relation of center to circumference, the inner to the outer, so urgently needing to be kept in motion by the Romantic theorists of the mind-world relation, has now become so firmly fixed in an *identity* of inner and outer that redetermination can no longer occur."[23] And so the question arises: what positive force can narration play if it has been deprived of its power or capacity to redetermine its "raw materials"?

This problem can be explored further through an examination of the central paradox in "An Outpost of Progress": Africa is characteristically represented as unknowable and fixed, but by the same token the European self, which assumed it could master or change this inscrutable landscape, is itself reduced to the same "inert duplication."[24] Conrad begins his story by calling the idea of progress—and a civilized subjectivity—into question: the two men at the outpost of progress are, as we have already seen, victims of their own society's mechanistic desire, symptoms of the decline of civilization. At the same time, however, Conrad refuses to associate the colonial space with redemptive value: for if Kayerts and Carlier have left Europe deprived of their autonomy, no redetermination can occur in Africa. The continent is not the utopian space in which Europe can be regenerated; on the contrary, Africa is the locality in which the workings of the mind are challenged and ultimately reduced to the inert will of the world:

They lived like blind men in a large room, aware only of what came into contact with them (and of that only imperfectly), but unable to see the general aspect of things. The river, the forest, all the great land throbbing with life, were like a great emptiness. Even the brilliant sunshine disclosed nothing intelligible. Things appeared and disappeared before their eyes in an unconnected and aimless kind of way. The river seemed to come from nowhere and flow nowhither. It flowed through a void. Out of that void, at times, came canoes, and men with spears in their hands would suddenly crowd the yard of the station. They were naked, glossy black, ornamented with snowy shells and glistening brass wire, perfect of limb. (218)

What we have in this kind of passage, apart from the obvious crystallization of the themes of fragmentation and fetishism discussed earlier, is a certain homology between Conradian style and the reified culture of late colonialism. The impressionistic style and the fragmentary sentence are the most obvious examples of this homology, but there is also the disjunctive perspective of the subjects and their loss of a totalizing vision; in addition, the description is driven by what one may call its negative intentions, its hankering for what cannot be perceived and its desire to level peoples and things, the animate and inanimate into one fetishistic mass.

There are other reasons why the above passage is central to the changing discourse on representation in early modernism; in several ways, it reverses some of the central tenets of imperial mastery discussed in the previous chapters. Described as blind, the European subjects have no control over their surroundings and no capacity to reorganize their social spaces; without imperial agency, such subjects cannot manage the colonial landscape to secure domestic identities. Indeed, they are imprisoned in a world full of material objects whose presence does not yield intelligibility. The forest, like the river in *Heart of Darkness*, is a powerful presence whose primary narrative function, however, is to call attention to equally powerful absences, namely, culture and civilization.

What we have here, then, is a radical skewing of temporal relationships and the conjunctive moments of closure that we witnessed in earlier narratives. Whereas such writers as Froude or Kingsley use the moment of return to reflect on the imperial experience, now seen in its totality and closure, Conrad's narrative ends in what can best be described as a demented moment of insight. After killing his associate, Carlier, in a state of insane rage, Kayerts finds solace in hermeneutic delirium:

> The violence of the emotions he had passed through produced a feeling of exhausted serenity. . . . He sat by the corpse thinking; very actively, thinking very new thoughts. He seemed to have broken loose from himself altogether. His old thoughts, convictions, likes and dislikes, things he respected and things he abhorred, appeared in their true light at last! (231)

In the face of insights acquired only in delirium and confirmed by death, can we talk of a redemptive force in Conrad or the utopian compensation of his modernist aesthetic?[25] It would be tempting here to reopen the whole question of his relation to imperialism, or even to modernism, but

I want to take a different tack: I want to examine these relationships some-how indirectly by reexamining Conrad's tenuous revision of hegemonic notions on representation and temporality as they are developed in *Heart of Darkness*. I want to argue that to read this novella as an uneven challenge to hegemonic theories of representation, we need to connect it more clearly with the cultural debates surrounding late colonialism. We can do so if we begin with an axiom and a working hypothesis: if the culture of colonialism, industrialism, and bourgeois hegemony in the nineteenth cen-tury demands and establishes a "realistic" style that depends on the exis-tence of an intelligible world, the capacity of language to represent this world, and a linear temporality, then the modernism of Conrad's novel is an attempt to narrate the failure of this hegemonic style.

My assumption here is that the relative stability we seem to detect in the great "realistic" narratives of the nineteenth century arises from the writers' confidence in the stability of the world they represent, its sense of time, and its cartography; this style is predicated on the hope that the cri-sis of culture and consciousness triggered by radical historical change can be redetermined in narrative form. And thus, until colonialism enters the period of crisis discussed earlier in this chapter, no one doubts what Eng-land signifies and what its relation to the rest of the world is; the concern with topographic representation in novels such as George Eliot's *Middle-march* or the travel narratives discussed earlier in this book is premised on the belief that social and physical boundaries can be confirmed, social for-mations made visible, and ideological norms secured in writing.[26]

Conrad's novel opens by challenging such a topographical schema and the philosophy of representation that underwrites it. The London that is celebrated by Victorian writers as the uncontested center of the world—and the visible symbol of a thriving Englishness—is now qualified by "a mournful gloom brooding motionless" over it; the subjects who gaze over the city are bound by the sea, the insignia of displacement, and appear to us as truncated, fetishistic figures (7). If the Thames functions in popular and official imperial discourse as the waterway to civilization and progress, in Conrad's tale it stands for either a belated historicism ("The dreams of men, the seed of commonwealths, the germs of empires" [8]) or an inscrutable signifier of the mysterious or incomprehensible (10). Readers of the novel can tell, even in its first few pages, that it evokes the narrative of historicism—of temporal progress and hermeneutical understanding—only to negate it. What may not be apparent, however, is how the tale similarly conjures up geographical figures to question the social formation that has secured the identity of empire in the last fifty years. This simultaneous evocation and displacement of geographical figures is most apparent in the parallel representation of the Thames and the Congo, a presentation that undoes the center/periphery configuration that we saw in older imperial narratives: both rivers are pathways into the mysterious and the unknown, into barbarism.

A more complex form of spatial displacement, however, occurs when Africa is represented as a blank space. And while numerous commentators have seen this blankness as a form of semiotic emptiness that, nevertheless, confirms preexisting images of the continent, I would like to suggest that its intention (unsuccessful, perhaps) is to undermine the authority of topographic representation, the efficacy of the cartographic.[27] In other words, while Africa in the nineteenth century is the space of alterity ready to be inscribed on the European grid of knowledge and representation, it is now conceived as something larger than the existing grammar of spatial representation or cultural values: "It had ceased to be a blank space of delightful mystery—a white patch for a boy to dream glorious over. It had become a place of darkness" (12). But what does Marlow seek beyond the unrecoverable romance of blankness and colonial darkness?

My contention here is that Marlow hankers not for the empty space into which the European imagination might project its fears and desires, or the locality in which empire reproduces or displaces domestic anxieties, but for a place of excess, of a hermeneutical surplus that goes beyond binomialism: "The best way I can explain it to you is by saying that for a second or two I felt as though instead of going to the centre of a continent I were about to set off for the centre of the earth" (16). While Said is right in reading Marlow's journey up the river as a temporal process propelled by "Europeans performing acts of imperial mastery and will in (or about) Africa"[28], Conrad's subject and narrator seeks to transcend and ultimately resolve the opposition between Europe and Africa through acts of allegorization.

This allegory relies heavily on the evocation of a surplus of meaning.[29] Neither Europe nor Africa is a stable geographic figure: as the ending of the novel confirms, Kurtz is ultimately a product of both European "civilization" and African "barbarism." When the allegories of Europe and Africa seem to have the same import, our critical attention should not perhaps be on where Conrad stands in relation to the culture of colonial-ism—we can assume he is both for it and against it—but on why his nar-rative abrogates distinctions that his acquired English identity considers fundamental to its existence and uniqueness. The focus here should be on both the relation between temporality and epistemology and Conrad's departure from his immediate precursors and contemporaries.

For illustrative purposes, let us compare the deployment of the gesture of naming and denomination, itself an important act of imperial mastery, as it emerges in two representative moments, one from Mary Kingsley's *Travels in West Africa*, the other from *Heart of Darkness*. In Kingsley's elaborate descriptions of the West African coast, the emphasis is on both the dis-tinctiveness of the rivers and the trading posts that line them and the impressions they leave in the observer's mind; but even where the accent is on the impressionism, the reader is never allowed to question the reality of the objects of representation:

> Lagos is a marvellous manifestation of the perversity of man cou-pled with the perversity of nature, being at one and the same time one of the most important exporting ports on the West African seaboard, and one of the most difficult to get at.[30]

The same coast becomes, in Conrad's narrative, a series of transferable fetishistic figures:

> Every day the coast looked the same, as though we had not moved, but we passed various places—trading places—with names like Gran' Basam, Little Popo, names that seemed to belong to some sor-did farce acted in front of a sinister back-cloth.[31]

In Kingsley, the act of representation is clearly connected to a kind of mas-tery: trading posts are insignias of the European mission in Africa; locali-ties exist in an intelligible geographical schema and temporal scale. Con-rad's description, in contrast, negates some of the most important schemes in the traditional narrative of travel: the pluralization of the observer negates its claim to unique subjectivity; represented as unrelentingly uni-form, the coast is denied both its uniqueness and its sense of wonder; dis-connected from a clear system of values or even a cultural grammar, place names become marks of disembodiment. Add to this disembodiment the images of decay, death, and atrophy that populate Conrad's narrative, and you can see how he deliberately subverts traditional temporality.

Indeed, where earlier writers on Africa see their narratives as proof of what Fabian has called "the power to name, to describe, to classify,"[32] Conrad's narrative exhibits what Jameson aptly calls the "bravura effect"—a display of the gap between the sign and its performance.[33] Temporality is certainly a central motif in Marlow's narrative, but as Peter Brooks and Christopher Miller have observed, time and its passage are enclosed in repetition, circularity, and reversion; time is deployed in the cause of anti-temporality.[34] And if temporality is the enabling condition of epistemology and consciousness in the Western tradition, then we can read Conrad's narration of time as the undoing of knowledge and consciousness and thus their condition of possibility.[35] In short, temporality in *Heart of Darkness* is haunted by fetishism, which the narrative compels to function as the radical opposite of knowledge and consciousness.

Now, let us recall that Marlow's journey up the river is cast in the form of a quest motif or a pilgrimage: it promises revelation and significance at the end of the voyage. But the more Marlow moves deeper and deeper into the "heart of darkness" and hence closer to Kurtz, the more he is confronted by the gap between signs and their meaning: Kurtz's figure hovers over the trading posts of the Congo, but for the narrator, he is just a word—"I did not see the man in the name any more than you do" (29)—and not even time will reveal who he is or what he means. The problem that Marlow faces at this stage, as both a narrator and a subject, is one that he presents to his interlocutors succinctly: "Do you see anything?" (30). And if we accept Roland Barthes's basic premise that temporality provides narrative with its logic, the more immediate problem here is how to represent experience when it has lost the logic of time, the "adequate motive" that in Brooks's words secures its meaning.[36]

Alternatively, we could argue that Conrad's novel asserts its modernity by renouncing the Benjaminian notion of redemptive or messianic time.[37] The journey up the river becomes, in these circumstances, regressive: "'Going up the river was like travelling back to the earliest beginnings of the world, when vegetation rioted on the earth and the big trees were kings'" (35). Regressive time, which takes us to a time before temporality, is also empty time, and empty time doesn't secure knowledge: "Were we to let go our hold of the bottom, we would be absolutely in the air—in space. We wouldn't be able to tell where we were going to—whether up or down stream or across—till we fetched against one bank or the other—and then we wouldn't know at first which it was" (43). Far from helping us negotiate the miasma engendered by the African landscape, the narrative revels in its capacity to muddy the waters, so to speak! We cannot turn to the narrator or temporality for assurance or anchor.

This kind of reading of temporality in the novel, however, creates a problem of its own: if Marlow's narrative is about the dislocation of words from their referents, signs from their performance, and temporality from its logic, how do we explain the dynamism of the narrative? Does the bravura effect function as a compensation for the missing temporal sequence? Does the novel derive its momentum from its capacity to empty itself of time? Or is Said right in his conclusion that the novel's numerous dilatory moments are compensated for by "the narrative's sheer historical movement, the temporal forward movement—with digressions, descriptions, exciting encounters, and all"?[38] But how can we define the narrative's momentum as temporal when it is driven by an anti-temporal imperative? One way out of this paradox is to take the high modernist path and argue that when temporality can no longer be read as a historical phenomenon we have to seek the logic of the narrative in its aesthetic effect. In this reformulation, temporality is connected to epistemology only in a negative relationship—one of disavowal.[39]

Said's influential reading of *Heart of Darkness*, of course, takes a different path, one that leads us to the problem of late colonialism: "This narrative . . . is connected directly with the redemptive force, as well as the horror, of Europe's mission in the dark world," argues Said.[40] It is tempting to endorse this claim for a simple reason: even as the narrative renounces imperial temporality, it also seems to be motivated by the ideals of empire enunciated early in the novel (what redeems imperialism is "the idea only" [10]). And although I have suggested that the journey up the river retards the subject's capacity for knowledge, Marlow does come out of his adventures enlightened—he has discovered the power of the horror and its empty echo.

But the situation is slightly more complicated. The knowledge Marlow has discovered is simply affective—it cannot be transferred to others in a systematic and rational manner. And since his enlightenment emerges from impressions that only he, the privileged observer, can see, it can be narrated only in a phantasmological discourse that calls the narrator's authority into question. It is only in such a discursive formation, for example, that Kurtz can be reimagined and be performed for the interlocutors: "He lived then before me, he lived as much as he had ever lived—a shadow insatiable of splendid appearances, of frightful realities, a shadow darker than the shadow of the night, and draped nobly in the folds of a gorgeous eloquence" (72). But Kurtz cannot live before the interlocutors the same way he lives for Marlow. The narrator's encounter with the ivory god remains an original moment that cannot be reproduced; he can only try to convey the affect of the first encounter. The narrative of late colonialism is, like the historical process itself, belated, alienated from both its agents and its ideals; the telling of this story of failure demands that both the narrator and his interlocutors be alienated from Kurtz, their object of reflection.

If we take Kurtz to be the embodiment of the new imperialist, the narrative nudges, even forces, us to conclude that he presides over an enterprise whose ideologies have degenerated into empty language: "Kurtz discoursed. A voice! a voice! It rang deep to the very last. It survived his strength to hide in the magnificent folds of eloquence the barren darkness of his heart" (67). The reader, then, is not a witness to any redemptive force in imperialism but of its staging in that gap between its ideality and reality, of its disarticulation on the cusp where Europe and Africa threaten to collapse into each other. And thus the process of time in the "heart of darkness" is neither the "medium of a sacred history" nor a "negative modernity."[41] Narrative still affirms the distance between Europe and its dark other, but the trope of travel no longer seems to ascribe a positive value to either entity; sometimes Africa and Europe seem to be defined by the same negativity, but their modes of darkness are not entirely the same; the glitter of European greed (represented by Kurtz's ivory) is pitted against the ominous shadows of African barbarism. And thus we are left to operate in a state of temporal limbo, in which neither Africa nor Europe can provide the European subject, be it Marlow or Kurtz, with secure places of emplacement or a set of redemptive values.

The Uses of Primitivism

This situation seems to change dramatically in the period after World War I when, with the consolidation of high modernism as the normative literary style, Africa suddenly begins to be associated with a certain kind of redemptive primitivism. The idea of Africa as a possible sanctuary for the lost souls of civilization is particularly appealing when the idea of Europe enters into a state of terminal crisis in the years between the two world wars. It is indeed ironic that at the very moment when modernism is consolidated as the hegemonic European art form, it is forced to renegotiate its relationship with the colonial other. And it is because the works of writers of the interregnum, novelists such as Graham Greene, do not seem to fit in either the modernist norm or what will later come to be called the postmodern moment, that they come to provide the best illustrations of the relationship between modernism and colonial culture in the age of imperial decline, which is also the beginning of decolonization.[42] In such works, Africa is both the self and the other of Europe, connected to it by a long history of colonial rule and conquest but separated from it by the persistence of what is considered its residual primitivism. The important change from the narratives of nascent modernism such as *Heart of Darkness* is that there is a concerted attempt by some European writers, such as Greene or André Gide, to valorize this primitivism.

Indeed, in narratives such as Greene's *Journey Without Maps* (1936), the social and cultural codes that mark the continent as the depository of alterity—danger, eroticism, and the unknown—are now sought after and represented as desirable alternatives to European civilization. Africa itself becomes a key integer in what Greene calls the "method of psychoanalysis"—the mechanism for understanding forms of alterity hidden beneath the veneer of civilization:

> The method of psychoanalysis is to bring the patient back to the idea which he is repressing: a long journey backwards without maps, catching a clue here and there, as I caught the names of villages from this man and that, until one has to face the general idea, the pain or the memory. This is what you have feared, Africa may be imagined as saying, you can't avoid it, there it is creeping round the wall, flying in at the door, rusting the grass, you can't turn your back, you can't forget it, so you may as well take a long look.[43]

In temporal terms, Greene's formulation of Africa is a clear echo of Conrad's notion of regressive time, but with important qualifications: instead of cutting us off from comprehension, the journey back in time is a journey of discovery, one that yields useful clues to self-understanding; instead of confronting us with the innate emptiness in the center of our being, the encounter with Africa affords us a mirror in which we can discover and gaze at hidden selves. In addition, if Greene's Africa is neither utopic nor dystopic it is because, as we shall see in greater detail below, the continent is conceived as the heterotopic space in which the European subject comes to terms with its repressed self.[44]

To journey without maps is to travel to a place that is no longer defined by inherited cultural norms but is described by the subject's own inclinations or projections. In these circumstances, argues Greene, Africa cannot be defined by its radical alterity—"you couldn't talk of darkest Africa with any conviction when you had known Nottingham well" (100–101)— but by the human emotions we invest in it and our modes of possessing it (157–58). As for those who would prefer to define the continent as a blank darkness, or as the depository of decay and death, Greene reminds us that the joy he derives from traveling in Africa is secured by the knowledge that the more he journeys into the continent, the closer he gets to an unadulterated racial self:

But it was only fair, I suppose, that the moments of extra-ordinary happiness, the sense that one was nearer than one had ever been to the racial source, to satisfying the desire for an instinctive way of life, the sense of release, as when in the course of pyscho-analysis one uncovers by one's effort a root, a primal memory, should have been counterbalanced by the boredom of childhood too, that agonizing boredom of "apartness" which came before one had learnt the fatal trick of transferring emotion, of flashing back enchantingly all day long one's own image, a period when other people were as distinct from oneself as this Liberian forest. I sometimes wondered whether, if one had stayed longer, if one had not been driven out again by tiredness and fear, one might have re-learned the way to live without transference, with a lost objectivity. (158)

From this passage, which is typical of many in Greene's book, we can see that although the categories that define Africa have remained the same— the continent is associated with instinctiveness and enchantment rather than reason and reflection—they are no longer conceived as the negative axiologies against which European reason and order are measured. The continent is conceived, on the contrary, as a figure of desire, especially the desire for cognitive and aesthetic values that transcend the prisonhouse of modernity and civilization. And thus the African other is now the figure through which the European subject simultaneously expresses its disenchantment with civilization and its desire for its lost moment of origins and innocence. My concern here, then, is how this colonial space whose alterity was, as we saw in previous chapters, often represented as the very condition of impossibility of the English self (remember the Haitian dystopia in chapter 3?), becomes transformed into a place of knowledge and insight.

Freud's 1913 essay "Totem and Taboo" provides us with a useful starting point. As readers will recall, Freud's primary argument in this essay was that the primitive subject, often represented in Western thought as a figure of difference, was a useful medium for self-understanding in civilized cultures: the mental life of "those whom we describe as savages or half-savages" must "have a peculiar interest for us if we are right in seeing it as a well-preserved picture of an early stage of our own development."[45] In this context, the primitive was not the counterpoint of civilization but the condition of understanding the ideals that modernity had negated in the name of progress and self-fulfillment. Our relationship to the space of the savage, Freud would assert, was equivalent to the notion of taboo—something simultaneously sacred and dangerous, defined by both desire and prohibition (18, 22). As modern subjects, we could not become savages again; indeed, savagery posed one of the greatest threats to the idea of culture. But, at the same time, primitivism provided the only mirror through which we could gaze at the original moments of this culture. It is in this sense that primitivism was to become modernism's alter ego.[46] More significantly, Freud would suggest that there was a general agreement between "taboo usages and obsessional symptoms" (28), going so far as to say that there was a direct collation between the child's primitive psychology and the psyche of primitive cultures. If understanding the psyche of childhood was central to the modernist project, a turn to primitive cultures provided a temptation that few modern writers, influenced by psychoanalysis as they were, could resist.

Given the analogy between the child and the primitive in the foundational moments of psychoanalysis, then, post-Freudian writers like Greene would posit the reading of the bodies and cultures of the other as mirror images of the Western subject before the taint of civilization and of the individual self before the traumas of childhood and adolescence.[47] These authors would come to invest in the other for both cultural and private reasons: because it took them far away from the culture of the father and his law, the journey into the world of the primitive was conceived as a form of transgression; if the fathers had created and valorized the culture of modernity, the sons would seek their *dédoublement* from this culture by striving—through narrative—to possess its radical opposite.

And yet what these writers would come to read on the face of the other was their own ambivalence toward modernity and modernism, their simultaneous rejection of and identification with the culture of the father. It is precisely because of this ambivalence that Africa, for many proponents of modernism, came to be figured primarily by its masks; indeed, Africa would enter modernism as a mask, the symbol of the most primal and yet most frightful meanings.[48] The important point, though, is that such meanings were now valued because they defied the laws of culture and reason—perhaps the two most important insignias of European modernity. And as Freud was to observe in his 1927 essay on civilization and its discontents, one major source of the European disenchantment with modernity was that "what we call civilization is largely responsible for our misery, and that we should be much happier if we gave it up and returned to primitive conditions."[49]

As Greene was to put it aptly at the beginning of *Journey Without Maps*, his travels in West Africa—the modern writers' entry into the body of the other—represented "a distrust of any future based on what we are" (20). Greene may have been in Africa for many reasons, but they all revolved around the question of transgression and excess. In other words, while the identity of the English subject in the high imperial period depended on maintaining the opposition between England and its colonies, between colonial masters and subjects, we now seem to have entered a period (in late colonialism and modernism) in which the reversal of such binaries was seen as the precondition for identity. In a situation in which the relation between centers and margins was being defined by what Zizek calls "a chiasmic exchange," the concept of identity had become *"the result of a certain 'transgression.'"*[50] Indeed, Greene represents his encounter with Africa

as a transgressive and contingent operation driven by the force of necessity: the continent is thus described as a place where the author "never
meant to find myself" (15), but also as a locality that attracts the alienated
European subject because of its purported dangers. For Greene, then, the
blank map of Liberia (16) and the country's dystopic representation in
British diplomatic literature (18) make it an attractive destination: "There
seemed to be a seediness about the place you couldn't get to the same
extent elsewhere, and seediness has a very deep appeal. . . . It seems to sat-
isfy, temporarily, the sense of nostalgia for something lost; it seems to represent a stage further back" (19).

Greene is, of course, never in doubt that in its essence Africa is a temporal category embodied in the figure of the primitive: the Africa he
prefers is that which has yet to be touched by civilization; the primitivism
of this Africa seems to have the capacity to "act strongly on the unconscious mind" (20). But because an essentialized African temporality is
sought as a counter to the modern English culture from which the author
is fleeing, Africa is, in both its positivity and its negativity, a measure of
the failure of colonial modernity itself. In the space where modernity was
supposed to have proved its ability to rationalize culture and civilize the
savage, Greene is quick to note that we were going back in time "from what
we have come, to recall at which point we went astray" (21). If Conrad's
Africa was a place of danger and death, Greene's "dark continent" is a
place of desire, and it is particularly desirable when it is most dangerous.

The consequence of this merging of danger and desire is the transformation of Africa from the epic stage on which imperial grandeur is played
out (the colonialists in Greene suffer from ennui and disenchantment)
into a lyrical discourse in which the human spirit transcends its sordid
materiality to revel, momentarily, in "a sense of warm and sleepy beauty,
of enjoyment divorced from activity and the weariness of willing" (33). If
the subject of modernity was defined by will and reason, Africa is the
place of sentimentality and desire; indeed, the continent appears to
Greene as not a particular place "but a shape, a strangeness, a wanting to
know"; and the cartography of the unknown and the compulsive is "that
of the human heart" (37). Greene's writing of Africa seems to be motivated by the belief that as an aesthetic object, the continent has a value that
transcends its bleak materiality.

A mark of Greene's indebtedness to high modernism, then, can be detected in his contention that while reality cannot be represented simply as it is, and it cannot be repressed completely, it can be suspended in the numerous instances of lyricism proffered by Africa. There are two consequences to this shaping of Africa according to the dictates of the sentimental heart and the unconscious mind. First, the continent comes to be mediated through the category of *aisthesis*—through sensation rather than rationality. If civilization is associated with material cognition and linear temporality, the African primitive is desired because of its capacity to defy such materiality. As an aesthetic object, Africa is an embodiment of the aesthetic space in which our corporal and sensate lives are conjoined. This aesthetic space, says Terry Eagleton in a different context, is "nothing less than the whole of our sensate life together—the business of affections and aversions, of how the world strikes the body on its sensory surfaces, of that which takes root in the gaze and the guts and all that arises from our most banal, biological insertion into the world."[51] Compared to the corrupt civilization of coastal Sierra Leone, the Republic of Liberia attracts the traveler because it exists outside formal modes of cognition: "It would have been easier if I had been able to obtain maps. But the Republic is almost entirely covered by forest, and has never been properly mapped" (45). Travel, then, is no longer motivated by the desire to map unknown territory, to bring unknown spaces under the control of a rational grid; on the contrary, travel seeks to defy cartographical notions such as borders and boundaries and to show how culture can be organized and represented outside the taxonomies we have inherited from modernity (62).

Second, when it is rescued from its materiality (which is conceived as entirely European) and is turned into an aesthetic object, Africa becomes indispensable to Greene's own notion of a modernist subjectivity, one liberated from the demands of custom and tradition. This is what prompts Greene to represent his entry into Liberia, what he considers to be the savage slot, as a form of liberation: "It was a relief to enter the Republic and no longer feel that I was a member of the ruling class" (52). And thus, in dystopic Liberia, the land without borders, the place where civilization had collapsed on its foundations, the subject reconstitutes himself as a free agent, liberated from the dominant ideology and temporality: "I was vexed by the delay at Kailahun. I had not yet got accustomed to the idea that time, as a measured and recorded period, had been left behind on the coast. In the interior there was no such thing as time; the best watches couldn't stand the climate. Sooner or later they stopped" (65).

In late colonialism, then, subjects of modernism are constituted beyond inherited temporality. As Peter Bürger has observed in another context, the articulation of a new subjectivity now depends on the writer's ability to create a work that transcends time.[52] We can push this claim even further and assert that if for Greene and his contemporaries the subject that exists beyond European time and space is an aesthetic subject, traveling in Africa enables the narration of the process in which the aesthetic self is produced and, conversely, provides the mechanics by which the old self rejects bourgeois culture. The subject that is produced in Africa is defined as aesthetic precisely because of its transcendental ambition—its desire to exist beyond time and space in general and beyond the boundaries of the nation-state in particular. Thus, if Greene seems to reserve most of his scorn for England and transplanted English culture, it is because he is in Africa to escape Englishness itself.

He scorns Freetown, the capital of Sierra Leone, not merely because it is a caricatured version of civilization but also because its truncated Anglo-Saxonism reminds him so much of England: "One could see the Anglican cathedral, laterite bricks and tin with a square tower, a Norman church built in the nineteenth century, sticking up out of the early morning fog. There was no doubt at all that one was in home waters" (37). Home is no longer the privileged place of return valorized by earlier travelers, however; it is now the corrupt depository of the insignias of civilization. Transplanted to the colonial space, Englishness seems fake and incomplete. What "darkest" Africa offers in exchange for this incomplete Englishness—and the corrupt insignias of civilization—is the possibility of a transcendental subjectivity, a subjectivity beyond race and creed, a sense of identity that returns us, as it were, to what we were before we embraced the crude materialism of civilization and its divisive taxonomy. This is Greene in western Liberia casting a long gaze at the eight wives of a dead chief being smeared with clay as part of a "pagan" funeral rite:

The majority were old and hideous anyway, but now, the pale colour of the pit in which they sat, they looked as if they had been torn half decomposed from the ground. They had lost with their colour their mark of race and might have been women of any nation who had

been buried and dug up again. . . . There must have been scenes very
like this, I thought, in the last days of pagan England.   (87)

Yes: Africa is the place where "pagan England"—the raw and pure state of
cultural being—can be recuperated.

And so Greene is with Conrad when he turns his attention to the decay
and decomposition he sees on the tropical landscape, but he is perhaps a
step ahead when he sees the value of that decay not so much as lying in its
atavistic inevitability, but in both its transcendentalism and its historicism:
it is in their most horrifying moment that the widows lose the mark of race
and become human beings in their most pure form; it is in the hideousness
of their rites that we glimpse what England was before modernity. Consequently, if Conrad's claim to be one of the pioneers of modernism lies in
his ability to merge the self/other dichotomy in such a way that it is no
longer possible to tell where civilization begins and barbarism ends, Greene,
the late modernist, goes a step further and represents Africa as the mirror
in which England must gaze at itself if it is to recover its essential values.

Does this mean that we can now talk of a European identity whose sig-
nification no longer depends on the evocation of the dark figure of alterity?
Do Nottingham and Africa exist on the same level of representation, unified by a certain "negative universality"?[53] In textual terms, Greene travels in
Africa not in the company of the ancients (or their imperial successors) but
with advocates of modernism such as Baudelaire and Gide, authors whose
projects are driven by the need to collapse the existing topoi of modernity,
the topoi that divides societies into civilized and primitive, rational and irrational, progressive and timeless. But his project is written within a paradox
that Bürger has located in the heart of the aesthetic of modernism:

> Insofar as the polemical rejection of bourgeois culture merely adds
> another chapter to its history, so too the existential interpretation of
> aesthetic autonomy is tied to what it turns against. Neither the self-
> realization of the artist as one who ascetically denies life, nor the
> polemical cultural gesture of the work of art allows us to break out
> of the "nature park" of bourgeoisie culture.[54]

Greene is, of course, not traveling in Africa to deny life; rather, his goal is
to establish alternative configurations of experience, of living, as it were.

But if his ultimate goal in *Journey Without Maps* is to establish a discursive terrain in which the inherited European structures are declared null and void, he is still located somewhere, still writes from an established culture and tradition and a given subjectivity. His challenge, then, is how to represent Africa inside the prism of inherited bourgeois culture, the culture of modernism, and yet present it as the embodiment of an alternative value system. As we have already observed, Greene uses several techniques to circumvent this problem: he celebrates the primitiveness of Africa as the (desirable) polarity of Europe; he collapses the paradigm of cultural difference that posits Africa as the scene of radical alterity; he even reads Africa as transcendentalizing, as the site of infinite freedom, the place in which the writing self finds the power of *aisthesis*. And yet in none of these situations is Greene able to circumvent the power of the Englishness he writes against. He obviously prefers the primitivism of Africa to its civilized enclaves, but he celebrates the primitive under two perhaps inescapable anxieties: first, that the insignias of the primitive are already inscribed in the European mind as symbols of horror and second, that to evoke the notion of the primitive, even in the most positive way, is to sustain one of modernism's dread notions—the idea of progress.

Greene finds it difficult, especially in the latter respect, to free the notion of the primitive from the category of progress. For while he sets out to debunk the idea of an imperial mission and its informing vision of civilization, his belief that primitive Africa mirrors Englishness at an earlier historical period already presupposes the topos of progress. True, the whole book displays how negative and corrupt this progress is, but still, the journey is structured by a certain progressive temporality and mentality. Now, while this claim certainly goes against Greene's overt intentions (after all, he has already informed us that the journey into Africa is "a long journey backwards without maps" [97]), his representation of the continent is mediated by a cultural map that precedes his journey. The issue here is not only Greene's self-projection onto Africa—remember, he uses the continent as a mechanism for confronting his own troubled childhood—but the way the "journey without maps" mirrors or parallels two previous ideological and theoretical journeys: (a) a trip through the new Soviet Union in which Greene's expectations of the "new country" ushered in by socialism quickly melt into disillusionment (99); and (b) the journey of the author's conversion to Catholicism, in which the advent of a new faith quickly leads to cynicism ("In Nottingham I was instructed in Catholicism, travelling here and there by tram into new country with the fat priest who had once been an actor" [101]).

The modernist excursion—and excursus—into Africa will take the form of a narrative journey defined by circularity—a movement from disillusionment to expectation to disillusionment. What this means, among other things, is that in the end, not even the most "primitive" and "uncontaminated" of African cultural institutions—the Secret Society—can be apprehended outside the language Greene has acquired from the civilization he had sought to leave behind: the world of masked "devils" is described as "a curiously Kafka-like situation" (175). This feeble attempt to recuperate one of the most secretive and complex West African institutions using the language of modernism is a mark of the author's awareness of the failure of his own project, of the exhaustion and ennui that set in when the world of the primitive refuses to be contained by the cultural grammar of modernism and the author discovers that he cannot speak the language of the other.

For if Greene's ideological intention throughout the book is to establish a certain discursive equality between Africa and England, as I have already suggested, his encounter with the continent seems to make him even more aware of the simple fact that the world of the primitive has no value without its claim to some measure of difference. Greene sets out to escape the Europeanized enclaves of the West African coast, in search of the cradle of mankind, so to speak, but this journey leads backward to its original sites, to the places from which its author sought to escape. And significantly, as Greene makes his way back to the coast, he is relieved to encounter the sites of civilization that he set out to negate, sites that now serve to counter the fatigue and disillusionment triggered by an encounter with the bush: "I was happy with the sense that every step was toward home, there was something peculiarly English about the fish, the pond, the quite small trees" (182).

Are we now dealing with a Lacanian scenario in which the object of desire, once encountered, loses its allure? If we remember the dictum that the meaning of the journey ultimately depends as much on the mechanism of writing as it does on the desire that propels it, we will see that the "authentic primitivism" the author celebrates at the beginning of his journey is no different from the "corrupted primitivism" of coastal Liberia that he seems to be fleeing at the end of the book. While Greene may not accept this assertion, he seems to have discovered that the boundary between England and its colonial other is not as pronounced as he thought at the beginning of his journey; in cultural terms, Englishness and the "African forest" are separated by a "quarter of a mile"; in temporal terms, there is a continuous two-way movement across the now amorphous border that separates civilization and barbarism:

> A quarter of a mile away the forest wall set a limit to England, and across the stream in a single file came a few men, naked except for their loin-cloths, carrying bows and steel-tipped arrows. It was like the world of Miss Nesbit, where odd savage people appear in the country lanes; they might have been coming through the Amulet out of the African forest into an English park. We passed them, going ourselves into Africa, while they with their bows and arrows, their naked cicatrized bodies, went on into the park, toward the great house and the butler's pantry. (182)

Greene's journey began with the supposition that civilization and barbarism were separated as much by time as by space; he assumed that although the primitive other represented our culture at an earlier age, the insignias of civilization and modernity were clear marks of the gap between England and Africa as cartographic and cultural categories. The trajectory of his journey was intended to trace difference by evoking indelible temporal and spatial gaps. In the end, however, he seems to struggle (and his prose is a mark of this struggle) to sustain cultural difference in a situation in which, he laments, "the true primitive source" seems hard to discover or grasp. What brings the exhaustion that plagues the end of the voyage is the recognition that the "journey without maps" has been pre-mapped all along, that the journey back in time actually leads to the dreaded present the author sought to escape. Does this circularity mean that colonial culture, even in crisis, continues to replay tropes and ideologies conceptualized in the high noon of colonialism? Does modernism mark any radical transformation in the symbolic economy that gave us an idea of culture and identity imprisoned in the moment of colonialism and its discourse of power?

⊰ 6 ⊱

Beyond Empire and Nation: Writing Identity After Colonialism

Identity is formed at the unstable point where the "unspeakable" stories of subjectivity meet the narratives of history, of a culture.

Stuart Hall, "Minimal Selves"

The migrant suspects reality: having experienced several ways of being, he understands their illusionary nature. To see things plainly, you have to cross a frontier.

Salman Rushdie, "The Location of Brazil"

※

If the movement of my book from the high noon of imperialism (the nine-teenth century) to the modernist period (the early twentieth century) seems to underscore the emerging crisis in the nature of the colonial ref-erent, it is because I have sought to understand what Richard Terdiman calls the "shadowing of notions of objective reality by the overwhelming force of individual and collective subjectivity."[1] My presupposition here is similar to Terdiman's theoretical position on the function of alterity in the narrative of identity: if the "lability and the fugacity of the referent" are what condition the discourse of the other, and if empire is one of the most important and visible historical and geographical referents in British culture in the nineteenth and early twentieth centuries, then the study of the narratives of English and colonial identities must concern itself with both the changing fortunes of this referent and the ways in which this change affects the modes and forms of what I have called Englishness.[2] The question that still needs to be considered—and this is the question that concerns me in this chapter—is about the colonized subject's own relation to the culture of colonialism once the imperial referent has collapsed. How do postcolonial writers represent identity when the empire is dead but the long shadow cast by the culture of colonialism continues to haunt them in the name of modernity and the new nation? In short, what happens to culture after colonialism?

Clearly, to understand postimperial writing as a discourse that exists under the shadow of the experience it seeks to negate (the colonial project), we must begin by reflecting on the historical and discursive cusp that marks the shift from imperial authority to modernist atrophy. While one hesitates to endow this shift with the power of an epistemic revolution, it has an unprecedented bearing on the forms of postimperial literatures. For one of the great ironies of the imperial century, as we saw in the introduction to this study, was its promulgation of cultural forms that brought together colonizer and colonized under the totality of the same. Empire robbed colonial subjects of their identities (this goes without saying), but it also conferred new forms of identity on native peoples, identities that stretched, albeit in uneven ways, all the way from British Columbia in Canada to the Malaysian Peninsula.

In terms of consciousness, ideology, and even language, the imperial experience invented a referent (empire) and a culture (that of colonialism) that became the conditions of possibility for metropolitan and colonial subjects and cultures alike. And if both colonizer and colonized assumed an imperialized identity in the nineteenth century—in either affiliation or resistance—we can perhaps assume that both metropolitan and colonial subjects understood that, within the hermeneutical circle established by the *imperium*, England and its colonies existed under the same theoretical and political schema, even as they invoked their differences in the name of biology or tradition. And thus if the reconstructive agency of postcolonialism is to have any effect in its attempts to displace colonial institutions from their hegemonic positions in both the metropolis and the former colonies, it has to begin by recognizing the force of the totality of empire.

Whether we read this schema in official texts (administrative documents and commission reports) or in the travelogues of colonized subjects (Sir Apolo Kagwa or Mary Seacole), we are never left in doubt that the imperial idea is driven by notions of cultural difference framed by the ideology of the same, that the encounter of colonizer and colonized provided "a new world in which to deploy a critical cartography of the history and effects of power."[3] True, all those imbricated in the culture of empire—and those who studied this imbrication—understood what differentiated England from its colonial possessions. Perhaps few people were in doubt about where colonial subjects stood in relation to the ideologies of power and domination that generated the imperial project; nevertheless, the resonance of empire lay in its ability to evoke a horizontal identity for both the colonizer and the colonized even when they were imprisoned in strict racial and economic hierarchies. In addition, as we saw in previous chapters, the narrative of imperial rule assumed that England's ability to manage and control her colonial spaces was a commentary on the character of the nation itself.

With the advent of modernism and in its aftermath, however, the notion that colonial control and rule reflect the moral character of the domestic space is vigorously contested, for the colony has become a space of crisis, the mirror for truncated European subjectivities and a stillborn modernity. Indeed, the binary opposition between the inherent moral character of the "home" country and the indisputable barbarism of the imperial frontier becomes increasingly frayed. We have seen, for example, how Greene's African travelogue is generated by the idea of homelessness: to travel without maps is to reject the traditional notion of home as an absolute point of origin and meaning. The idea of modernist travel as a kind of *dédoublement* from one's natal spaces is, nevertheless, limited by the traveler's ultimate resort to the very ideologies he sought to negate, ideologies that are deeply rooted in the domestic economy of representation. For instance, Greene posits his journey into Africa as a critique of Western civilization, but he still finds it difficult to abandon the cultural grammar of Englishness, which remains his primary point of reference. His narrative thus comes to depend on a split structure: a rhetoric of overt anti-Englishness is communicated through the idiom of the public school. The author labors to convince his readers that his destination (Africa), rather than his point of departure (England), proffers what Abbeele calls "a transcendental point of reference," but African primitivism becomes intelligible—and hence valuable—only when it is interred on the altar of Englishness.[4]

When African phenomena are translated into the cultural idiom of Englishness, England becomes, even against the author's best intentions, his teleological point of departure and reference. And thus the journey without maps, a journey that opens by rejecting conventional views and cultural signposts, winds its way back to where it began—in the familiar landscapes of England. True, the tone of irony and melancholy with which Greene concludes *Journey Without Maps* seeks to sustain the radical gap between Africa (the preferable axis) and England (the place of disenchantment). But by translating Africa into explicitly English or European terms, Greene has brought back the continent and fitted into it an economy of representation that precedes his journey: standing in "the cold empty Customs shed" at Dover, he concludes that the only loot he has brought back from Africa is "the innocence, the virginity, the graves not yet opened for gold, the mine not broken with sledges."[5]

What does a colonial reader of this text—or Greene's African novels, for that matter—conclude about an ending in which the innocence and virtue of Africa are valorized from the vantage point of Englishness? Such a reader would have to direct several questions to this ambivalent economy of travel. Although England has lost its virtue and energy, doesn't its ultimate "oikorization" reinstate its primacy even in the face of the author's harsh critique of imperialism? Doesn't Africa have value only as the opposite of what Europe has become? Doesn't Africa function as more than an insignia of what European intellectuals lack and thus desire—a premodern consciousness and subjectivity? Where in this discourse, then, is the slippage that colonial subjects can revert to their own critique of imperialism, a critique that is a precondition for their own narratives of identity? Indeed, do modernist narratives have any oppositional function? What kind of spaces do they open up for colonized subjects who are beginning to construct their own narratives of identity at precisely the same time when the modernists are writing about the failure of the imperial narrative?

Well, the oppositional potential of Greene's narrative would seem to lie in the author's equivocal deployment of England as both his point of reference and the source of his disenchantment: the traveler's return to England is not prompted by any renewed desire for the culture of Englishness but is propelled, as we have already seen, by melancholy and cultural angst. Greene returns home because he realizes that he has nowhere else to go, that he is just as alienated from the Africa he desires as he is from the England he detests: "It isn't that one wants to stay in Africa: I have no yearning for a mindless sensuality, even if it were to be found there" (249). Thus while *Journey Without Maps* is a travel narrative marked by the "transgression of losing or leaving the home," the ending of the journey is not mediated, to borrow Abbeele's terms, "by a movement that attempts to fill the gap of that loss through a spatialization of time."[6]

Indeed, the modern travel narrative ends and calls attention to the persistence of this gap (witness the last image of England as a wasteland). This temporal gap, the distance between Africa and England, is also the mark of a double crisis: a crisis in the economy of a narrative that is no longer structured by the positivity of home and a crisis in the teleology of empire that, without its power, prestige, and authority, can be mediated only by a rhetoric of decline and decay. If, as Nicholas B. Dirks has asserted, "what we now recognize as culture was produced by the colonial encounter, the concept itself was in part invented because of it," then the whole debate on postcoloniality and the politics of identity is about what happens to the idea of culture in the face of decolonization.[7]

Writing in the Postimperial Aporia

My thesis here is simple: the crisis in colonialism, so latent in the period of nascent and high modernism, presented postcolonial writers with a productive cultural space, for it was in their exploitation of this crisis (especially in the period after World War II) that colonized peoples began to chart alternative narratives of their own histories and experiences against the pressures of what Frantz Fanon once called a dying colonialism.[8] Nationalist intellectuals and writers positioned themselves in this space of crisis—what I have termed the postimperial aporia—and reinvented their national identities either as a self-willed return to precolonial traditions or as a conscious rejection of an imposed European identity. And while the project of nationalist retour has been questioned rigorously in postcolonial theory, the desire for a national space outside the culture of colonialism often resulted in a radical transformation of the idea of home and related spaces of emplacement.

For if imperial travelers and colonial writers alike assumed that England was the *oikos*—the place of return and the depository of domestic ideals—anti-imperial nationalism came to be propelled by a narrative that insisted on retour as a necessary condition for alternative identities.[9] Thus the narratives of the nationalist period came to be defined by the call for a return to the native land, a return that was posited as a radical departure from the colonial culture that had created nationalist writers in the first place. The totality of empire and its grand narratives was going to be undermined by the very instrumentalities that the process of colonization had globalized—the European language, the idea of the nation, invented traditions, and economic and cultural rationalization.

But at the heart of the narrative of nationalism lay some basic questions: What was the native land? Where was home? And could the former colony reinvent itself as a nation and transform its "subaltern" cartography into a new transcendental point of reference independent of the colonial experiences of the preceding century and a half? Could the culture of colonialism be translated into the discourse of the decolonized nation? Could modernity, once an agency of imperial control, now be turned into an instrument of liberation? If answers to these questions seem to elude readers of the postcolonial experience, it is because, increasingly, the temporality of the postcolonial nation and that of the empire it sought to transcend are hard to differentiate. There is, as Homi Bhabha has observed, a significant conflation between empire and nation, a conflation that is manifested, ironically enough, in the temporal disjunction that defines modernity itself: "This temporal disjunction is the ambivalent and antagonistic construction of civil society, state, modernity, the notion of the nation, the notion of the citizen, which occurred at the same time as the creation of the colony, colonial subjects, racist disciplinary forms, modes of discriminatory and prejudicial government policies."[10] Is the space of the nation, then, to be characterized as identical to that of empire? Or are postimperial identities possible only in a temporality and cartography that transcend empire and nation and their founding mythologies of origins, of home, of unique subjectivities?

Postcolonial intellectuals, especially those who have lived through, or witnessed, the disenchantment of nationalism, have evolved at least two basic theoretical and narrative responses to these questions. The first response seeks to locate the postimperial subject in what Salman Rushdie has called "Imaginary Homelands." The writers' tack here is to appeal to the authority of migration and displacement (and the imagination that emerges from those experiences) and to empower themselves, through negation, by rejecting the mythologies of nationalism and the nationalist cartography.[11] As Rushdie notes in his reading of *Brazil*, the condition of migrancy is essentially transcendental—it propels the subject beyond the "shackles of nationalism" and "its ugly sister, patriotism" (124).

Although Rushdie's novels are read as exemplars of postmodern historiography, his aesthetic seems to come out of the blue book of modernism: the imagination thrives in a world rooted in transcendental ideas rather than places. "Having experienced several ways of being," the migrant subject suspects, and thus writes against, reality; to be a migrant is to be compelled to establish "a new relationship with the world, because of the loss of familiar habitats" (124–25). My concern here, however, is not the relation between this modernist aesthetic and Rushdie's postmodernist fictional techniques. Rather, as I will show in my reading of *Satanic Verses* later in this chapter, I am interested in the ways in which his desire to locate the postimperial subject in an ideal place beyond given (national) time and space comes against the weight of imperial history and its institutions, including the idea of the nation itself. My focus, then, is on the implicit conflict between the staging of a unique migrant subjectivity (written beyond boundaries), and national myths of origins and foundations.

This is the kind of conflict that is represented in Joan Riley's *The Unbelonging*,[12] one of the most haunting novels of postcolonial migration and return. What makes this novel memorable is not merely its naturalistic representation of England as a place that destroys or devours black selves but also its refusal to concede either the mythology of the metropolitan center as the mother country or the decolonized nation as the place of ultimate refuge and gratification, the destination of a narrative retour. True, the power of the novel depends on its violent metaphorical opposition between English winters and Jamaican summers; true, its heroine, Hyacinth, inscribes her ancestral memories with a power that she will never summon to represent her place of migration; and yet this opposition is constantly thwarted by an ironic undercurrent that calls attention to the illusionary nature of the binarism sought by the subject. In other words, if Hyacinth's pastoral image of Jamaica cannot ward off exile (memories of summer cannot erase the reality of winter), it is because Riley foregrounds the character of the homeland as phantasmic, either by representing it as part of the heroine's daydreams or by juxtaposing idyllic memories and dreams of a Jamaican childhood with the "clammy wetness" of her bed, a wetness that we are invited to read as a symptom of deep-rooted anxieties about home and retour. Hyacinth is hence caught between the empty and dreary culture of Englishness and its institutions—especially the school and the social welfare department—and the passion for a Jamaica that she has invented as the supplement for her lack of home and family.

And if in the earlier narratives of retour it was easy to invoke images of a precolonial, pre-Oedipal home to counter the hegemony of empire, Riley's novel systematically calls into question the efficacy of memory and the imagination. The key narratorial question for Riley is this: "What happens when memory comes up against reality?"[13] The answer is to be found, unequivocally, in the novel's moment of closure, when Hyacinth, determined to return all "the sordid evil she had found in England" to "the realm of her nightmares, where [it] should have stayed," decides to go back to her native Jamaica. But no sooner has she returned to what used to be her habitus than she is struck by its strangeness and estrangement. The place of return is represented by corrosion, decay, and a sense of sheer terror; the crowds she encounters in the streets frighten her because they now seem so different from what she thought they were, from the way she remembered them. Sensing the hostility from the people who used to be her neighbors, Hyacinth "thought longingly of the taxi, the hotel, England, all so far away and safe" (138). In what was anticipated as a moment of commemoration, memory has become an intractable prisonhouse, a mark of the gap between the desire for a home and the reality of homelessness.

And thus Hyacinth's epiphanic moment becomes one of radical negativity and *ressentiment*. Rejected in England because she is a black West Indian, she is detested in Jamaica because she has "been to" England. As she is being chased away from her old neighborhood, where, because she is unremembered, she is despised like any other foreigner, Hyacinth comes to understand the real implications of being unhomely:

"Go back whe you come fram." The words whirled about inside her head. How many times had she heard that since coming to Jamaica, or was it since she had gone to England? She felt rejected, unbelonging. Where was the acceptance she had dreamt about, the going home in triumph to a loving, indulgent aunt? Was this what she had suffered for? It was all so pointless, all for nothing. There was a wringing pain in her chest, and tension made her jaw ache as tears refused to fall from burning eyes. But inside she cried, pain-racked sobs that made breathing hard and walking a labored thing. She wondered if they all noticed her pain, the people in the street glaring their hate, the curious taxi-driver. She felt exposed, her blackness ugly and rejected even among her own kind. . . . She remembered England as a child, the beatings, the jeers. "Go back where you belong," they had said, and then she had thought she knew where that was. But if it was not Jamaica, where did she belong?   (142)

No one can read a passage like this—and this surely is a metacritical function of postcolonial testimony—without recalling the celebratory narratives of return to the native land written at the height of the nationalist movement. Hyacinth's rejection by the native land, and her alienation in both the metropolitan center and the postcolonial nation, must be read as a parody of the fictions of retour: unlike narratives, such as Césaire's *Cahier*, that affirm the power of home to counter deracination, Riley ends her novel by simultaneously positioning Hyacinth in a world of dreams and nightmares and overpowering her with the ugly materiality of both England and Jamaica, not merely to suggest that the two entities are similar in their capacity to alienate but to foreground their common genealogy:

So she sat there, full of guilt and horror, not knowing what to do. It was safe there, in the little green cave. Safe and lonely and sad. But was there anything out there but rejection and all the uncertainty she had hidden from? Safe inside her cave, Hyacinth lay back in the sweet-smelling grass and cried.   (144)

There is no hybridity here; being unhomely cannot be reverted into a mode of existential identity. Indeed, at the end of Riley's novel, neither an attempted return to natal spaces nor the ostensibly transgressive act of migrancy is posited as a resolution to the sense of disjunction engendered by the uneasy relation between empire and nation. And thus writing the self takes place in an aporia that, as I will argue often in this chapter, is a common response to the problem of staging identity after colonialism.

The haunting ending of *The Unbelonging* suggests a second response to the problem of locating postimperial subjectivities: the kind of myths of origin that Rushdie's aesthetic and Riley's novel deconstruct are already inscribed in the postimperial subject. As Spivak observes, because the myth of origins is part of the grounding that makes identity possible, the only way to argue for origin "is to look for institutions, inscriptions and then to surmise the mechanics by which such institutions and inscriptions can stage such a particular style of performance."[14] How then can we deconstruct, in the name of identity, the grounds on which this identity is constructed? Toward the end of her essay on the staging of identity, Spivak raises a series of intriguing questions: "What are we choosing today when we choose an identity, which is different from an echoing or a counter-echoing of Western discourse? Is there a difference between the choice of this counter-echo and the choice of programmed madness? Or are we in the place where we can choose something ex-orbitant?"[15] Once again, questions of origins and foundations lead to an aporia, as if this figure of evasion and ambiguity is the most appropriate mechanism for responding to the problem of origins and location in the postimperial scene.

Maybe it is: for how else can we talk about a situation—postcolonialism and postimperialism—that does not yet exist? My contention is, however, that if we cannot go beyond the colonial aporia, we can perhaps push it to its limits. Since the writing of identity, for example, can no longer be structured by the myth of return to origins, and since postcolonial narrative cannot escape the weight of the history of colonialism that enables it, narrative can function as a mechanism for deconstructing the epistemology of the sources themselves, or as a metacommentary on previous narratives of return and identity. Indeed, the myth of return in postcoloniality is more complex than the simple opposition between home and exile beloved of an earlier generation of nationalists—it is plagued by conflicts and pluralities that emerge from the histories that migrancy seeks to leave behind.

A simpler way of positing this problem is to argue that our response to the questions of identity and alterity that concern me in this chapter—questions of home and emplacement, origins and agency, and the transformation of imperial identities—depend not so much on where one chooses to go but where one comes from. To choose to transcend nation and patriotism, à la Rushdie, is to claim some choice in the staging of one's identity, but this choice does not implicitly negate the agency of nation and *patria*. Going away from home and the law of the father does not change the constitutive force of the nation. Indeed, the deployment of narrative as a mechanism for transcending nation and *patria* is, as Rushdie's case demonstrates so well, inevitably driven by anxieties about both, for even when we deploy the reconstructive powers of the imagination to call the grand narratives of empire and nation into question, even when we reject the nationalist myth of return, we are—unconsciously, perhaps—restaging it.

Consider, for example, Rushdie's return to his native Bombay after years of migrancy in England. The novelist refuses to call the city home; he has been away too long, and memories of partition and repatriation are hardly pleasant. He prefers to label the place of his birth the "lost city." The author's attempt to detach himself from the city and its memories is, however, negated by what he encounters in its streets and archives:

> Shortly after arriving, acting on an impulse, I opened the telephone directory and looked for my father's name. And amazingly, there it was; his name and our address, the unchanged telephone number as if we had never gone away to the unmentionable country across the border. It was an eerie discovery. I felt as if I were being claimed, or informed that the facts of my faraway life were illusions, and that this continuity was real. (9)

The name of the father, an address and phone number—these are the facts that narrative may seek to deconstruct, and possibly to nullify, but ends up restaging (sometimes against the author's overt intentions). And thus the persistence of the name of the father in narratives that seek to do away with the *patria* would seem to confirm Stuart Hall's conclusion that the self, even in its fragmentation and displacement, has "a real set of histories"—that "narratives of displacement have certain conditions of existence, real histories in the contemporary world, which are not only or exclusively psychical, not simply 'journeys of the mind.' "[16] But if these real histories are, at the same time, the sources of the denial and repression of the self that generate the narrative of identity in the first place, are they of any use in the construction of a postimperial identity? Shouldn't narrative function as the mechanism that transcends ugly histories and realities? Must a narrative of postcolonial futures realize its authority by confronting the colonial archive?

An examination of the "communicational circumstances" that generate these texts is a worthy undertaking.[17] In the case of postcolonial texts, the most important of these communicational circumstances is the split of the writing subject between metropolitan and postimperial identities. What does it mean to figurate or establish a discursive space in the place in between, let's say, London and Karachi, Bombay, or Kingston?

Let us compare Rushdie's return to Bombay with Hanif Kureishi's encounter with Karachi. Rushdie's journey, as it is represented in *Imaginary Homelands*, is structured by the anxiety of a belated return: Bombay is a place he has known in its "materiality" and also a space of mind, associated with the anxieties that emerge when nostalgia accompanies trauma but also impelled by the desire for recovery and commemoration. Although Rushdie insists that his commitment as a writer is to cultural spaces that transcend national boundaries and interests, there is no doubt that he revels in his childhood memories of Bombay (and indeed India) even as he relates the historical traumas that separated him and his family from the city (and country) of their birth. If a photograph of the family's Bombay home—viewed in exile—provides the author with "monochromatic" images of the native land, "seeping" the colors of his history out of his "mind's eye," a view of the actual house restages the past as inexorable and desirable:

Now my two other eyes were assaulted by colours, by the vividness of the red tiles, the yellow-edged green of cactus-leaves, the brilliance of bougainvillaea creeper. It is probably not too romantic to say that that was when my novel *Midnight's Children* was really born; when I realized how much I wanted to restore the past to myself, not in the faded grays of old family-album snapshots, but whole, in CinemaScope and glorious Technicolor.   (9)

But for Kureishi, whose only connection to Pakistan is the simple fact that his father was born there and he still has relatives who inhabit the spaces of the postcolonial state, the narrative of return is a movement in the empty time of two postimperial cultures and nations—England and Pakistan—and the representation of an identity that cannot fit into the spaces associated with either entity. In all matters cultural and social, Kureishi notes in "London and Karachi," he is English to "the backbone";

nevertheless, he is traumatized by his interpellation into a Pakistani identity that, in racist English discourse, has become the symbol of abjection and abomination:

In the mid-1960s, Pakistanis were a risible subject in England, derided on television and exploited by politicians. They had the worst jobs, they were uncomfortable in England, some of them had difficulties with the language. They were despised and out of place. From the start I tried to deny my Pakistani self. I was ashamed. It was a curse and I wanted to be rid of it. I wanted to be like everyone else.[18]

Kureishi's dilemma—later to be narrativized in *The Buddha of Suburbia*—is that he is a natural-born English subject and his mother is actually English, but he is abused in the streets because, as a nonwhite person, it is assumed that he is part of the alien swamp that is threatening the purity of Englishness. In response, he simultaneously internalizes this imposed alterity and tries to exorcize it: "I was desperately embarrassed and afraid of being identified with these loathed aliens. I found it almost impossible to answer questions about where I came from. The word 'Pakistani' had been made into an insult. It was a word I didn't want used about myself. I couldn't tolerate being myself" (272). It is logical, given the choice between an "ontology of lack" and a degenerative alterity, that the author should seek to encounter Pakistani in "its reality" and thus come to terms with, or exorcize, the source of his shame and self-hate.

But in trying to understand the implications of Kureishi's journey to Pakistan, we need to look beyond its compensatory function and see how it moves in intangible temporal situations. In other words, compared to Rushdie's journey to Bombay, Kureishi's travel in Karachi is not a journey to real places encountered before but a sojourn in an imaginary place, a place that is conjured simultaneously by notions of ancestry and English racist discourse. Now, Karachi is not the source of any kind of trauma, because it has not been experienced before; on the contrary, it is the symbol of an imaginary repressed that must be encountered if a nonalienated identity is to be secured.[19]

The point I am making here is that postcolonial writers experience nation and empire differently, and this difference depends more on their places of origin than on their metropolitan locations and identities. For while Rushdie, in the passage above, sees Bombay as the geographic space that triggers the imaginary force that creates *Midnight Children*, Karachi generates a radically different response in Kureishi's mind. One could even speculate that for Kureishi, Karachi cannot be the source of the kinds of fictions Bombay has given Rushdie. Simply put, once in Pakistan, moving in a culture defined by the tense relation between postimperial secularism and the ideologies of Islamic fundamentalism, Kureishi begins to have "a little identity crisis":

> I'd been greeted so warmly in Pakistan, I felt so excited by what I saw, and so at home with all my uncles, I wondered if I were not better off here than there. And when I said, with a little unnoticed irony, that I was an Englishman, people laughed. They fell about. Why would anyone with a brown face, Muslim name and a large well-known family in Pakistan want to lay claim to that cold little decrepit island off Europe where you always had to spell your name? Strangely, anti-British remarks made me feel patriotic, though I only felt patriotic when I was away from England. (276)

How does one inscribe oneself between here and there? Kureishi rejects simple answers. Refusing to yield to the "falsity and sentimentality" of a compensatory identity, he accepts the fact that he feels out of place in Pakistan; he accepts the reality of his English identity but realizes that to the extent that this identity is based on *dédoublement* and self-alienation, it is essentially negative. At the end of his journey, Kureishi returns, predictably, to England, a place he had never wanted to identify with but one that, after the encounter with Pakistan, demands "some kind of identification": "It is strange to go away to the land of your ancestors, to find out how much you have in common with people there, yet at the same time realise how British you are," he concludes (284). And one is not merely British because "the suet puddings and the red-pillar boxes have entered the soul," Kureishi says, quoting Orwell (284). In an uncanny way, Britishness seems to have become a cultural value that transcends the British Isles, a value that is encapsulated by the logic of the colonial and postcolonial experience. Britishness is the sum total of the culture created in the colonial encounter, and it seems to have survived empire in the name of modernity.

Indeed, every time Kureishi tries to seek alternative identities to his troublesome Englishness, it is the ideal of modernity that pulls him back. As a young man in the 1960s, Kureishi is appalled by racist discourse, not simply because it has imposed a false identity on him and victimized him on the basis of this but also because racism seems to go against the ideals of reason and common sense—"I saw racism as unreason and prejudice, ignorance and a failure of sense; it was Fanon's incomprehension" (274). He seeks alternative communities in the discourse of black Islam only to be repelled by what he sees as its "unreason" and "abdication of intelligence" (274). And finally, one of the things that makes Pakistan so alien to him is what he sees as the "fatherland's" negation of secular culture: "In England I was a playwright. In Karachi this meant little. There were no theatres; the arts were discouraged by the state—music and dancing are un-Islamic—and practically ignored by everyone else" (276). Originally founded on the ideals of modernity—rationalization, progress, and a secular culture—the postcolonial state has regressed, as it were, to "theocracy" and charismatic authority. Kureishi's belief that Britain secures the ideals of modernity may be naive, but it is reinforced by his Pakistan uncles who were not simply educated in England but were influenced as well by the secular tradition of the Fabians; for these men, "the new Islamisation was the negation of their lives" (277).

And thus Kureishi's reticent identification with Englishness is based on the belief that, in England, he can valorize the logic of a secular and enlightened English culture and use it against the unreason of the racists. This way he will posit himself as the true Englishman and cast the racists as aberrations from the national norm—and the national norm is assumed to be secular and reasonable, revisionary and self-reflective:

> It is the British, the white British, who have to learn that being British isn't what it was. Now it is a more complex thing, involving new elements. So there must be a fresh way of seeing Britain and the choices it faces: and a new way of being British after all this time. Much thought, discussion and self-examination must go into seeing the necessity for this, what this "new way of being British" involves and how difficult it might be to attain.   (286)

This new reconceptualization of the culture of Englishness (for, as I noted in the first chapter, Britishness is the cartographic container for this culture) must begin by acknowledging that the futures of Britain and Pakistan are, like their histories, intermixed. But how are we to read Britishness anew against the powerful mechanisms that have been established to represent it as it was before empire, before decolonization? And how are new British identities—postimperial, postcolonial—to be represented inside and outside the culture of modernity, especially when, as Homi Bhabha has noted, "the place of identification" is also "a space of splitting"?[20] Where is the postcolonial subject to be located?

Masks of Englishness: Postcoloniality in The Satanic Verses

These questions lie at the heart of Salman Rushdie's novel *The Satanic Verses* and the contentious debates surrounding it. Indeed, two hermeneutical moments at the beginning of the book can help us clarify the problems of locating the postcolonial subject outside bounded spaces, imperial epistemologies, or even national allegories, and the impossibility of renouncing such entities altogether. The novel thus invites us to read it as a metacommentary on two of the questions that opened this study—what does it mean to exist inside and outside Englishness? and what does it mean to be a postcolonial subject in between the spaces of empire and nation?

At the opening of the novel, as readers will recall, Rushdie systematically offers us a dramatic rendering of the explosive scene of postcoloniality: the moment is explosive not only on a thematic level (the catastrophe that plummets Gibreel into the sacred spaces of Englishness is a plane crash) but also as an epistemological unpacking of the binaries that have hitherto defined the relation between the imperial center and its colonial margins. As he falls down from the sky, Gibreel directs a reversed gaze on England, a gaze that also needs to be read as the radical questioning of the immigrant's paradigmatic encounter with the metropolis, the mother country, the projected depository of colonial desires. From the shattering sky, England is now seen not simply as a site of fulfillment but as a place of unclarified beginnings, a locality in which binaries and definitions are set askew as the remnants of the plane mingle with "equally fragmented, equally absurd . . . debris of the soul, broken memories, slough-off selves, severed mother-tongues, violated privacies, untranslated jokes, extinguished futures, lost loves, the forgotten meaning of hollow, booming words, land, belonging, home."[21]

In this short excerpt alone, the narrator succinctly questions some of the key tenets of colonial—and, indeed, nationalist—modernity: the notion of a unified subject whose cogito comes to self-recognition and consciousness at its moment of reconciliation with the *imperium*; the idea of a unique subjectivity; the logic of historicism and the doctrine of progress; and, ultimately, the central integers of identity itself—land, belonging, home. In *Satanic Verses*, England is not a space in which a divided consciousness is reconciled to its defining other; on the contrary, the appointed zone of the immigrants' reincarnation is the waters of the English Channel—liminal zones between countries and continents—and an "air-space," an "imperceptible field" that is "insecure, transitory . . . illusionary, discontinuous, metamorphic" (4). Under these circumstances, the hybrid and metamorphic spaces of postimperial culture would seem to be part of the postmodern condition, which, according to Lyotard, is defined by an "incredulity toward metanarratives"; the explosion that opens the novel would seem to be a telling dispersal of the singular narrative function "in clouds of narrative language elements."[22] This dispersal of narrative authority is matched only by Rushdie's desire to call all totalized explanatory systems into question: Englishness, Indianness, even Thatcherism.

But for such explanatory systems to be called into question they must, at the same time, function as an integral part of the narrative itself, for it is not enough to narrate reincarnated—and dispersed—identities without also ruminating on the foundational moments that they try to transcend. Indeed, if postcolonial identities in the metropolis are sought through negation, the discourse in the postcolony itself is about meanings and interpretations couched in the language of modernity. It is perhaps true that all metaphors "are capable of misinterpretation" (537), but, as the sections of the novel dealing with the "satanic verses" illustrate so well, when the secular grammar of modernism becomes pluralized, it provides cultural fundamentalism some powerful gatekeeping concepts. In other words, you cannot disperse the authority of modernity and its narratives except in the languages they have established—the languages of history, destiny, and the heroic. And yet to use such terms ipso facto is to be caught right in the middle of the cultural politics of both English patriotism and Islamic fundamentalism. We will return to this question later.

For now, let us reflect more on the problem that opened this chapter, and indeed this book—the question of positionality and location. Where are we to place the postcolonial moment, caught as it is between the imperative of colonial modernity and the genealogy of postmodernism? What are the signifiers of the new *epocha* in which empire is inscribed in the heart of the postcolonial periphery as much as the postcolony has come to define the organic crisis in the postimperial locality? And what narrative and interpretive modes do we require to read experiences—and subjectivities—that can no longer be defined by national boundaries? Here we need to recall Rushdie's basic premise in regard to positionality: "It is not easy . . . to be precise about the location of the world of the imagination," Rushdie says in "The Location of Brazil" (118). The migrant sensibility, he goes on to argue, transcends the shackles of nationalism and patriotism. But freedom from the cartographical is also construed as "burdensome" because while the migrant is a new type of human being—"people who rooted themselves in ideas rather than places" (124)—migrancy is already a condition defined by loss.

In these circumstances, if migrants are forced to create a new imaginative relationship with the world, as Rushdie asserts in the quote I use as my epigraph in this chapter, it is because of "the loss of familiar habitats" (125). In addition, as Spivak has observed, the migrant imagination, which appears to be Rushdie's preferred cognitive mode, is not paradigmatic of the "historical case of postcoloniality." Indeed, migrancy (in its ideality) could be defined as "the name of the institution that in-habits the indifferent anonymity of space and dockets climate and soil-type and the inscription of the earth's body"; once it is historicized, however, it cannot but be derived from the national spaces it seeks to renounce.[23] Rushdie's problem, then, is how to locate and narrate migrancy in this duality—as a new place of identity and as a condition outside national boundaries, but also as an experience that is overdetermined by the historical and cartographical claims of the postcolony and the metropolis. The problem posed by *The Satanic Verses* is not simply that it displaces national histories and their narratives, or even subverts the epistemology of empire. It also valorizes such histories, narratives, and epistemes as the very condition of existence of postcoloniality and migrancy. If the novel seems to abrogate its own authority to celebrate the schizophrenia that generates it, as numerous critics have suggested, it is not simply because of its divided thematic intentions or the conflictual identities it seeks to sustain but also because it is condemned, as it were, to reinscribe the very normativities— nation and empire—that it seeks to negate.[24]

Clearly, if it seems imperative to read *The Satanic Verses* as the paradigmatic text of postcolonialism, it is not merely because it dramatizes the problems that define modern culture after the collapse of the empire but also because it straddles the landscape of colonial modernism discussed in previous chapters, and what has come to be known as the postmodern condition.[25] More significantly, as I hope to show in greater detail below, Rushdie's work is self-consciously performative in its engagement with the cultural politics of postcoloniality, spaciously deploying many of the tropes discussed in previous chapters but also undermining the authority of such tropes in its many self-referential moments. If Englishness is defined by Enoch Powell in terms of its racial purity, pastoral landscape, and metaphysics of national belonging (as we saw in chapter 2), Rushdie's subjects inscribe their identities through mutation and metamorphosis, renunciation and ultimate denial. Rosa Diamond's England, the spot on which Gibreel Farishta falls from the sky, is written as a parody of the English myth of origination, a violation of its sacredness and telos. For the demented woman on the shoreline, the moment of William the Conqueror—the foundational scene of Englishness—is a shifting mirage that needs to be secured by continuous self-assurance: "Repetition had become a comfort to her antiquity; the well-worn phrases, *unfinished business, grandstand view,* made her feel solid, unchanging, sempiternal, instead of the creature of cracks and absences she knew herself to be" (130).

And if the notion of a black threat is what gives Englishness cohesion in times of crisis, as we saw in our discussion of Carlyle and Mill (chapter 2), Rushdie's novel mocks the very apparatus in which this threat is constructed. But he also parodies the rhetoric of black power, which, instead of serving a liberating function, actually empowers the dominant's vision of "dark" alterity by turning resistance into a fetish. "We have been made again," says the mother of the would-be black activist, Sylvester Roberts, renamed Dr. Uhuru Simba. But renewal speaks the old language of alterity: "I say that we shall also be the ones to remake this society, to shape it from the bottom to the top. We shall be the hewers of the dead wood and the gardeners of the new. It is our turn now" (414).

And if the typical response to the imperial management of the colonized subject has been to invent or narrate a *patria* or *matria* for the new nation, as is often the case in the narratives of return mentioned earlier, Rushdie's novel appears to be an uncompromising narration of the impossibility of the national project, in both the postimperial center and the postcolonial margin. Thus, in the heart of London, Hind, the Bangladesh woman, sees her location in the metropolis as her husband's revenge "for preventing you from performing your obscene acts upon my body" (248). Here, everything she valued "had been upset by the change; had in this process of translation been lost" (249). But what precisely has Hind lost?

> Her language: obliged, now, to emit these alien sounds that made her tongue feel tired, was she not entitled to moan? Her familiar place. . . . Where now was the city she knew? Where the village of her youth and the green waterways of home? The customs around which she had built her life were lost, too, or at least were hard to find.
>
> (249)

It is significant that the response to the question of loss or lack is represented in a long series of rhetorical questions that seem to suggest that while Sid is quite clear of the alienness of London, she is not quite so sure about the palpability of the world left behind: her evocation of the terminology of identity—language, place, and custom—is more complicated than it might first appear, for the languages, places, and customs she evokes have, through colonization, been contaminated by Englishness. In effect, Hind's idea of a home left behind—it now doesn't matter whether this home is in the city of Dhaka or the rural village of her youth—acquires use-value only in the face of the overwhelming alterity of Englishness. If the colonial other made England conscious of itself through negation, Hind's cognition of that unstable and contested entity called Bangladesh is possible only against the pressures of migration and hybridity. In other words, if England could only be defined in relation to others (my argument in chapter 3), postcolonial others can now define themselves only in relation to Englishness.

It should be apparent by now that I'm arguing against some of the critical claims made for *The Satanic Verses* as a text that calls into question, or even consumes, the properties that have so far defined the relation between the colonial other and the imperial self.[26] While the novel seems to destabilize such properties as modern temporality, the space of the nation, and the foundational moments of culture, its power of critique—its oppositionality—also seems to be dependent on such categories. Rushdie cannot, in other words, write except from within the spaces he critiques— England, Islam, India. Indeed, there is a sense in which the enabling condition of narration is the impossibility of detaching oneself from such compromised axioms as empire, cultural nationalism, and the postcolony. And yet—and this is the great irony of *The Satanic Verses*—the whole momentum of the novel, at least until its moment of closure, is toward the transcendence of such categories.

The novel, in fact, poses its generative problem simply: "How does newness come into the world? How is it born? Of what fusions, translations, conjoinings is it made?" (8). But as we have already seen, willing newness—or narrating or translating it—is compounded by the instability of the situation in which postcolonial writers like Rushdie write, caught as they are in the liminal space between empire and nation, England and its others. And if we agree with Spivak's definition of postcolonialism as a situation of catachresis—"A concept-metaphor without an adequate referent"[27]—then we must ask not only how a catachrestical narrative is authorized but how it is to be read.

Rushdie's response to this problem is to confront the attendant problem of catachresis itself: narrate the impossibility of engendering newness and thus unpack the objective metaphors of colonialism and nationalism by confronting them with more subjective and ambivalent, even metonymic, narratives of identity. Let us examine some of the strategies he uses in this process. There is, first of all, the author's self-inscription in his own text. While Rushdie's novel cannot be described as autobiographical in the strict sense of the word, clearly recognizable references are written into the narrative so that the figure of the author—his experience of migrancy and his reading of the Western canon, in particular—is an unmistakable presence in a novel in which the authorial voice is largely absent. From the reference to Defoe in the epigraph, the constant deployment of Kafka-esque metaphors, the playful re-creation of Borges's Argentina, to the grammar of metamorphosis in Ovid and García Márquez, Rushdie seems to insist on the essentially intertextual nature of the postcolonial text. Rushdie the writer is first and foremost a reader.

And then there is the parodic—and again unmistakable—presence of the author in both the figure of Saladin Chamcha and Salman, the Persian, the prophet's scribe. The experiences of the former mirror Rushdie's migrancy—his rejection of a troubled Indian patrimony and difficult assimilative desires; the latter's skepticism toward received doxa can be read as defining the author's critical stance toward both empire and nation. But the most obvious example of the author's self-encodement in his text is Saladin's struggle with the kipper in an English public school, an episode that comes right out of Rushdie's autobiography:

One day soon after he started school he came down to breakfast to find a kipper on his plate. He sat there staring at it not knowing where to begin. Then he cut into it, and got a mouthful of tiny bones. And after extracting them all, another mouthful, more bones. His fellow-pupils watched him suffer in silence; not one of them said, here, let me show you, you eat it this way. It took him ninety minutes to eat the fish and he was not permitted to rise from the table until it was done. (44)

For Saladin, as for Rushdie, this episode comes to represent the primal scene in relation to the acquired English identity. The kipper provides both migrants with a permanent metonym for their adopted homeland— "England was a peculiar-tasting smoked fish full of spikes and bones, and nobody would ever tell him how to eat it" (44). England is at once the scene of originality, of becoming new ("The eaten kipper was his first step in his conquest of England"), and the scene of revolt (since it provides the stage on which he seeks to assert his autonomy from the paternal authority represented by Changez Chamchawalla). But Englishness is also the source of adolescent trauma and the place where the colonized self discovers the pain of separation both from the father (India) and from the imaginary mother (England).

An important caution here: such autobiographical codes and scenes are by no means valorized, and even if we didn't know about them from Rushdie's nonfictional texts, they would still function well in the novel's thematic scheme. And yet it is precisely because they have a self-evident autobiographical authority that they must be read as important indicators of the extent to which the postcolonial text is, above everything else, a text of psychoanalysis in a generic sense: it seeks to understand the genealogy of what we have already labeled the divided localities of postcolonial identities, caught between doctrines of a "natural home" and the grand narratives of the nation-state (537). It is in such autobiographical moments that the novelist inscribes the troubled relation between the imperial center and the postcolony, both identified with a hegemonic patrimony. Let us recall, then, that the primal scene of Englishness (the "kipper" episode) is preceded by a rape scene, which Saladin reads, importantly enough, as the moment of estrangement from the *Heimat*: "It seemed to him that everything loathsome, everything he had come to revile about his hometown, had come together in the stranger's bony embrace, and now that he had escaped the evil skeleton he must also escape Bombay, or die" (38).

Significantly, the description of the rapist as "a creature of the bone" (38) foreshadows Saladin's father's final atrophy ("Cancer had stripped Changez Chamchawalla literary to the bone" [523]). So, when we discuss how London becomes Saladin's "novel metropolis" later in this chapter, we should keep in mind how his flattering (hence self-appreciating) image of Englishness is generated by his rage against his Indian patrimony. In addition, the narrative reminds us that Saladin's flight from Indianness to Englishness is psychological, not cartographic: "The distance between cities is always small; a villager, travelling a hundred miles to town, traverses emptier, darker, more terrifying space" (41). The distance becomes immeasurable when we recognize the feelings and desires that underwrite Saladin's "mutation" into a proper Englishman—

> that implacable rage which would burn within him, undiminished, for over a quarter of a century; which would boil away his childhood father-worship and make him a secular man, who would do his best, thereafter, to live without a god of any type; which would fuel, perhaps, his determination to become the thing his father was-not-could-never-be, that is, a goodandproper Englishman.   (43)

But what exactly is a good and proper Englishman? What is the postimperial meaning of Englishness? Or rather, how does the formerly colonized redefine the cartography of empire, in its postmortem, in order to claim a space in the metropolis? Well, given the complexity and indeterminacy of this problem in the novel, we can best see any responses to these questions as always provisional, ready to be overturned by each successive episode. We can, for example, argue that Englishness is defined by the various masks that Saladin wears to appear English, "the thing his father was-not-could-never-be" (43), or his sometimes desperate gestures to reinvent himself in the metropolis (50). Or we could argue that Englishness is the condition of being of the ventriloquist, that Salman, like most migrants, had learned numerous disguises to counter the falsehoods invented by the dominant (49).

There are, however, many instances in which the narrative restages the axiom that opened this study—that we cannot speak of an English identity outside the history of empire and the culture of colonialism. In this respect, then, we have to underscore the extent to which *The Satanic Verses* performs elaborate acts of metacommentary on the postcolonial condition. Such interpretative gestures, it seems, are intended to call into question the idiom of the nation as a hermetic space. Thus, if in the language of both the new English racist (Powell) and the founding father of the postcolony (Nehru), this idiom is flaunted as the precondition for national identity and subjectivity, Rushdie's narrative uses metacommentary to call attention to "the strangeness, the unnaturalness" of a discredited nationalist hermeneutical situation.[28] Thus, where the nationalists would insist on the integrity and fixity of the national space and its boundaries, and the sacredness of its genealogy, Rushdie's text valorizes transiency and migrancy, blasphemy and fictionality (292); the certainties of symbolic and pedagogical language are replaced by the indeterminacy of parody and performativity (281); the dream of polyglossia is undermined by the reality of heteroglossia and the challenge of translation (58, 249); and the idea of home is replaced by the reality of exile.

Now, such reversals are not unique to Rushdie's text—*migrancy, exile, hybridity* have become stock terms in postcolonial literature. The originality of *The Satanic Verses*, however, lies in its jettisoning of even such alternative (postcolonial) terms as *migrancy* and *hybridity*. The ideal of home, for example, is not simply displaced by the trope of exile in a dialectic in which the illusionary identity preferred by the former is contrasted to the painful and yet authorizing moments of the other. On the contrary, neither term is endorsed or negated entirely. The novel insists on being read as a set of irresolvable oxymorons or as a series of what Fredric Jameson has defined as antinomies.[29] There is, in fact, a crossing over from home to exile, exile to home.

For example, as an assimilated Englishman, Saladin can no longer feel at home in Bombay, nor can he negate it completely: "This isn't home. It makes me giddy because it feels like home and is not. It makes my heart tremble and my head spin" (58). But as most of the novel makes apparent, the same condition is repeated in England, the place that he calls home but that never completely feels like home. Furthermore, if in the discourses of modern identity, exile is posited as an ideal mode of escape from an authoritative patrimony, this doesn't make it unequivocally liberating in Rushdie's novel, certainly not in relation to the nation and its grand narratives. In the case of the Imam, for example, exile is a precondition for cultural fundamentalism: "Exile is a dream of glorious return. Exile is a vision of revolution: Elba, not St. Helena. It is an endless paradox: looking forward by always looking back" (205). *Paradox*, then, is the operative word in Rushdie's narrative.

And within the terms established by this figure, even the sacred grammar of postmodernity is questioned. For those who would insist that the postmodern denial of the grand narrative of history—and thus historicism—is a coveted mark of an epistemic rupture, Rushdie insists that temporal agnosticism can also be deployed in the service of the absolute spirit of cultural fundamentalism—after all, doesn't the Imam in exile read history as the enemy of belief itself (210)? We can now see why all readings of *The Satanic Verses* are condemned to be provisional and incomplete. In the absence of a stable postcolonial or postimperial referent that can invite modes of interpretation that depend on the totalizing agency of temporal or spatial configurations, national allegory or agency and subjectivity, we do not have any other way of reading this novel except through its aporic moments and narrative ellipses.

Consider, for example, the problem of time and space in the novel. *The Satanic Verses* opens, as we have already seen, by unsettling the traditional temporal and spatial relation between England and India: we don't have those metaphorical passages, intelligible journeys, or teleological transitions from margin to center that are so obvious in modernist imperial texts such as Forster's *A Passage to India* or colonial texts such George Lamming's *The Emigrants*. On the contrary, the explosion of the Baston burlesques metaphorized notions of ordered entries and beginnings, and the emphasis on the metamorphic and hybrid, as Homi Bhabha has observed, structures the narrative of identification through "incommensurability."[30] In addition, presumed spaces of emplacement, such as Saladin Chamcha's

England, are represented in a language that foregrounds discontinuity and fragmentation rather than the organism of polis and eros beloved of an earlier generation of nationalists. If the central question of the first part of the book is about beginnings—"How does newness come into the world?"(8)—incipiency is not generated by clearly ordered temporal or spatial configurations. On the contrary, the spaces that were thought to connote the brave new world promised by Englishness are simply a place in which old anxieties are restaged in uncanny and ironic moments. Thus, while Chamcha's five-story mansion in Notting Hill appears, on the one hand, to be the mark of his arrival, it is, on the other hand, situated in a locality that has become, since the "riots" of 1959, the site of the innumerable ways in which immigrants have "contaminated" and "criminalized" English culture (59).

We know, of course, that temporality appears to be most destabilized in the novel when such key cartographic signifiers as India and England resist their allegorical or their institutionalized meaning. Consider, for example, the trope of retour: in the grand narratives of national identity and reconstruction, as I argued earlier, the colonized subject's return home is lyricalized as a gesture of self-affirmation and absolute identification with the national landscape. In *The Satanic Verses*, however, Saladin's first return to India is described as a form of regression: "It was an unnatural journey; a denial of time; a revolt against history; the whole thing was bound to be a disaster" (34). Home is not that classical nationalist *epos* in which the deracinated subject recovers its disalienated self, voice, and origins. On the contrary, India "jumbled things up" (54); even the paternal home is described as "that place of lost time" (64). More significant, because he cannot create a new identity for himself by appealing to the postcolonial narrative of Indianness, Saladin can only engage the *Heimat* in negative terms: he sees the country "measuring him against her forgotten immensity, her sheer presence, the old despised disorder" (54). What, then, is the alternative? While Saladin might sustain the illusion that England is the locale that has provided him with agency, the whole narrative seems to resist his belief that he has, as a result, acquired a positive (allegorical) identity; the England of Rosa Diamond is not "allegory but entertainment" (64). As a matter of fact, Saladin has no English identity except as an entertainer or performer.

What are the implications of these unstable national cartographies on subjectivity and agency in the novel? How can agency be generated in the absence of allegorized national spaces? And why has agency, which in the past used to be discussed primarily in temporal terms, come to be overdetermined by cartography? As we saw earlier in this chapter, there was a time when nationalist writers saw their claim to the grand narratives of history and patrimony as the precondition of national identity. But after the pitfalls of national consciousness, postcolonial writers began to realize that an evocation of historicity and tradition could not provide a detour around the imperial past. Far from providing usable pasts, the histories and traditions recovered by nationalism tended to be variations on the imperial normativity.

Under these circumstances, a subject derived from the "ideal location" of the "imaginary homeland"—which Rushdie excavates beyond nationality and locality—would seem to be a detour around such compromised paradigms as nation and *Heimat*. A postnational subjectivity would thus seem to be derived from a cartography with the power to break down what Suleri has called "static lines of distinction between the indigenous and the foreign" but at the same time continually question "any synthesizing conflation of this duality."[31] But if the idiom of subjectivity cannot be derived from indigenous traditions, historical experiences, or bounded territories, how are we to locate a postnational and postimperial identity?

We can begin to address this question by calling attention to the centrality of subjectivity and agency in *The Satanic Verses* and by noting, with Spivak, that Rushdie's concern with national and migrant agency locates the philosophical concerns of his novel within the parameters of modernism—especially its concern with the production of subjects—rather than postmodernism, which has come to be associated with "industriously de-centered subjects and radicalized citationality."[32] But this kind of demarcation, as Spivak realizes, raises questions more than it provides answers:

> Are we obliged to repeat the argument that, as metropolitan writing is trying to get rid of a subject that has too long been dominant, the post-colonial writer must still foreground his traffic with the subject-position? Too easy, I think. Not because the migrant must still consider the question of identity, plurality, roots. But because fabricating de-centered subjects as the sign of the times is not necessarily these times de-centering the subject.[33]

There are even preliminary questions to consider: is the subject, as it emerges in this novel and other postcolonial texts, actually decentered or simply located at conflicting sites of self-articulation? And if this subject is decentered, is it decentered the same way as the postmodern subject? In other words, is what appears to be Rushdie's decentering of the subject an effect of his fabrication (narration) or a condition of postcolonial migrancy?

Let us examine the way agency and subjectivity are coded through the personalities of Gibreel and Saladin, especially in their varied relation to both national and metropolitan spaces. While many critics of the novel have concentrated on the obvious differences between the two subjects— one is easily associated with blasphemy and insurgency and the other with imperial sycophancy—their variegated desires for national agency are marked, in equally significant ways, by contiguousness and displacement. It is particularly important to note that the differences in affiliation that mark the two characters are only noticeable retrospectively, for when we encounter them at the present (on the moment of narration), they are either involved in comical acts of male bonding or forced into transgressive moments against their best intentions. They come to be defined by misrecognition. In other words, if Rushdie's novel is primarily concerned with national and migrant agency, then the coding of the two characters within the English and Indian spaces is similar, although it appears to be staged differently.

Consider, for example, the ways in which both characters are defined in terms of reincarnation and metamorphosis. "Reincarnation was always a big topic with Gibreel," we are told (11). As a movie star of mythical proportions, Gibreel carries an inscription as an Indian that is performative rather than essentialist. The magic of his persona, we are reminded, lies in his capacity to transgress theological conventions and "religious boundaries" (16): "For many of his fans, the boundary separating the performer and his roles had long ago ceased to exist" (17). Thus while the whole of India celebrates Gibreel because they assume that he is an incarnation of the national spirit—"If Gibreel dies, could India be behind?" (29)—his reincarnation begins on the day he renounces belief and the allegorical fiction that he is the embodiment of India: "On that day of metamorphosis the illness changed and his recovery began. And to prove to himself the nonexistence of God, he now stood in the dining-hall of the city's most famous hotel, with pigs falling out of his face" (30). Thus, rather than being a form of somatic rebirth, this reincarnation is conceived in terms of performative (semiotic) codes. Gibreel is not the figuration of the Indian body but a phantasmal and fabricated image, which not even the vastness of India can contain.

Gibreel's relation to England is marked by similar acts of metamorphosis, of dissociation between bodies and national spaces. When he falls from the sky near the Dover coast, for example, he appears to Rosa Diamond as a "satyrical" and Dionysian figure. And at this moment of unexpected arrival in England, which is no longer defined by the archetypal migrant desire for the metropolitan experience, the subject is located in a "universe of nightmares" (144), dreams, and Kafkan and Borgean geography (153). The evocation of Borges and Kafka here is important, for the two novelists seem to provide Rushdie with "a sense of the modern," in which, as he argues in "The Location of Brazil," imagination is opposed to reality. In the unreal world of comedy and fantasy, we are able to "break down our conventional, habit-dulled certainties about what the world is and has to be. Unreality is the only weapon with which reality can be smashed, so that it may subsequently be reconstructed" (122). If Gibreel is, in thematic terms, the figure of dissonance and insurgency, he is also a narratological agent of disruption—he allows the author to break down our conventional notions of language and cognition and the boundaries that define them.

Rushdie provides an excellent example of this semantic and cognitive dissonance in his description of Gibreel's entry into London. Now, we have to remember that Gibreel's journey into the city—the journey from Dover to Victoria Station—is the *arché* of the migrant's encounter with Englishness, the moment in which colonial desires are supposed to be fulfilled. In the imagination of colonized peoples, the train journey into Victoria Station is usually the beginning of the process by which imperial subjects are ostensibly transformed into Englishmen and Englishwomen, the moment when they enter the world of Englishness, its law and modes of cognition. Gibreel's Kafkan journey into London is, however, a systematic negation of received notions of the law and cognition:

Mr. Gibreel Farishta on the railway train to London was once again seized as who would not be by the fear that God had decided to punish him for his loss of faith by driving him insane. . . . The terror of losing his mind to a paradox, of being unmade by what he no longer believed existed, of turning his madness into the avatar of a chimerical archangel, was so big in him that it was impossible to look at it for long; yet how else was he to account for the miracles, metamorphoses and apparitions of recent days? (189)

Gibreel might be soothed, momentarily at least, by "manifestations of law." He might even "invent rationalizations" for his behavior, but whichever way he looks at his relationship with the imperial city, Gibreel cannot encounter London except as an imaginary construct—"All the London he wanted was right there, in his mind's eye" (190). When it is finally encountered in its materiality, however, London— the city of many colonial desires—turns out to be a figuration of the twilight zones and repressed histories that the subject had sought to leave behind, or of a female agency—Rekha Merchant and Alleluia Cone— that cannot be encapsulated by the law of the father: "The city—Proper London, yaar, no bloody less!—was dressed in white, like a mourner at a funeral. . . . That day Gibreel Farishta fled in every direction around the Underground of the city of London and Rekha Merchant found him wherever he went" (200–201). It is in this obvious disjunction between the migrant and the city, and between patriarchy and female subjectivity, that we can read Rushdie's unsettling of the imperial gaze; Gibreel's encounter with England becomes, as Bhabha has noted, a site of mimicry and ambivalence.[34] Here, Gibreel's metamorphic turn—as his blasphemy later in the novel—allows the author to simultaneously invalidate the colonial and postcolonial spaces and their boundaries. In the world of fantasy, reality itself is fatally undermined.

And yet, Rushdie constantly worries about the institution of value in a novelistic world in which the referent has been smashed: "Can a work of art grow into anything of value if it has no roots in observable reality?" he asks in "The Location of Brazil" (123). The truth is, in spite of the theorization of migrancy as a condition beyond spatial boundaries and national histories—beyond "reality," as it were—it cannot be narrativized without an authoritative representation of recognizable referents, antecedents, and histories.[35] It is important, in this regard, to recognize the limitations of Gibreel's agency, for while Bhabha is right to argue that "narrative sorcery" allows this new migrant to represent "the bleak history of the metropolis,"[36] the resulting knowledge cannot be complete or authoritative, because it is associated either with dementia (319) or with the dream world:

> Even the serial visions have migrated now; they know the city better than he. And in the aftermath of Rosa and Rekha the dream-worlds of his archangelic other self begin to seem as tangible as the shifting realities he inhabits while he's awake. . . . Who is he? An exile. Which must not be confused with, allowed to run into, all the other words that people throw around: émigré, expatriate, refugee, immigrant, silence, cunning. Exile is a dream of glorious return. Exile is a vision of revolution: Elba not St. Helena. It is an endless paradox: looking forward by always looking back. (205)

If Gibreel's mission is to break away from Indianness and remake Englishness, his authority—the authority of the exile—is compromised by its entrapment in a temporality that cannot evoke the vision of the new except by looking back at the spaces and histories it sought to transcend. In addition, if Gibreel's knowledge arises from his dementia, which allows him to reconceptualize the postimperial frontier in what Bhabha has called "the menacing agonistic boundary of cultural difference that never quite adds up,"[37] his absolute alienation from this frontier makes it impossible for him to represent the metropolis outside the "asymmetries of his imagination."[38] Who can narrate what Gibreel cannot grasp except Saladin Chamcha, the compromised figure of assimilative Englishness who is, nevertheless, subjectively anchored, if not in "observable reality," at least in figures of "the real" world, figures that may not always be recognizable referents but that still point to familiar ethnographic fields—India and England?

The more immediate problem that concerns me here, however, has to do with the relation between narrative agency and cultural or cognitive value. It is, first and foremost, a problem of the postcolonial subject's relation to the spaces it claims, occupies, or even negates. For if Spivak is right in her assertion that we take positions "in terms not of the discovery of historical or philosophical grounds, but in terms of reversing, displacing, and seizing the apparatus of value-coding," then Saladin, rather than Gibreel, is the subject best equipped to marginalize and singularize the national culture.[39] The most important point to note here is that Saladin simultaneously seizes the apparatus of Englishness and fails to deploy it. We can see this doubleness in the subject's unceremonious return to England after the explosion abroad the *Baston*, a moment whose mixture of comedy and irony is underlined by two facts: first, he has become so deformed that his well-cultivated image of Englishness (signified by his bowler hat) is now a big joke; second, his claim to the authority of the law and the codes of Englishness falls short of the doctrines of nationality espoused by English law, represented here by police and immigration officers (163).

The point is, it is through the figure of Saladin that Rushdie's narrative undermines Englishness by reducing its allegorical axioms to *la bêtise*: "He found himself dreaming of the Queen, of making tender love to the Monarch. She was the body of Britain, the avatar of the State, and he had chosen her, joined with her; she was his Beloved, the moon of his delight" (169). At the same time, however, such utterances are shown to be delirious, cut off from any body of value or meaning, hence deprived of the authority of cultural critique. Saladin's naive claim to an English identity not only directs the reader to the emptiness that lies at the heart of national allegories and metropolitan identities but also proceeds to undermine the fabricated *epos* of the imagined community of Englishness— "The place never stopped being a picture postcard to him. You couldn't get him to look at what was really real" (175). Thus, if the discourse on Englishness is anchored in the ideal of home and domesticity, as I argued in earlier chapters, there is no greater gesture of ironic reversal in the novel than Saladin's return to his English home not as the conquering hero but as "a figure out of a nightmare or a late-night TV movie, a figure covered in mud and ice and blood, the hairiest creature you ever saw, with the shanks and hoofs of a giant goat" (189).

My argument here is that while Saladin cannot be accredited with subversive agency, he is indispensable to Rushdie's attempt to redraw the frontiers of Englishness. For if the reconceptualization of Englishness cannot be achieved through absolute negation—postcoloniality, I have argued, is a condition that draws from the bounded spaces of both the postcolony and the postempire—then Saladin must eventually be read as the agent of the new cartography. Consider, in this regard, his agonistic relationship with London and the transformation that this relationship undergoes in the course of the novel. A useful starting point here is to compare Saladin's ambivalent relation to London with Gibreel's ultimate rejection of the city. For Gibreel, as we have already seen, London is an object of unrequited love. It is out of the despair generated by his inability to penetrate and embrace the metropolis that he sets out to transform the city into a projection of his abjection:

> The city's streets coiled around him, writhing like serpents. London had grown unstable once again, revealing its true, capricious, tormented nature, its anguish of a city that had lost its sense of itself and wallowed, accordingly, in the impotence of its selfish, angry present of masks and parodies, stifled and twisted by the insupportable, unrejected burden of its past, staring into the bleakness of its impoverished future. (320)

While some readers of *The Satanic Verses*, most notably Bhabha, have seen this rendering of the city as evidence of Gibreel's ability to see through "the bleak history of the metropolis,"[40] the narrative seems to be pointing away from cognition and gnosis: the visions the subject acquires, in the guise of the archangel, are visions that question his capacity for knowledge and a sense of cartography; he seeks to roll back "the frontiers of the adversary's dominion," but his conquest of the city depends on his adversary's maps; and inevitably, the city "in its corruption refused to submit to the dominion of the cartographers, changing shape at will and without warning, making it impossible for Gibreel to approach his quest in the systematic manner he would have preferred" (327). More significantly, Gibreel's "proposed metamorphosis of London into a tropical city" (354) cannot be read as a serious attempt to redraw the frontiers of the metropolis. On the contrary, it is reduced to nonsense. Clearly, Gibreel cannot be the agent of any positive knowledge about the postcolonial condition.

Saladin's images of the metropolis are equally represented as romantic abstractions—his rhapsodic celebrations of empire and England ("this islet of sensibility, surrounded by the cool sense of the sea") come out of Tennyson, Ruskin, and other Victorian apologists for empire (398). But at this stage in the novel, when Saladin has lost everything he thought he owed to England—"culture, city, wife" (400)—the reader cannot but read such rhapsodies as examples of a certain kind of romantic irony, one that calls attention to the inherent, even existential, gap between the subject and his cultural context.[41] Saladin may not see through the deracinated history of the metropolis, but it is through him that the reader can acquire knowledge about the gap that separates the ideality of Englishness from its bleak realities. Indeed, if Gibreel is an agent of performativity, Saladin is an agent of pedagogy.[42]

Nowhere are these two contrasting modes of agency as apparent as in the novel's last section, a section that has posed problems for many readers because it seems to undermine the whole ideological thrust of Rushdie's project. In other words, if the identity and power of *The Satanic Verses* depend on its ability to question modern and colonial notions of identity, including the ideals of home and return, why does it end with a kind of begrudging affirmation of such ideals? Gibreel's return to Bombay is easy to explain, simply because it doesn't seem to be driven by any ethical or political reconsideration of his previous position. The Gibreel who returns to Bombay from London to "pick up the threads of his film career" may not be "the old, irresistible Gibreel" to his fans, but to the readers of the novel he is still the old demented performer who writes his identity—and *ressentiment*—in acts of blood and fire. Saladin's return, on the other hand, has great import to the meaning of *The Satanic Verses* precisely because it calls into question (a) the modes of Englishness that the subject has tried to sustain throughout the novel and (b) the author's earlier critique of the *Heimat*. In both cases, it is significant that Saladin's desire to see his father before the latter dies is both imperative (it is something he must do to be born again, as it were) and dangerous (the journey back is haunted by the terror of repetition).

Up until this moment of return, Saladin's life has been an attempt to escape from inherited ideas of the *Heimat*. Saladin's fervent desire for Englishness has been matched only by his need to escape from Bombay, India, and the law of the father. Now, at the end of the novel, we see him embracing his inheritance (533), occupying defunct spaces, and reestablishing old relationships in what he sees as a process "of renewal, of regeneration, that had been the most surprising and paradoxical product of his father's terminal illness" (534). At this moment of retour, even the subject's notions of temporality have changed: if the old Saladin saw time as the process that would enable him to reinvent himself as a good and proper Englishman, and if he believed that this new identity depended on a radical break with the past, the moment of retour reasserts the power of con-flated time—he realizes that he was living in "the *present moment of the past*" (535). Two questions emerge from this return to the past: Is this discourse of retour—and the identity it presupposes—different from the narratives of home espoused in the nationalist period? And what does it mean to be living in the "present moment of the past"?

⊰ Epilogue ⊱

The political movements in the New World in the twentieth century have had to pass through the re-encounter with Africa. The
African diasporas of the New World have been in one way or
another incapable of finding a place in modern history without
the symbolic return to Africa.

> Stuart Hall, "Negotiating Caribbean Identities"

You know the passport forms
or even some job applications noo-a-days?
well, there's nowhere to write
Celtic-Afro-Caribbean in answer to the "origin" question;
they think that's a contradiction.

> Jackie Kay, "Kail and Callaloo"

§

This book has been following a trajectory on which the writing of English and
colonial identities becomes more complicated the greater the interac-
tion between the two entities, their cultures and cartographies, and as
fixed modes of alterity collapse in the face of shared ideologies and
desires. My argument has been that writing colonial identities used to
be simple when the metropolis and the colony were defined by binary
tropes, intelligible temporalities, and stable cartographies. Now that the
categories that authorized the colonial relationship have collapsed, the
politics and poetics of cultural identity seem pretty messed up. And yet,
as the ending of *The Satanic Verses* illustrates so well, we cannot dismiss
the authority that such categories as metropole and nation have just
because we are able—or eager—to deconstruct their epistemological
and cultural claims. For when all the deconstruction is done, and when
all the tropes and figures have been split and hybridized, England and
India, like the political realities they have come to represent, insist on

their historicity, their social meaning, and configuration of memories and desires.[1]

At the same time, however, in reading Chamcha's unexpected return to India, one might even be tempted to argue that the more complicated the boundaries that demarcated Englishness and its others became, the more entrenched the institutions and ideals established by colonialism became. As the controversy surrounding Rushdie's novel has come to signify, we cannot talk about England without invoking India, nor can we initiate a discourse on Indianness without coming to terms with its inscription within a discourse of colonial Englishness. And thus, if my book was triggered by the disputes on the meaning and efficacy of postcoloniality as a theoretical and epistemological category, and if my inaugural point was an attempt to sort through the debates that have surrounded works such as Aijaz Ahmad's *In Theory: Classes, Nations, Literatures*, my focus has changed in the course of trying to come to terms with the culture of colonialism.[2]

Indeed, what at first appeared to be a huge chasm separating empiricist students of colonialism such as Ahmad and poststructuralist critics such as Homi Bhabha appears now to be a strategic rather than an epistemological gap. In retrospect, what brings these respective positions closer is the fact that whether we take the long historical view and read imperialism within the positivist myths that it established—the myths of progress, of empiricism, and civilizational authority—or within the splits and slippages that were engendered by imperial conquest and rule, we are still caught within the orbit of colonial culture itself. The times we live in are both colonial and postcolonial times. As I argued in chapter 1, for both the colonizer and the colonized, the culture of colonialism came to provide the terms in which the idea of a modern culture took shape, both in the metropolis and in the colonies. Colonialism was the foundation on which modern (and hence also postcolonial) thoughts, actions, and debates were built.

This point needs to be emphasized because many of the misunderstandings that surround the notion of a postcolonial condition emerge when we dissociate the cultural and philosophical consequences of colonialism from its genealogy. Indeed, it is time to admit that one of the reasons why the discourse of decolonization failed to break away from its colonial past was its failure to recognize how its grammar of radical critique was already inherent in colonial culture itself. Consider, for example, the notion of *tradition*, one of the key terms in the lexicon of the discourse against colonialism. For many nationalists and writers in the period of decolonization, an explicit appeal to a historical past and culture that ante-dated colonialism—what many of them considered to be the core of tradition—was the key to undermining the hegemony of colonial rule. An appeal to tradition was the instrument for valorizing an alternative civilizational authority. What was forgotten in this appeal to a usable precolonial past, however, was how the notion of tradition it valorized was predicated on the authority of Englishness itself. Not only were the traditions deployed against imperialism invented by colonialism itself, as Terence Ranger and others have argued,[3] but the category that came to be known as "tradition" derived its moral authority from its association with bourgeois civility.

As it emerged in the eighteenth and nineteenth centuries in England, the notion of tradition was closely tied to the ideals of a new middle-class culture based on moral restraint and social civility, a culture that, as we have already seen, was a key ingredient in the making of colonial societies. It was in relation to the colonial context, as much as the revolutionary events in France, that Edmund Burke would invoke tradition as what Talal Asad has called the ultimate defense against the forces that threatened Englishness in the era of revolution:

> What made justice, and coherent social life itself, possible, was "tradition," and "tradition" consisted in a reverence for unbroken continuity, for the prejudices of the past, and it *was* indeed antithetical to the irresponsibility of free reason and the disruption of radical change.[4]

It is perhaps true that when nationalist leaders such as Nehru or Kenyatta invoked the word *tradition* they had something else in mind, but they valued the concept precisely because their English education and experience had convinced them of its centrality in imagining nations and communities.

But where do notions such as culture, tradition, and nation stand in the postcolonial moment? The difference between the nationalist and postcolonial reading of colonialism, I have argued, is ultimately about our strategies for reading and appropriating colonial culture and its institutions, including the discipline of English studies. A postcolonial reading is not one that inscribes the temporal and spatial distance between metropolis and colony but one that reinstitutes their mutual imbrication at that moment of rupture (decolonization), when they were supposed to have been finally separated. One of the issues that I have tried to understand in this book, then, is how metropole and colony, having been conjoined in the nineteenth century, found it difficult to conjugate or write their identities except in their mutual discourses of identity and alterity.

As I argued in chapters 2 and 3, projects intended to contain the dangers posed by the colonial subject—disorder, immorality, and the lack of respect for private property—were also attempts to deal with questions that were essentially English. The invocation of colonial alterity was one of the conduits into which anxieties about Englishness were channeled. The questions that concerned me here—and in chapter 4—were also about the fate of preexisting discourses transferred or translated to specific colonial spaces: "What concepts of dominant power did they assume, modify, or reject, as they tried to observe and represent the lives of 'traditional' populations being transformed in a 'modern' direction."[5] Imperial writers such as Carlyle and Froude took the ideals espoused by the dominant power as self-evident, superior, and natural, but in many cases, such concepts were subjected to unforeseen pressures in the colonial scene itself. An outstanding feature of the imperial narrative was how to contain such pressures.

Under these circumstances, as I argued in my discussion of imperial femininity (chapter 4), the story of a triumphant Englishness had different meanings for women and colonized subjects. More attuned to the slippages in the categories that defined colonial culture, women and colonial subjects existed both inside and outside Englishness, committed to the ideals of the dominant culture but also aware of their tenuous emplacement in it. The narratives that emerged out of this liminal situation both reinforced the civilization mission of Englishness and promoted a relativist notion of culture and tradition. Writers such as Mary Kingsley would thus posit cultural difference not as a force of contamination that Englishness had to purge in order to clarify its own meanings but as an alternative mode of cultural expression. And in the culture of late colonialism, as I argued in chapter 5, the emergence of a modernist style would be directly connected to a certain sense that the concepts of the dominant power were no longer tenable, and yet Englishness still continued to have a residual authority. Rather than deploy the other as the unequivocal figure of transgression, modernism promised to rewrite cultural difference as the topological manifestation of the European subject's desire for affirmative alterity; narrative and discourse thus became instruments of representing both the crisis of colonialism and the concomitant slippage in European modes of cognition.

In writing this book, and in trying to figure ways of connecting events that seem to be separated by time and space—Morant Bay in 1865 and the Rushdie affair in the 1990s, for example—I could not help asking myself questions that Ann Stoler has preempted at the end of *Race and the Education of Desire*:

What issues are being expressed and spoken through the contemporary study of colonialism and race? Can we account for the resurgence of interest in these topics as the response of postcolonial intellectuals now positioned to interrogate official wisdom about the colonial past, as they create and verify subjugated knowledges long repressed? Or does that resurgence also signal a verbose response to the crisis and anxieties of securing bourgeois identity in a rapidly shifting transcultural world in which "core" and "periphery" no longer look different in familiar ways or even map on to the same geopolitical entities?[6]

My response to these questions can be found in the last chapter of *Maps of Englishness*, where I argue that a questioning of the colonial past is intractably tied to the crisis of securing identity in an age of collapsing boundaries. As the two epigraphs I use for this chapter illustrate, the postcolonial journey to Africa, India, or the Caribbean is the first stage in a rite of passage back to the maps of Englishness. Indeed, the most repressed knowledge that postcolonial writers need in order to secure their authority as writing subjects (and thus also to claim their subjectivities in the maps of Englishness) is about their own place in the metropolis. For black subjects in the new Europe, where the old cultural models of citizenship and paternity will not do, the imaginary return to the past is an attempt to "name the unnameable, to speak about the possibilities of cultural identification."[7] And as one can see from Sonia Boyce's reconfiguration of

FIGURE EPILOGUE.1.
Sonia Boyce, *She Ain't Holding Them Up, She's Holding On
(Some English Rose)* (1986).
Courtesy of Cleveland Gallery, Middlesbrough.

the meaning of one of the central symbols of pastoral Englishness—the English rose—acts of naming the unnameable are also forms of renaming the already named (figure epilogue.1).

And thus, too, reading the scriptures of Englishness, which are also the texts of English-language literatures produced in the former colonial localities, is one of the most important ways of bearing what Spivak has called "the burden of English."[8] For if English literature was read by critics as diverse as F. R. Leavis and Raymond Williams as an attempt to secure a sense of tradition or to denote a knowable community in times of crisis, rereading Englishness from the vantage point of decolonization is one way of coming to terms with its interruptive authority. A book on the maps of Englishness is about both claiming a space in the culture that colonialism built and acknowledging our alienation in this cartography.

Notes

Preface

1. Nairn, *The Break-Up of Britain*.
2. The key texts in this tradition are Césaire, *Discourse on Colonialism*; Fanon, *The Wretched of the Earth*; and Lamming, *The Pleasures of Exile*.
3. R. Williams, *Culture and Society*, pp. 304–23.
4. Ibid., p. 38.
5. Ibid., p. 314.
6. Ibid., p. 17.
7. Dirks, "Introduction," p. 3.
8. The key debates on colonialism and postcolonial theory can be found in two anthologies: Ashcroft, Griffiths, and Tiffin, *The Postcolonial Studies Reader*, and Williams and Chrisman, *Colonial Discourse and Postcolonial Theory*.
9. Prakash, "Introduction," p. 3.
10. For resistance as a category in the emergence of colonial and postcolonial discourse, see the general introduction to Ashcroft, Griffiths, and Tiffin, *The Postcolonial Studies Reader*, pp. 1–4.
11. Bhabha has an elaborate discussion of the idea of colonial mimicry in *The Location of Culture*, pp. 66–84.
12. See Mukasa, *Sir Apolo Kagwa*; Mary Seacole, *Wonderful Adventures of Mrs. Seacole in Many Lands*, in the Schomburg Library of Nineteenth-Century Black Women Writers (New York: Oxford University Press, 1988); J. J. Thomas, *Froudacity*.
13. Thomas, *Froudacity*, p. 53.
14. Mukasa, *Sir Apolo Kagwa*, p. 91.
15. For Thatcherism as an intellectual and ideological category, see S. Hall, "The Great Moving Right Show."
16. P. Anderson, *English Questions*, p. 15.
17. Ibid., p. 7. The allusion here is to Tom Nairn and Benedict Anderson.

18. The whole notion of nations as imagined communities calls attention to the close relation between the narrative of identity and subjective desire. See B. Anderson, *Imagined Communities*, especially chapters 2 and 3.

19. R. Williams, *The Country and the City*, pp. 197–99, 264–71.

20. The figure of F. R. Leavis is central to understanding postcolonial theory not only because of the hegemony he exercised on the study of literature in England after World War II but also because of the even greater influence he had on literary studies in the colonial universities in the age of decolonization. The key text here is *The Great Tradition*.

21. Colley, *Britons*, p. 6.

22. For a critique of this kind of aestheticizing, see Dirks, "Introduction," p. 5.

23. N. Thomas, *Colonialism's Culture*, p. x.

24. Some powerful images of the function of the book can be found in Wole Soyinka's childhood memoir, *Akè*, p. 79; and Chinua Achebe speaks about his parents' "almost superstitious reverence" for books in "Named for Victoria, Queen of England," in *Morning Yet on Creation Day*, pp. 65–70. I am exploring the phenomenon of the book in colonial society in "The Colonial Library: Reading, Textuality, and the Making of Modern Subjects" (in progress).

25. See "On the Abolition of the English Department," collected as an appendix in Ngugi wa Thiong'o's *Homecoming*, p. 146.

26. Ibid. Cf. *The Great Tradition*, where Leavis connects literariness to Englishness (pp. 9–18). The irony, of course, is that the Leaviate tradition that Thiong'o and his colleagues were fighting against had already set the terms of this debate by connecting literature to tradition, community, and nation. The point of debate, then, was not whether these colonial categories were valid but whether they could be localized.

1. Colonial Culture and the Question of Identity

1. Said, *Culture and Imperialism*, p. 161.

2. My formulation here is indebted to Jacques Derrida's notion of *différence* as it relates to space and temporality: "An interval must separate the present from what it is not in order for the present to be itself, but this interval that constitutes it as present must, by the same token, divide the present in and of itself, thereby also dividing, along with the present, everything that is thought on the basis of the present, that is, in our metaphysical language, every being, and singularly substance or the subject" (*Margins of Philosophy*, p. 13).

3. Appadurai, "Playing with Modernity," p. 23.

4. See the essays collected in Crick, *National Identities*.

5. For a discussion of the imbrication of colonial and postcolonial cultures, see Suleri, *The Rhetoric of English India*, pp. 1–10, and Dirks, "Introduction," pp. 1–25.

6. Cooper and Stoler, *Tensions of Empire*.

7. On the notion of the past as a specter that haunts the present, see Derrida, *Specters of Marx*, p. xix.

8. According to Johannes Fabian, imperialized discourse, by defining the temporal relation between the self and the other as "exclusive and expansive," seeks to repress the fact that the two entities are "coeval"—that is, they "share the same Time" (*Time and the Other*, pp. 28, 30–31).

9. This kind of literary reorientation was initiated by Edward Said; it is part of the project that informs his reading of canonical writers such as Jane Austen and Joseph Conrad. See *Culture and Imperialism*.

10. Chambers, *Room for Maneuver*, p. 15.

11. Ibid. The most glaring absence in colonial and postcolonial studies—in literary and cultural studies, especially—is research in the colonial library or archive. For pioneering and challenging work in this direction, see Viswanathan, *Masks of Conquest*, and Spivak, "The Ranir of Sirmur."

12. Said, *Culture and Imperialism*, p. 83.

13. Roland Barthes, *S/Z: An Essay*, trans. Richard Miller (New York: Hill and Wang, 1974), pp. 15–16.

14. Mudimbe, *The Invention of Africa*, p. 151. For the larger implications of this new order of alterity, see Sandra Harding, *Whose Science? Whose Knowledge? Thinking from Women's Lives* (Ithaca: Cornell University Press, 1991), p. 16.

15. Ahmad's claim, in essence, is that the turn to abstract theory, especially in literary studies dealing with questions of empire, colony, and nation, has had "peculiarly disorienting effects": "In one kind of pressure, politics as such has undergone remarkable degrees of diminution. Any attempt to *know* the world as a whole, or to hold that it is open to rational comprehension, let alone the desire to change it, was to be dismissed as a contemptible attempt to construct 'grand narratives' and 'totalizing (totalitarian) knowledges' "(*In Theory*, p. 69).

16. Dipesh Chakrabarty, "Marx After Marxism: History, Subalternity, and Difference," *Meanjin* 52, no. 3 (1993): 422.

17. Ahmad, *In Theory*, p. 2.

18. Bal, "The Politics of Citation," p. 44.

19. Fanon, *The Wretched of the Earth*, p. 39.

20. In his famous description of the spatial organization of the colonial landscape as Manichaean, Fanon makes the important point that understanding the way the colonial world is divided into compartments enables us to understand not

only the "lines of force" that colonialism establishes but also "the lines on which a decolonized society will be reorganized" (*The Wretched of the Earth*, pp. 37–38).

21. Cf. Ahmad's argument against the kind of rupture I propose here: "For human collectivities in the backward zones of capital . . . all relationships with imperialism pass through their own nation-states, and there is simply no way of breaking out of that imperial dominance without struggling for different kinds of national projects and for a revolutionary restructuring of one's own nation-state" (*In Theory*, p. 11). My argument, however, is that (a) the binary opposition between centers of capital and its backward zones no longer holds true (as students of postcoloniality in the Pacific realm may point out, the centers of capital are no longer in Europe) and (b) where Ahmad sees a revolutionary restructuring as already overdetermined by the nation-state, I see postcolonial theory and writing as an attempt to critique and detour the project of the nation, both at home and abroad.

22. Cooper and Stoler, *Tensions of Empire*.

23. Dirks, "Introduction," p. 3. See also Fabian, *Time and the Other*, p. 7.

24. Mehta, "Liberal Strategies of Exclusion," p. 428.

25. Sandiford, *Cricket and the Victorians*, p. 1.

26. James, *Beyond a Boundary*, p. 252.

27. Orlando Patterson, "The Ritual of Cricket," in Beckles and Stoddart, *Liberation Cricket*, p. 144.

28. Hilary McD. Beckles and Harclyde Walcott, "Redemption Sounds: Music, Literature, and the Popular Ideology of West Indian Cricket Crowds," in Beckles and Stoddart, *Liberation Cricket*, p. 376.

29. See Richard D. E. Burton, "Cricket, Carnival, and Street Culture in the Caribbean," in Beckles and Stoddart, *Liberation Cricket*, p. 90.

30. See Appadurai, "Playing with Modernity," p. 46.

31. This formulation comes from a conversation with Ross Chambers.

32. Ama Ata Aidoo, "Conference presentation," in Philomena Mariani, ed., *Critical Fictions: The Politics of Imaginative Writing*, p. 152 (Seattle: Bay Press, 1991).

33. For the notion of "arrested decolonization," see Biodun Jeyifo, "The Nature of Things: Arrested Decolonization and Critical Theory," *Research in African Literatures*, Special Issue, *Critical Theory and African Literature* 21, no. 1 (Spring 1990): 33–46. A fascinating discussion of the "altered states" of the postcolonial state in Africa can be found in chapter 8 of Kwame Anthony Appiah's *In My Father's House: Africa in the Philosophy of Culture* (New York: Oxford University Press, 1992).

34. Cf. Spivak's argument that "the political claims that are most urgent in decolonized space are tacitly recognized as coded within the legacy of imperialism: nationhood, constitutionality, citizenship, democracy, even culturalism" (*Outside in the Teaching Machine*, p. 60).

35. For a discussion of the notion of *trace*, see Derrida, *Margins of Philosophy*, p. 18.

36. "Postcoloniality and the Artifice of History," pp. 1–4.

37. Aidoo, "Conference presentation," p. 154.

38. Jameson, *The Seeds of Time*, p. xii.

39. What I have in mind here is something akin to what V. Y. Mudimbe calls *reprendre*—the act of taking up an interrupted tradition and reading it in the context of the present and as a methodological assessment "of the tools, means, and projects of art within a social context transformed by colonialism." See "Reprendre: Enunciations and Strategies in Contemporary African Arts," in Susan Vogel, ed., *Africa Explores: Twentieth-Century African Art*, p. 276 (New York: Center for African Art, 1991).

40. Patrick Taylor, *The Narrative of Liberation: Perspectives on Afro-Caribbean Literature, Popular Culture, and Politics* (Ithaca: Cornell University Press, 1989), p. 54.

41. Fanon, *The Wretched of the Earth*, p. 43.

42. Taylor, *The Narrative of Liberation*, p. 81.

43. On the nationalist evocation of modernity as the path to freedom, see Kenyatta, *Facing Mount Kenya*, pp. 305–6, and Césaire, *Discourse on Colonialism*, p. 25.

44. See Dipesh Chakrabarty, "Marx After Marxism," p. 422, and Rafael, *Contracting Colonialism*, p. x.

45. On the contradiction between nation and empire, see Bhabha, "Interview," *Stanford Review* 3, no. 1 (Winter 1993): 1. The point here is that if the relation between empire and nation is now read as a contradiction that, according to Fredric Jameson, is productive in the sense that it generates new perspectives, we should not forget that nationalist discourse always reads empire and nation as antinomies, as "clearly and unequivocally two separate things" (Jameson, *The Seeds of Time*, p. 2).

46. The notion of "horizon of expectation" is borrowed from Reinhart Koselleck, *Futures Past: On the Semantics of Historical Time*, trans. Keith Tribe (Cambridge: MIT Press, 1985).

47. Kenyatta, *Facing Mount Kenya*, p. 305.

48. Quoted by Homi Bhabha in "Conference presentation," in Mariani, *Critical Fictions*, p. 64.

49. Said, *Culture and Imperialism*, p. 161.

50. For the possibility that the colonized might be in control of the imperial gaze, see Bal, "The Politics of Citation," p. 43.

51. For the relation between Thatcherism and the crisis of English identity, see Stuart Hall, "The Emergence of Cultural Studies and the Crisis in the Humanities," *October* 53 (Summer 1990): 21.

52. The changing character of Englishness can be discerned in the transformation of the portraits at the National Portrait Gallery in London, which have perhaps become more diverse in response to some of the questions raised by the debate on the national character. See Susan Foister et al., eds., *The National Portrait Gallery Collection* (London: National Portrait Gallery Publications, 1988).

53. Asad, *Genealogies of Religion*, p. 241.

54. Colley, "Britishness and Otherness," p. 311; Peter Scott, *Knowledge and Nation* (Edinburgh: Edinburgh University Press, 1990), p. 167. Other significant studies on the crisis of English identity include Colley, *Britons*; Gerald Newman, *The Rise of English Nationalism: A Cultural History, 1740–1830* (New York: St. Martin's, 1987); Nairn, *The Break-Up of Britain*; and P. Anderson, *English Questions*.

55. B. Anderson, *Imagined Communities*, p. 201.

56. Roland Barthes, "Mythology Today," in *The Rustle of Language*, trans. Richard Howard, p. 65 (New York: Hill and Wang, 1986).

57. Ann Williams, *The English and the Norman Conquest* (Woodbridge, Eng.: Boydell Press, 1995), p. 1.

58. George Lamming, *In the Castle of My Skin* (Ann Arbor: University of Michigan Press, 1991), p. 58. Further page references will be made in the text.

59. Although the culture of colonialism is conceptually a modern phenomenon, empire always presents itself as something akin to what Benedict Anderson calls a classical community; it is conceived "as cosmically central" and is represented "through the medium of a sacred language linked to a superterrestrial order of power" (*Imagined Communities*, p. 13).

60. Salman Rushdie, *The Satanic Verses* (New York: Viking, 1988), p. 129.

61. See Terry Castle, *The Apparitional Lesbian: Female Homosexuality and Modern Culture* (New York: Columbia University Press, 1993), pp. 28–65.

62. R. Williams, *Politics and Letters*, p. 65.

63. Ibid., p. 26.

64. Colley, "Britishness and Otherness," p. 325.

65. B. Anderson, *Imagined Communities*, p. 7.

66. Colley, *Britons*, p. 365. Important background to Wilkie and his art can be found in the following catalogs: Lindsay Errington, ed., *Tribute to Wilkie* (Edinburgh:

National Galleries of Scotland, 1985); and *Sir David Wilkie of Scotland, 1785–1841,* organized by William Chiego (Raleigh: North Carolina Museum of Art, 1987).

67. B. Anderson, *Imagined Communities,* p. 26. Cf. Bhabha's critique of Anderson's position in interview in *Stanford Humanities Review* 3, no. 1 (Winter 1993): 1.

68. Scott, *Knowledge and Nation,* p. 167.

69. See Spivak's reading of *The Satanic Verses* in *Outside in the Teaching Machine,* p. 226.

70. B. Anderson, *Imagined Communities,* p. 22.

71. Ibid., p. 14.

72. Hobsbawn, *The Age of Empire,* pp. 8–9.

73. Stoler presents this issue succinctly: "If we accept that 'whiteness' was part of the moral rearmament of bourgeois society, then we need to investigate the nature of the contingent relationship between European racial and class anxieties in the colonies and bourgeois cultivations of self in England, Holland, and France" (*Race and the Education of Desire,* p. 100).

74. Hobsbawn, *The Age of Empire,* p. 10.

75. Jan P. Nederveen Pierterse, *Empire and Emancipation: Power and Liberation on a World Scale* (London: Pluto Press, 1990), p. 354.

76. Cf. Jürgen Habermas, "Modernity—An Incomplete Project," in Hal Foster, ed., *The Anti-Aesthetic: Essays on Postmodern Culture,* pp. 3–15 (Port Townsend, Wash.: Bay Press, 1983).

77. Colley, "Britishness and Otherness," p. 315.

78. Muriuki, *A History of the Kikuyu,* p. 178.

79. For a discussion of the relation between education and the colonial situation in Kenya, see John Anderson, *The Struggle for the School* (London: Longman, 1970), pp. 1–32.

80. Samuel G. Kibicho, "The Continuity of the African Conception of God Into and Through Christianity: A Kikuyu Case Study," in Edward Fasholé-Luke, Richard Gray, Adrian Hastings, and Godwin Tasie, eds., *Christianity in Independent Africa,* p. 384 (Bloomington: Indiana University Press, 1978).

81. In one significant way, the use-value of the culture of colonialism in Africa lies in its temporal paradox: it marks a short historical period that nevertheless revolutionizes the structures of society. As Mudimbe has observed, although the history of the colonial experience in Africa was brief, "it signified a new historical form and the possibility of radically new types of discourses on African traditions and cultures" (*The Invention of Africa,* p. 1).

82. Sahlins, *Boundaries,* p. 8. Colley discusses the effect of peripheries in the constitution of Englishness in *Britons,* pp. 101–46.

83. Terence Ranger, "The Invention of Tradition in Colonial Africa," in Hobsbawn and Ranger, *The Invention of Tradition*, pp. 211–62.

84. My argument here follows Ranger's claim that "European invented traditions offered Africans a series of clearly defined points of entry into the colonial world, though in almost all cases it was entry into the subordinate part of a man/master relationship" (ibid., p. 227).

85. See Mukasa, *Sir Apolo Kagwa* (further references to this edition will be made in the text); I provide a context for this text in my introduction to a new and complete edition of Mukasa's text, *Uganda's Katikiro in England* (Manchester: Manchester University Press, forthcoming).

86. For *similitude*, see Michel Foucault, *The Order of Things: An Archeology of the Human Sciences* (New York: Vintage, 1973), pp. 17–25; for *thoma*, see François Hartog, *The Mirror of Herodotus*, trans. Janet Lloyd (Berkeley: University of California Press, 1988), p. 230.

87. These questions are discussed thoroughly in chapters 1 and 3 of Rafael's *Contracting Colonialism*.

88. Mukasa, *Sir Apolo Kagwa*, p. 75.

89. See Viswanathan, *Masks of Conquest*, p. 45.

90. R. Radhakrishnan, "Cultural Theory and the Politics of Location" (p. 289), and Gauri Viswanathan, "Raymond Williams and British Colonialism: The Limits of Metropolitan Cultural Theory" (p. 220), both in Dworkin and Roman, *Views Beyond the Border Country*. See also Said, *Culture and Imperialism*, pp. 82–83; and Stuart Hall, "Politics and Letters," in Eagleton, ed., *Raymond Williams*, p. 54.

91. Williams, *The Country and the City*, p. 196. Williams reads the postcolonial novel as symptomatic of what he calls the "new metropolis" (pp. 279–88).

92. Williams, *Politics and Letters*, p. 25.

93. Ibid., p. 26.

94. Williams, *The Country and the City*, p. 299.

95. Stuart Hall, "Old and New Identities, Old and New Ethnicities," in Anthony D. King, ed., *Culture, Globalization, and the World System*, p. 53 (Binghamton, N.Y.: Department of Art History, 1991).

96. Hall's explanation for leaving Jamaica is fascinating precisely because of the symbolic and real returns he has since had to make as a way of coming to terms with his Englishness: "The truth is, I am here because it's where my family is not. I really came here to get away from my mother. Isn't that the universal story of life?" ("Minimal Selves," p. 44). See also his "Negotiating Caribbean Identities."

97. Williams, *Politics and Letters*, pp. 295–96.

98. Gilroy, "One Nation Under a Groove," p. 266.

99. Chambers, *Room for Maneuver*, p. 18. For a discussion of the location of the black subject in the discourse of Englishness, see Gilroy, "Art of Darkness," and Kobena Mercer, "Black Art and the Burden of Representation," *Third Text* 10 (Spring 1990): 61–79.

100. Gilroy, "Art of Darkness," p. 51.

101. Peter Conrad, "The Englishness of English Literature," *Daedalus* 112, no. 1 (Winter 1983): 157.

102. Ibid., p. 160.

103. My argument here—as my whole discourse on cartography and identity—is indebted to Peter Stallybrass: "The mapping of space was of crucial significance both literally and symbolically in the formation of the nation. . . . Mapping was thus an instrument in the charting of ideological as well as geographical boundaries" ("Time Space and Unity: The Symbolic Discourse of *The Faerie Queene*," in Raphael Samuel, ed., *Patriotism: The Making and Unmaking of British National Identity*, 3:204–5 [London and New York: Routledge, 1989]).

104. Certeau, *The Writing of History*, p. 2.

105. Cf. Bhabha's discussion of the temporality of postcolonialism in *The Location of Culture*, pp. 177–78.

106. Under the circumstances, the strategies available to a heterological countertradition are, as Wlad Godzich has argued, limited: "Either it must deconstruct the epistemology from within, a rather arduous task that constantly runs the risk of becoming one more specialized language on the verge of institutionalization . . . or it must critique this epistemology from the outside, and then it runs the risk of relying upon the ethical and the figure of the other and its possible religious overtones." See "The Further Possibility of Knowledge," foreword to Michel de Certeau, *Heterologies: Discourse on the Other*, trans. Brian Massumi, pp. xvii–xix (Minneapolis: University of Minnesota Press, 1986). My book is an attempt to explore the possibilities of forms of discourse that are located both inside and outside the dominant epistemology.

107. Said, *Culture and Imperialism*, p. 187.

108. See Trotter, "Modernism and Empire."

109. Gillian Beer, "The Island and the Aeroplane: the Case of Virginia Woolf," in Homi K. Bhabha, ed., *Nation and Narration*, p. 265 (New York: Routledge, 1990).

2. *Through the Prism of Race*

1. Etienne Balibar, "Racism and Nationalism," in Etienne Balibar and Immanuel Wallerstein, *Race, Nation, Class: Ambiguous Identities*, p. 54 (London: Verso, 1991).

2. S. Hall, "Racism and Reaction," p. 23.

3. The paradox of Englishness, argues Paul Gilroy, is that it draws upon a metaphysics with racial referents and yet insists on the radical opposition between blackness and the national character, which it rewrites as "mutually exclusive categories, incompatible identities" ("The End of Anti-Racism," in James Donald and Ali Rattansi, eds., *"Race," Culture, and Difference*, pp. 53–54 [London: Sage Publications, 1992]).

4. Gillian Beer, "The Island and the Aeroplane: the Case of Virginia Woolf," in Homi K. Bhabha, ed., *Nation and Narration*, p. 265 (New York: Routledge, 1990). See also Said, *Culture and Imperialism*, pp. 82–83.

5. Semmel, *Jamaican Blood and Victorian Conscience*. Further references to this edition will be made in the text.

6. For a general background to the politics of the Eyre controversy, see Geoffrey Dutton, *In Search of Edward John Eyre* (Melbourne: Macmillan, 1982).

7. The relation between the nation and the rhetoric of the law is discussed by Paul Gilroy in *There Ain't No Black*, p. 74.

8. S. Hall, "Racism and Reaction," p. 30.

9. For some influential ("canonical") commentaries on Carlyle's pamphlet, see R. Williams, *Culture and Society*, p. 98; Basil Wiley, *Nineteenth Century Studies: Coleridge to Matthew Arnold* (New York: Harper, 1966), p. 102; John D. Rosenberg, *Carlyle and the Burden of History* (Oxford: Clarendon, 1985), p. 151; and Walter E. Houghton, *The Victorian Frame of Mind 1830–1870* (New Haven: Yale University Press, 1957), p. 54.

10. Thomas Carlyle, "Occasional Discourse on the Nigger Question," in Eugene R. August, ed., *Thomas Carlyle, The Nigger Question, and John Stuart Mill, The Negro Question*, p. 2 (New York: Appleton-Century-Crofts, 1971). Further references to this edition will be made in the text. On the changes in Carlyle's rhetoric in the *Latter-Day Pamphlets*, see Chris R. Vanden Bossche, *Carlyle and the Search for Authority* (Columbus: Ohio State University Press, 1991), pp. 133–35.

11. R. Williams, *Culture and Society*, p. 85.

12. Ian Campbell, "Carlyle and the Negro Question Again," *Criticism* 13, no. 3 (Summer 1971): 279–90.

13. Aileen Christianson, "On the Writing of the 'Occasional Discourse on the Negro Question,'" *Carlyle Newsletter*, no. 2 (March 1980): 15.

14. Campbell, "Carlyle and the Negro Question Again," p. 290.

15. Catherine Hall, "Missionary Stories: Gender and Ethnicity in England in the 1830s and 1840s," in Grossberg, Nelson, and Treichler, *Cultural Studies*, p. 242.

16. Houghton, *The Victorian Frame of Mind*, p. 37. See also Mary Desaulniers, *Carlyle and the Economics of Terror: A Study of Revisionary Criticism in the French Revolution* (Montreal and Kingston: McGill-Queen's University Press, 1995), p. 9.

17. John Stuart Mill, "The Negro Question," in August, *Carlyle and Mill*, p. 38. Further references to this edition will be made in the text.

18. Gilroy, *There Ain't No Black*, p. 78.

19. Homi K. Bhabha, "A Question of Survival: Nations and Psychic States," in James Donald, ed., *Psychoanalysis and Cultural Theory: Thresholds*, p. 100 (London: Macmillan, 1991).

20. Mehta, "Liberal Strategies of Exclusion," p. 441. For Mill and empire, see Eileen P. Sullivan, "Liberalism and Imperialism: J. S. Mill's Defense of the British Empire," *Journal of the History of Ideas* 44 (October/December 1983): 599–617. For Mill and India, see Zastoupil, *John Stuart Mill and India*.

21. For an insightful discussion of the distinction between pedagogical and performative functions in narrative and discourse, see Homi K. Bhabha, "DissemiNation: Time, Narrative, and the Margins of the Modern Nation," in Homi K. Bhabha, ed., *Nation and Narration*, p. 299 (New York: Routledge, 1990).

22. Mehta, "Liberal Strategies of Exclusion," p. 441.

23. For how metaphors "visibilize the invisible," see Barbara Maria Stafford, *Body Criticism: Imagining the Unseen in Enlightenment Art and Medicine* (Cambridge: MIT Press, 1991), p. 4.

24. For a study of the deployment of the Irish and Jews in the discourses of English, see Eagleton, *Heathcliff and the Great Hunger*, and Shapiro, *Shakespeare and the Jews*. For Powellism as a cultural formation, see S. Hall, "Racism and Reaction," pp. 29–30; Kobena Mercer, " '1968': Periodizing Postmodern Politics and Identity," in Grossberg, Nelson, and Treichler, *Cultural Studies*, p. 432. The ideological manifestations of the politics of Thatcherism are discussed by Stuart Hall in "The Emergence of Cultural Studies and the Crisis of the Humanities," *October* 53 (Summer 1990): 19–22, and in "The Great Moving Right Show," pp. 30–34.

25. For this post-Hegelian notion of identity, see Slavoj Zizek, *For They Know Not What They Do: Enjoyment as a Political Factor* (London: Verso, 1991), p. 37.

26. This quote is used as an epigraph by Paul Foot in *The Rise of Enoch Powell* (Harmondsworth: Penguin Books, 1969).

27. Mercer, " '1968,' " p. 432.

28. Hall, "The Emergence of Cultural Studies," p. 21.

29. J. Enoch Powell, *Freedom and Reality*, ed. John Wood (London: Batsford, 1969), p. 248.

30. Angus Maude and J. Enoch Powell, *Biography of a Nation: A Short History of Britain*, rev. ed. (London: John Baker, 1970), p. 7. Further references to this edition will be made in the text.

31. M. Barker, *The New Racism*, p. 45.

32. Nairn, *The Break-Up of Britain*, p. 269.

33. Jean-Paul Sartre, *Being and Nothingness: A Phenomenological Essay on Ontology*, trans. Hazel E. Barnes (New York: Pocket Books, 1966), p. 317; for a discussion of the "Other" as a mediator of the "Self," see pp. 301–15.

34. Ibid., p. 317.

35. Nairn, *The Break-Up of Britain*, p. 258.

36. M. Barker, *The New Racism*, p. 16.

37. See Gilroy, *There Ain't No Black*, chapter 3; M. Barker, *The New Racism*, passim.

38. For the ideological imperatives of this argument, see Nairn, *The Break-Up of Britain*, p. 258, and M. Barker, *The New Racism*, p. 45.

39. Hall, "Racism and Reaction," pp. 29–30.

40. Mercer, " '1968,' " p. 435.

41. My definition of ideology here comes from Louis Althusser: "Ideology represents the imaginary relationship of individuals to their real conditions of existence" ("Ideology and Ideological State Apparatuses," in *Lenin and Philosophy and Other Essays*, p. 162 [New York: Monthly Review Press, 1971]).

42. Gilroy, "The End of Anti-Racism," p. 53.

43. Ibid.

44. Gilroy, "Cultural Studies and Ethnic Absolutism," in Grossberg, Nelson, and Treichler, eds., *Cultural Studies*, p. 190.

45. Gilroy, "Art of Darkness," p. 45. Further references to this essay will be made in the text.

46. On Englishness as a cultural and theoretical concept, see Brian Doyle, *English and Englishness*; J. McMurty, *English Language, English Literature* (Hamden, Conn.: Archon Books, 1985); D. J. Palmer, *The Rise of English Studies* (London: Oxford University Press, 1982); Peter Widdowson, *Re-Reading English* (London: Methuen, 1982).

3. *Englishness and the Culture of Travel*

1. James Anthony Froude, *The English in the West Indies: or The Bow of Ulysses* (London: Longman, 1888), p. 364. Further references to this edition will be made in the text.

2. J. J. Thomas, *Froudacity*, p. 51.

3. For the problem of periodizing postcoloniality, see some of the essays collected in

Ashcroft, Griffiths, and Tiffin, *The Postcolonial Studies Reader*, and P. Williams and Chrisman, *Colonial Discourse and Postcolonial Theory*.

4. Fabian, *Time and the Other*, p. 26.

5. For the historical context on the Tennyson/Gladstone feud over empire, see C. C. Eldridge, *England's Mission: The Imperial Idea in the Age of Gladstone and Disraeli, 1868–1886* (London: Macmillan, 1973).

6. J. W. Burrow, *A Liberal Descent: Victorian Histories of the English Past* (Cambridge: Cambridge University Press, 1981), pp. 231–86.

7. Fredric Jameson, "Metacommetary," in *The Ideologies of Theory*, 1:5 (Minneapolis: University of Minnesota Press, 1988).

8. Stocking, *Victorian Anthropology*, p. 234.

9. Jameson, *The Seeds of Time*, p. 112.

10. Abbeele, *Travel as Metaphor*, p. xv.

11. Ibid., p. 8. The relation between ethnography and the space of the other is discussed by Michel de Certeau in *The Writing of History*, pp. 209–43.

12. Abbeele, *Travel as Metaphor*, p. xviii.

13. Pratt, *Imperial Eyes*, p. 10.

14. The significance of travel narratives in the imperial project is discussed in works by James Buzzard, *The Beaten Track: European Tourism, Literature, and the Ways to "Culture"* (New York: Oxford University Press, 1993); Lisa Lowe, *Critical Terrains: French and British Orientalisms* (Ithaca: Cornell University Press, 1991); Pratt, *Imperial Eyes*; David Spurr, *The Rhetoric of Empire: Colonial Discourse in Journalism, Travel Writing, and Imperial Administration* (Durham: Duke University Press, 1993); and Ali Behdad, *Belated Travelers: Orientalism in the Age of Colonial Dissolution* (Durham: Duke University Press, 1994).

15. Anthony Trollope, *The West Indies and the Spanish Main* (1859; reprint, Gloucester: Alan Sutton, 1985), p. 166. Further references to this edition will be made in the text.

16. Fabian, *Time and the Other*, p. 9.

17. For an excellent philological discussion of the relation between theory and travel, see Bernd Jager, "Theorizing, Journeying, Dwelling," in Amedeo Giorgi, Constance T. Fischer, and Edward L. Murray, eds., *Duquesne Studies in Phenomenology Psychology*, pp. 235–60 (Pittsburgh: Duquesne University Press, 1975).

18. Thomas William Heyck, *Transformation of Intellectual Life in Victorian England* (New York: St. Martin's, 1982), p. 125.

19. Fabian, *Time and the Other*, p. 9.

20. Barbara Maria Stafford, *Body Criticism: Imagining the Unseen in Enlightenment Art and Medicine* (Cambridge: MIT Press, 1992), p. vii.

21. James Clifford, "Notes on (Field)notes," in Sanjek, *Fieldnotes*, p. 52.

22. The notion of "cognitive mapping" is borrowed from Fredric Jameson ("Cognitive Mapping," pp. 49–50).

23. As Trollope tells us in his autobiography, his principle reason for being in the West Indies was to organize the region's post office system. See Anthony Trollope, *An Autobiography* (London: Oxford University Press, 1950), pp. 118–31.

24. Clifford, "Notes on (Field)notes," p. 67.

25. The relation between ideas of the sublime and colonialism is discussed by Suleri in *The Rhetoric of English India*, pp. 44–48.

26. Jonathan Culler, *Flaubert: The Uses of Uncertainty* (Ithaca: Cornell University Press, 1974), p. 186.

27. Richard Lowell Howey, "Some Reflections on Irony in Nietzsche," *Nietzsche-Studien Band* 4 (1975): 46.

28. Charles Kingsley, *At Last: A Christmas in the West Indies*, vol. 14, *The Works of Charles Kingsley* (London: Macmillan, 1885), p. 1. Further references to this edition will be made in the text.

29. Stephen Greenblatt, *Marvelous Possessions: The Wonder of the New World* (Chicago: University of Chicago Press, 1991), p. 60.

30. Ibid., p. 75.

31. See Johannes Fabian, "Hindsight: Thoughts on Anthropology Upon Reading Francis Galton's Narrative of an Explorer in Tropical South Africa (1853)," *Critique of Anthropology* 7, no. 2 (1985): 45–47.

32. Arjun Appadurai, "Theory in Anthropology: Center and Periphery," *Comparative Studies in Society and History* 28 (1986): 358.

33. Ibid.

34. Michel Beaujour, "Some Paradoxes of Description," *Yale French Studies* 61 (1981): 32.

35. R. Williams, *Culture and Society*, p. 112.

36. Ibid., pp. 111–12.

37. Lowe, *Critical Terrains*, p. 31.

38. See Appadurai, "Theory in Anthropology," p. 358.

39. Michel-Rolph Trouillot, "Anthropology and the Savage Slot: The Poetics of

Otherness," in Richard G. Fox, ed., *Recapturing Anthropology: Working in the Present*, pp. 28–31 (Santa Fe: School of American Research Press, 1991).

40. See Bal, "The Politics of Citation," p. 4.

41. Cf. Homi Bhabha's argument that the subject of colonial discourse is "a subject of such affective ambivalence and discursive disturbance, that the narrative of English history can only beg the 'colonial' question. Deprived of its customary 'civil' reference, even the most historical narrative accedes to the language of fantasy and desire" (*The Location of Culture*, p. 97).

42. Fabian, "Hindsight," p. 42.

43. See Homi Bhabha, "The Other Question: Difference, Discrimination, and the Discourse of Colonialism," in Francis Barker, Peter Hulme, Margaret Iversen, and Diane Loxley, eds., *Literature, Politics, and Theory*, pp. 148–72 (London: Methuen, 1986).

44. J. J. Thomas, *Froudacity*, p. 179.

45. Fabian, "Hindsight," p. 43.

46. Michel Foucault defines heterotopias as places that are "something like counter-sites, a kind of effectively enacted utopia in which the real sites, all the other sites that can be found within the culture, are simultaneously represented, contested, and inverted" ("Of Other Spaces," *Diacritics* 16 [1986]: 24).

47. Edward Said argues for the synchronic nature of the imperial vision in *Orientalism*, pp. 238–42. The most succinct critique of what is seen as Said's representation of imperialism as a totalizing project is by John M. Mackenzie. See his "Edward Said and the Historians," *Nineteenth-Century Contexts*, Special Issue, *Colonialisms* 18 (1994): 9–25.

48. Fabian, "Hindsight," p. 38.

4. *Imperial Femininity*

1. R. Williams, *The English Novel*, p. 9.

2. Gauri Viswanathan, "Raymond Williams and British Colonialism: The Limits of Metropolitan Cultural Theory," in Dworkin and Roman, *Views Beyond the Border Country*, pp. 217–30.

3. R. Williams, *The English Novel*, p. 15.

4. Eagleton, *Heathcliff and the Great Hunger*, p. 4.

5. See Said, *Culture and Imperialism*, pp. 80–96.

6. C. Hall, *White, Male, and Middle-Class*, p. 75.

7. The critical literature on women and empire—and on women travelers in the

colonial space—is now extensive. I have drawn on the following texts in my discussion: Dea Birkett, *Spinsters Abroad* (Oxford: Blackwell, 1989); Nupur Chaudhuri and Margaret Strobel, eds., *Western Women and Imperialism: Complicity and Resistance* (Bloomington: Indiana University Press, 1992); Dorothy Middleton, *Victorian Lady Travellers* (London: Routledge and Kegan Paul, 1965); Sara Mills, *Discourses of Difference: An Analysis of Women's Travel Writing and Colonialism* (London and New York: Routledge, 1991); Mary Russell, *The Blessing of a Good Thick Skirt* (London: Collins, 1986); and Margaret Strobel, *European Women and the Second British Empire* (Bloomington: Indiana University Press, 1991).

8. The complicity/resistance thesis informs most of the essays in Nupur Chaudhuri and Margaret Strobel. A more complex exploration of the location of white women in colonial spaces can be found in Jenny Sharpe's *Allegories of Empire*, and Suleri, *The Rhetoric of English India*; for the difficult intersection of race and gender, see Frankenberg, *White Women, Race Matters*, and Ware, *Beyond the Pale*.

9. Spivak, "Imperialism and Sexual Difference," pp. 319–20.

10. Spivak, "Three Women's Texts and a Critique of Imperialism," *Critical Inquiry*, "Race," Writing, and Difference 12, no. 1 (Autumn 1985): 244.

11. Mills, *Discourses of Difference*, p. 23.

12. See Bhabha, *The Location of Culture*, pp. 80–84.

13. Anthony Trollope, *The West Indies and the Spanish Main* (1859; reprint, Gloucester: Alan Sutton, 1985), p. 6.

14. Ibid., p. 17.

15. Spivak, "Imperialism and Sexual Difference," p. 319.

16. Cf. Sandra Pouchet-Paquet, "The Enigma of Arrival: *The Wonderful Adventures of Mrs. Seacole in Many Lands*," *African American Review* 26 (1992): 651–63; and Faith Smith, "Coming Home to the Real Thing: Gender and Intellectual Life in the Anglophone Caribbean," *South Atlantic Quarterly*, Special Issue, *Materialist Feminism* 93, no. 4 (Fall 1994): 895–923. On the meaning and culture of the Creole in Jamaica, see Edward Brathwaite, *Creole Society in Jamaica*.

17. My notion of *différence* comes from Jacques Derrida. See *Margins of Philosophy*, pp. 9–16.

18. Mary Seacole, *Wonderful Adventures of Mrs. Seacole in Many Lands*, in the Schomburg Library of Nineteenth-Century Black Women Writers (New York: Oxford University Press, 1988), pp. 1–2. Further references to this edition will be made in the text.

19. For a discussion of Equiano and his relation to Englishness, see Keith A. Sandiford, *Measuring the Moment: Strategies of Protest in Eighteenth-Century Afro-English Writing* (Selingsgrove: Susquehanna University Press, 1988), pp. 118–48.

20. Spivak, *Outside in the Teaching Machine*, p. 60.

21. My general thesis here is that the so-called nationalist problem in the Caribbean region arises from the complexities of constituting a black subjectivity after slavery. See the essays in Franklin W. Knight and Colin A. Palmer, eds., *The Modern Caribbean* (Chapel Hill: University of North Carolina Press, 1989).

22. R. Williams, "Forms of English Fiction in 1848," p. 2.

23. Ibid., p. 3.

24. My argument here follows Williams (ibid., pp. 3–4), but some interesting qualifications about the production of the fiction of 1848 can be found in Nancy Armstrong's *Desire and Domestic Fiction: A Political History of the Novel* (New York: Oxford, 1987), pp. 176–86.

25. See Dea Birkett, *Mary Kingsley: Imperial Adventuress* (London: Macmillan, 1992).

26. Cf. Suleri's argument that the Anglo-Indian woman "performs a symbolic function that is closely aligned to that of her Indian counterpart" (*The Rhetoric of English India*, p. 77).

27. Peter de Bolla, *The Discourse of the Sublime: Readings in History, Aesthetics, and the Subject* (Oxford: Blackwell, 1989), p. 212.

28. See Henry Louis Gates, Jr., *The Signifying Monkey: A Theory of Afro-American Literary Criticism* (New York: Oxford University Press, 1988), pp. 127–69.

29. *Chromatism* is used, after Spivak, to refer to "the visible difference in skin color." See "Imperialism and Sexual Difference," p. 331.

30. Bhabha, *The Location of Culture*, p. 91.

31. Ibid.

32. This argument is elaborated in Gayatri Chakravorty Spivak's controversial article "Can the Subaltern Speak?" in Cary Nelson and Lawrence Grossberg, eds., *Marxism and the Interpretation of Culture*, pp. 271–313 (New York: Routledge, 1988).

33. Chambers, *Room for Maneuver*, p. 240.

34. Mary Kingsley, *Travels in West Africa* (1897; reprint, Boston: Beacon Press, 1982), p. 74. Further references to this edition will be made in the text. For a general account of Slessor's imperial mission (including her absolute regal authority in Okÿon), see W. P. Livingstone, *Mary Slessor of Calabar* (London: Hodder and Stoughton, 1934).

35. C. C. Eldridge, *England's Mission: The Imperial Idea in the Age of Gladstone and Disraeli, 1868–1886* (London: Macmillan), 1973), p. xvii. For the function of the aesthetic in the culture of late empire, see Said, *Culture and Imperialism*, pp. 186–90.

36. Melman, *Women's Orients*, p. 8.

37. Pratt, *Imperial Eyes*, p. 213.

38. Chambers, *Room for Maneuver*, p. 240. For Africanist discourse, see Christopher L.

Miller, *Blank Darkness: Africanist Discourse in French* (Chicago: University of Chicago Press, 1985), p. 5.

39. Kingsley occupies such a central role in discussions on feminism and empire that she has become a representative of the "white woman in the colonial sphere" paradigm. See the sections devoted to her in the books by Mills, Middleton, and Russell cited in note 7 above.

40. Pratt, *Imperial Eyes*, p. 214.

41. Ibid., pp. 215–16.

42. Mohanty, "Us and Them," p. 2.

43. Pratt, *Imperial Eyes*, p. 215.

44. See Talal Asad, "The Concept of Cultural Translation in British Social Anthropology," in James Clifford and George E. Marcus, eds., *Writing Culture: The Poetics and Politics of Ethnography*, pp. 141–64 (Berkeley: University of California Press, 1986).

45. James Clifford, "On Ethnographic Authority," *Representations* 1, no. 2 (Spring 1983): 121.

46. Ibid., p. 124.

47. See Bronislaw Malinowski, *The Dynamics of Culture Change: An Inquiry Into Race Relations in Africa* (New Haven: Yale University Press), pp. 1–20; see also George W. Stocking, Jr., "The Ethnographic Sensibility of the 1920s and the Dualism of the Anthropological Tradition," in George W. Stocking, Jr., ed., *Romantic Motives: Essays on Anthropological Sensibility*, vol. 6, *History of Anthropology*, pp. 208–76 (Madison: University of Wisconsin Press, 1986).

48. This dilemma, a defining characteristic of modernism, is explored by Peter Bürger in "Aporias of Modern Aesthetics," *New Left Review*, no. 184 (November/December 1990): 47–57.

5. Belated Englishness

1. Rubin, "Picasso," p. 254.

2. Brathwaite, *Roots*, p. 286.

3. Said, *Culture and Imperialism*, p. 187.

4. For an outstanding discussion of melancholy and modernist discourse, see Ross Chambers, *Writing of Melancholy: Modes of Opposition in Early French Modernism*, trans. Mary Seidman Troille (Chicago: University of Chicago Press, 1993).

5. This conceptualization of modernism and capitalism lies at the heart of Fredric Jameson's reading of Conrad in *The Political Unconscious*, pp. 236–38.

6. Ibid., p. 236.

7. The terminology here is borrowed from Mary Douglas's classic study of trans-

gression, *Purity and Danger*. For primitivism in high culture, the most comprehensive book is Marianna Torgovnick's *Gone Primitive*.

8. *The Political Unconscious*, p. 236. On the fetish and modernist discourse, see Simpson, *Fetishism and Imagination*, pp. 91–116.

9. Said, *Orientalism*, p. 240.

10. At the precise time when modernist writers are traveling in the imperial space to confront colonial atrophy, colonized writers such as Ham Mukasa (see chapter 1) are going to Europe to master metropolitan culture. It would be interesting to consider the implications of these kinds of cultural crossings.

11. Douglas, *Purity and Danger*, p. 94.

12. The important point, then, is that by the beginning of the new century, the epic of empire generated only anxiety and a sense of collective decline. As F. S. Oliver noted in 1909, the Edward generation was "the first of a new order, and look[ed] forward upon a prospect in which the ideas of conquest and expansion [found] no place"; the anxiety was aggravated by the sense that the empire had become a force of mechanization for which there was no escape. The quote from Oliver comes from Keith Robbins, "The Edwardians and Their Empire," in Donald Read, ed., *Edwardian England*, p. 128 (London: Croom Helm, 1982).

13. Said, *Orientalism*, pp. 236–40.

14. As Fredric Jameson notes, "the structure of imperialism also makes its mark on the inner forms and structures of that new mutation in literary and artistic language to which the term modernism is loosely applied." See "Modernism and Imperialism," in Terry Eagleton, Fredric Jameson, and Edward Said, *Nationalism, Colonialism, and Literature*, p. 44 (Minneapolis: University of Minnesota Press, 1990).

15. See Trotter, "Modernism and Empire."

16. Fredric Jameson, "Beyond the Cave: Demystifying the Ideology of Modernism," in *The Ideologies of Theory*, vol. 2, *Syntax of History*, p. 129 (Minneapolis: University of Minnesota Press, 1988).

17. Fredric Jameson, "Postmodernism and Consumer Society," in Hal Foster, ed., *The Anti-Aesthetic: Essays on Postmodern Culture*, p. 114 (Port Townsend, Wash.: Bay Press, 1983).

18. Joseph Conrad, "An Outpost of Progress," in *Eastern Skies and Western Seas: Two Complete Novels and Six Short Stories*, p. 214 (New York: Carroll and Graf, 1990). Further references to this edition will be made in the text.

19. An excellent discussion of the ideological and semiotic function of the appellation *nigger* can be found in James Snead, *Figures of Division: William Faulkner's Major Novels* (New York: Methuen, 1986).

20. Simpson, *Fetishism and Imagination*, p. 95.

21. *The Political Unconscious*, p. 250.

22. The debate on Conrad and impressionism was triggered by Ian Watt's classic study, *Conrad and the Nineteenth Century* (Berkeley: University of California Press, 1979). See pp. 168–80.

23. Simpson, *Fetishism and Imagination*, p. 108.

24. Ibid.

25. Said, *Culture and Imperialism*, p. 22. Cf. Jameson's argument that "modernism can at one and the same time be read as a Utopian compensation for everything reification brings with it" (*The Political Unconscious*, p. 236).

26. My notion of the nineteenth-century novel may appear somehow reductionist here, but it is a fair summary of how the novelists of the period conceptualized the epistemological function of their art. See R. Williams, *The Country and the City*.

27. See James Duncan and David Ley, introduction to *Place/Culture/Representation* (London and New York: Routledge, 1993), p. 1. The literature on Conrad and imperialism is quite extensive, but my rereading of his African texts builds on arguments presented by Said in *Culture and Imperialism*, pp. 19–31; Benita Parry, *Conrad and Imperialism: Ideological Boundaries and Visionary Frontiers* (London: Macmillan, 1983), pp. 1–32; Brantlinger, *Rule of Darkness*, pp. 255–74; and Taussig, *Shamanism, Colonialism, and the Wild Man*, pp. 3–36.

28. Said, *Culture and Imperialism*, p. 23.

29. On allegory and meaning, see Doris Sommer, "Allegory and Dialectics: A Match Made in Romance," *Boundary 2* 18, no. 1 (1991): 60–82.

30. Mary Kingsley, *Travels in West Africa* (1897; reprint, Boston: Beacon Press, 1982), p. 84.

31. Joseph Conrad, *Heart of Darkness*, ed. Robert Kimbrough, 3d ed. (New York: Norton, 1988), pp. 16–17. Further references to this edition will be made in the text.

32. Fabian is quoted in Duncan and Ley, introduction, p. 50.

33. Frederic Jameson, Hayward Kenison Lecture, University of Michigan, Ann Arbor, February 4, 1994. Jameson develops this argument in *The Seeds of Time*, pp. 73–128.

34. Brooks, *Reading for Plot*, p. 244; on the relation between temporality and Africanist narrative, see Christopher L. Miller, *Blank Darkness: Africanist Discourse in French* (Chicago: University of Chicago Press, 1985), p. 170.

35. See Genevieve Lloyd, *Being in Time: Selves and Narrators in Philosophy and Literature* (London and New York: Routledge, 1993), pp. 1–13.

36. Brooks, *Reading for Plot*, p. 244. See Roland Barthes's discussion of the relation between time and narration in "Introduction to the Structural Analysis of Narratives," in Susan Sontag, ed., *A Roland Barthes Reader*, pp. 269–76 (New York: Hill and Wang, 1982).

37. For an astute reading of Walter Benjamin and temporality, see Andrew Benjamin, "Time and Task: Benjamin and Heidegger Showing the Present," in Andrew Benjamin and Peter Osborne, eds., *Walter Benjamin's Philosophy: Destruction and Experience*, pp. 216–50 (London and New York: Routledge, 1994).

38. Said, *Culture and Imperialism*, p. 23.

39. My argument here follows Paul de Man, who argues in "The Rhetoric of Temporality" that the act of irony reveals "the existence of a temporality that is definitely not organic, in that it relates to its source only in terms of distance and difference, and allows for no end, for no totality" (*Blindness and Insight: Essays in the Rhetoric of Contemporary Criticism*, 2d ed. [Minneapolis: University of Minnesota Press, 1983], p. 222).

40. Said, *Culture and Imperialism*, p. 23.

41. Fabian, *Time and the Other*, pp. 6, 5.

42. My notion of late colonial culture builds on Fredric Jameson's concept of "cognitive mapping" ("Cognitive Mapping," pp. 249–51).

43. Graham Greene, *Journey Without Maps* (1936; reprint, London: Penguin Books, 1980), p. 97. Further references to this edition will be made in the text.

44. Michel Foucault, "Of Other Spaces," *Diacritics* 16 (1986): 22–27.

45. Sigmund Freud, *Totem and Taboo and Other Works*, vol. 13 (1913–1914), The Standard Edition, trans. James Strachey (London: Hogarth, 1955), p. 1. Further references to this edition will be made in the text.

46. Richards, *Masks of Difference*, p. 206.

47. There is now a critical consensus that Greene's literary works, both fictional and nonfictional, are motivated by a core of motifs central to the project of psychoanalysis: disillusionment, childhood trauma, and anxieties about the law of the father. See Marie-Françoise Allain, *The Other Man: Conversations with Graham Greene*, trans. Guido Waldman (London: Bodley-Head, 1983); and Judith Adamson, *Graham Greene: On the Frontier* (London: Macmillan, 1988).

48. On African art and the modernist aesthetic, see the essays collected in Rubin, *"Primitivism" in Twentieth-Century Art*.

49. Sigmund Freud, *The Future of an Illusion, Civilization and Its Discontents, and Other Works*, vol. 21 (1929–1930), The Standard Edition, trans. James Strachey (London: Hogarth, 1961), p. 86.

50. Slavoj Zizek, *For They Know Not What They Do: Enjoyment as a Political Factor* (London: Verso, 1991), p. 39.

51. Terry Eagleton, *The Ideology of the Aesthetic* (Oxford: Blackwell, 1990), p. 13.

52. Peter Bürger, *The Decline of Modernism*, trans. Nicholas Walker (Cambridge: Polity Press, 1992), p. 128.

53. Zizek, *For They Know Not What They Do*, p. 47.

54. Bürger, *The Decline of Modernism*, p. 131.

6. Beyond Empire and Nation

1. Richard Terdiman, "The Response of the Other," *Diacritics* 22, no. 2 (Summer 1992): 5.

2. Ibid.

3. Dirks, "Introduction: Colonialism and Culture," p. 5. Cf. John Frow, *Marxism and Literary History* (Cambridge: Harvard University Press, 1986), p. 223.

4. Abbeele, *Travel as Metaphor*, p. xviii. As Michel de Certeau aptly puts it, "The other is the phantasm of historiography, the object that it seeks, honors, and buries" (*The Writing of History*, p. 2).

5. Graham Greene, *Journey Without Maps* (1936; London: Penguin Books, 1980), p. 250. Further references to this edition will be made in the text.

6. Abbeele, *Travel as Metaphor*, p. xix. See also Behdad, *Belated Travelers*.

7. Dirks, "Introduction," p. 3.

8. Frantz Fanon, *A Dying Colonialism*, trans. Haakon Chevalier (New York: Grove Weidenfeld, 1967), passim.

9. The archetypal rhapsody of retour is, of course, to be found in Aimé Césaire's *Notebook of a Return to the Native Land*: "I would go to this land of mine and I would say to it: 'Embrace me without fear . . . And if all I can do is speak, it is for you I speak.' " See *The Collected Poetry of Aimè Cèsaire*, trans. Clayton Eshleman and Annette Smith (Berkeley: University of California Press, 1983), p. 45.

10. See Homi Bhabha, interview, *Stanford Humanities Review* 3, no. 1 (Winter 1993): 1.

11. Salman Rushdie, "The Location of Brazil," in *Imaginary Homelands: Essays and Criticisms, 1981–1991*, pp. 9–21 (New York: Viking, 1991). Further references to this edition will be made in the text.

12. Joan Riley, *The Unbelonging* (London: Women's Press, 1985). Further references to this edition will be made in the text.

13. Joan Riley, interview by Donna Perry, in *Back Talk: Women Writers Speak Out*, p. 270 (New Brunswick, N.J.: Rutgers University Press, 1993).

14. Gayatri Chakravorty Spivak, "Asked to Talk About Myself . . . ," *Third Text* 13 (Summer 1992): 3.

15. Ibid., p. 18.

16. S. Hall, "Minimal Selves," p. 45.

17. Chambers, *Room for Maneuver*, p. 15.

18. Hanif Kureishi, "London and Karachi," in *Patriotism: The Making and Unmaking of British National Identity*, vol. 2, Raphael Samuel, ed., *Minorities and Outsiders*, p. 272 (London: Routledge, 1989). Further references to this essay will be made in the text.

19. Homi Bhabha, "Interrogating Identity: The Postcolonial Prerogative," in David Theo Goldberg, ed., *Anatomy of Racism*, p. 196 (Minneapolis: University of Minnesota Press, 1990).

20. Ibid., p. 187.

21. Salman Rushdie, *The Satanic Verses* (New York: Viking, 1988), p. 4. Further references to this edition will be made in the text.

22. Jean-François Lyotard, *The Postmodern Condition: A Report on Knowledge*, trans. Geoff Bennington and Brian Massumi (Minneapolis: University of Minnesota Press, 1993), p. xxiv. Cf. Zeenat Vakil's theory in *The Satanic Verses*: "Society was orchestrated by what she called *grand narratives*: history, economics, ethics. In India, the development of a corrupt and closed state apparatus had 'excluded the masses of the people from the ethical project.' As a result, they sought ethical satisfactions in the oldest of the grand narratives, that is, religious faith" (p. 537).

23. Spivak, "Reading *The Satanic Verses*," in *Outside in the Teaching Machine*, pp. 221–22.

24. According to Spivak, the Bengali writer Mahasweta Devi "invites us to realize that . . . for the subaltern, and especially the subaltern woman, 'Empire' and 'Nation' are interchangeable names, however hard it might be for us to imagine" ("Woman in Difference," in *Outside in the Teaching Machine*, p. 78).

25. See Bhabha, "The Postcolonial and the Postmodern: The Question of Agency," in *The Location of Culture*, pp. 171–97.

26. My reading of *The Satanic Verses* is generally in response to the following critical and theoretical works: Spivak, "Reading *The Satanic Verses*"; Talal Asad, "Multiculturalism and British Identity in the Wake of the Rushdie Affair," *Politics and Society* 18 (December 1990): 455–80; Homi Bhabha, "DissemiNation: time, narrative, and the margins of the modern nation," in Homi K. Bhabha, ed., *Nation and Narration*, pp. 317–19 (New York: Routledge, 1990); and Sara Suleri, "Contraband Histories: Salman Rushdie and the Embodiment of Blasphemy," *Yale Review* 78 (1989): 604–24.

27. Spivak, "Marginality in the Teaching Machine," in *Outside in the Teaching Machine*, p. 60.

28. Fredric Jameson, "Metacommentary," in *The Ideologies of Theory*, 1:5 (Minneapolis:

University of Minnesota Press, 1988). My basic assumption here is that the nationalist project, rather than seeing itself as an appropriation of specifically European discourses—on modernity and nation, for example—presents itself as the recuperation of a *socius* that predates colonization and conquest; there is, however, an unresolved conflict between the forms of modern nationhood and the performance of precolonial traditions.

29. Here I'm adopting Jameson's suggestive differentiation of contradictions and antinomies: "Contradictions are supposed, in the long run, to be productive; whereas antinomies . . . offer nothing in the way of a handle, no matter how diligently you turn them around and around" (*The Seeds of Time*, p. 2).

30. Bhabha, "DissemiNation," p. 319.

31. Suleri, *The Rhetoric of English India*, p. 21.

32. Spivak, "Reading *The Satanic Verses*," p. 225.

33. Ibid.

34. Bhabha, "DissemiNation," p. 318.

35. Cf. Spivak's observation that "because the migrant as paradigm is a dominant theme in the theorizations of post-coloniality, it is easy to overlook Rushdie's resolute effort to represent contemporary India" ("Reading *The Satanic Verses*," p. 221).

36. Bhabha, "DissemiNation," p. 319.

37. Ibid., p. 318.

38. Spivak, "Reading *The Satanic Verses*," p. 221.

39. Spivak, "Marginality in the Teaching Machine," p. 63. Cf. Bhabha's conclusion that Gibreel Farishta is "the mote in the eye of history, its blind spot that will not let the nationalist gaze settle centrally. His mimicry of colonial masculinity and mimesis allows the absence of national history to speak in the ambivalent, ragbag narrative" ("DissemiNation," p. 318). My argument, however, is that it is precisely in the failure of mimicry, a failure represented by Saladin's quest for "proper Englishness," that Rushdie destabilizes the history of both England and India.

40. Bhabha, "DissemiNation," p. 318.

41. Spivak, "Reading *The Satanic Verses*," p. 225.

42. Bhabha, "DissemiNation," p. 318.

Epilogue

1. I take up some of these questions in "In the Shadow of Hegel: Cultural Theory in an Age of Displacement," *Research in African Literatures* 27, no. 1 (Spring 1996): 139–50.

2. For the debate triggered by Ahmad's book, see the special issue of *Public Culture* 6, no. 1 (Fall 1993).

3. Terence Ranger, "The Invention of Tradition in Colonial Africa," in Hobsbawn and Ranger, *The Invention of Tradition*, pp. 211–62.

4. Talal Asad, "Afterword: From the History of Colonial Anthropology to the Anthropology of Western Hegemony," George W. Stocking, ed., *Colonial Situations: Essays on the Contextualization of Ethnographic Knowledge*, History of Anthropology, p. 317 (Madison: University of Wisconsin Press, 1991).

5. Ibid., pp. 315–16.

6. Stoler, *Race and the Education of Desire*, pp. 197–98.

7. S. Hall, "Negotiating Caribbean Identities," p. 9.

8. Spivak, "The Burden of English," p. 151.

Selected Bibliography

Abbeele, Georges van den. *Travel as Metaphor: From Montaigne to Rousseau.* Minneapolis: University of Minnesota Press, 1992.

Achebe, Chinua. *Morning Yet on Creation Day: Essays.* London: Heinemann, 1975.

Ahmad, Aijaz. *In Theory: Classes, Nations, Literatures.* London: Verso, 1992.

Anderson, Benedict. *Imagined Communities: Reflections on the Origin and Spread of Nationalism.* Rev. ed. London: Verso, 1991.

Anderson, Perry. *English Questions.* London: Verso, 1992.

Appadurai, Arjun. "Playing with Modernity: The Decolonization of Indian Cricket." In Carol A. Breckenridge, ed., *Consuming Modernity: Public Culture in a South Asian World,* pp. 23–48. Minneapolis: University of Minnesota Press, 1995.

———. "Theory in Anthropology: Center and Periphery." *Comparative Studies in Society and History* 28 (1986): 356–61.

Asad, Talal. *Genealogies of Religion.* Baltimore: Johns Hopkins University Press, 1993.

Ashcroft, Bill, Gareth Griffiths, and Helen Tiffin. *The Postcolonial Studies Reader.* New York: Routledge, 1995.

Bal, Mieke. "The Politics of Citation." *Diacritics* 21, no. 1 (1991): 25–45.

Barker, Francis, Peter Hulme, Margaret Iversen, Diana Loxley, eds. *Europe and Its Others.* Proceedings of the Essex Sociology of Literature Conference. 2 vols. Colchester: University of Essex, 1985.

Barker, Martin. *The New Racism: Conservatives and the Ideology of the Tribe.* Frederick, Md.: University Publications of America, 1981.

Beckles, Hilary McD., and Brian Stoddart. *Liberation Cricket: West Indies Cricket Culture.* Manchester, Eng.: Manchester University Press, 1995.

Behdad, Ali. *Belated Travelers: Orientalism in the Age of Colonial Dissolution.* Durham: Duke University Press, 1994.

Bhabha, Homi. *The Location of Culture.* New York: Routledge, 1994.

Brantlinger, Patrick. *Rule of Darkness: British Literature and Imperialism, 1830–1914.* Ithaca: Cornell University Press, 1988.

Brathwaite, Edward. *The Development of Creole Society in Jamaica, 1770–1820.* Oxford: Clarendon, 1971.

—— [Kamau]. *Roots.* Ann Arbor: University of Michigan Press, 1993.

Brooks, Peter. *Reading for Plot: Design and Intention in Narrative.* New York: Vintage, 1985.

Certeau, Michel de. *The Writing of History.* Translated by Tom Conley. New York: Columbia University Press, 1988.

Césaire, Aimé. *Discourse on Colonialism.* New York: Monthly Review Press, 1972.

Chakrabarty, Dipesh. "Postcoloniality and the Artifice of History: Who Speaks for 'Indian' Pasts?" *Representations* 37 (Winter 1992): 1–26.

Chambers, Ross. *Room for Maneuver: Reading the Oppositional in Narrative.* Chicago: University of Chicago Press, 1991.

Colley, Linda. "Britishness and Otherness: An Argument." *Journal of British Studies* 31 (October 1992): 309–29.

——. *Britons: Forging the Nation, 1707–1837.* New Haven: Yale University Press, 1992.

Cooper, Frederick, and Ann Laura Stoler. *Tensions of Empire: Colonial Cultures in a Bourgeois World.* Berkeley: University of California Press, forthcoming.

Crick, Bernard, ed. *National Identities: The Constitution of the United Kingdom.* Oxford: Blackwell, 1991.

Derrida, Jacques. *Margins of Philosophy.* Translated, with additional notes, by Alan Bass. Chicago: University of Chicago Press, 1982.

——. *Specters of Marx: The State of Debt, the Work of Mourning, and the New International.* Translated by Peggy Kamuf. New York: Routledge, 1995.

Dirks, Nicholas B. "Introduction: Colonialism and Culture." In Nicholas B. Dirks, ed., *Colonialism and Culture,* pp. 1–26. Ann Arbor: University of Michigan Press, 1992.

Douglas, Mary. *Purity and Danger: An Analysis of the Concepts of Pollution and Taboo.* London: Routledge, 1988.

Doyle, Brian. *English and Englishness.* London: Routledge, 1987.

Dworkin, Dennis L., and Leslie G. Roman, eds. *Views Beyond the Border Country: Raymond Williams and Cultural Politics.* New York and London: Routledge, 1993.

Eagleton, Terry. *Heathcliff and the Great Hunger: Studies in Irish Culture.* London: Verso, 1995.

——, ed. *Raymond Williams: Critical Perspectives.* Cambridge, Eng.: Polity Press, 1989.

Eagleton, Terry, Fredric Jameson, and Edward Said, *Nationalism, Colonialism, and Literature.* Minneapolis: University of Minnesota Press, 1990.

Fabian, Johannes. *Time and the Other.* New York: Columbia University Press, 1983.

Fanon, Frantz. *The Wretched of the Earth.* Translated by Constance Farrington. New York: Grove Press, 1968.

Frankenberg, Ruth. *White Women, Race Matters: The Social Construction of Whiteness*. Minneapolis: University of Minnesota Press, 1993.

Gilroy, Paul. "Art of Darkness: Black Art and the Problem of Belonging to England." *Third Text* 10 (Spring 1990): 45–52.

———. "One Nation Under a Groove: The Cultural Politics of 'Race' and Racism in Britain." In David Theo Goldberg, ed., *Anatomy of Racism*, pp. 262–82. Minneapolis: University of Minnesota Press, 1990.

———. *There Ain't No Black in the Union Jack*. London: Hutchinson, 1987.

Grossberg, Lawrence, Cary Nelson, and Paula Treichler, eds. *Cultural Studies*. New York: Routledge, 1992.

Hall, Catherine. *White, Male, and Middle-Class: Explorations in Feminism and History*. Cambridge: Polity Press, 1992.

Hall, Stuart. "The Great Moving Right Show." In Stuart Hall and Martin Jaques, eds., *The Politics of Thatcherism*, pp. 19–39. London: Lawrence and Wishart, 1983.

———. "Minimal Selves." In Lisa Appignanesi, ed., *The Real Me: Post-Modernism and the Question of Identity*, pp. 44–46. London: ICA Documents, 1987.

———. "Negotiating Caribbean Identities." *New Left Review* 209 (January/February 1995): 3–14.

———. "Racism and Reaction." In *Five Views for Multi-Racial Britain*. Talks on Race Relations Broadcast by BBC TV, pp. 23–35. London: Commission for Racial Equality, 1978.

Hobsbawn, Eric. *The Age of Empire, 1876–1914*. New York: Vintage, 1987.

Hobsbawn, Eric, and Terence Ranger, eds. *The Invention of Tradition*. Cambridge: Cambridge University Press, 1983.

James, C. L. R. *Beyond a Boundary*. New York: Pantheon, 1983.

Jameson, Fredric. "Cognitive Mapping." In Cary Nelson and Lawrence Grossberg, eds., *Marxism and the Interpretation of Culture*, pp. 347–56. Urbana and Chicago: University of Illinois Press, 1988.

———. *The Political Unconscious: Narrative as a Socially Symbolic Act*. Ithaca: Cornell University Press, 1981.

———. *The Seeds of Time*. New York: Columbia University Press, 1994.

Kenyatta, Jomo. *Facing Mount Kenya*. New York: Vintage, 1965.

Lamming, George. *The Pleasures of Exile*. London: Allison and Busby, 1984.

Leavis, F. R. *The Great Tradition*. New York: New York University Press, 1973.

Mehta, Uday S. "Liberal Strategies of Exclusion." *Politics and Society* 18, no. 4 (December 1990): 427–53.

Melman, Billie. *Women's Orients: English Women and the Middle East, 1718–1918: Sexuality, Religion, and Work*. Ann Arbor: University of Michigan Press, 1992.

Mohanty, S. P. "Us and Them: On the Philosophical Bases of Political Criticism." *Yale Journal of Criticism* 2, no. 2 (Spring 1989): 1–31.

Mudimbe, V. Y. *The Invention of Africa: Gnosis, Philosophy, and the Order of Knowledge.* Indianapolis: Indiana University Press, 1988.

Mukasa, Ham. *Sir Apolo Kagwa Discovers Britain.* Edited by Taban lo Liyong. London: Heinemann, 1975.

Muriuki, Godfrey. *A History of the Kikuyu, 1500–1900.* Nairobi: Oxford University Press, 1974.

Nairn, Tom. *The Break-Up of Britain: Crisis and Neo-Nationalism.* London: New Left Books, 1977.

Nederveen, Pieterse J. P. *Empire and Emancipation: Power and Liberation on a World Scale.* London: Pluto Press, 1989.

Poovey, Mary. *Making a Social Body.* Chicago: University of Chicago, 1995.

Prakash, Gyan, ed. "Introduction: After Colonialism." In *After Colonialism: Imperial Histories and Postcolonial Displacements,* pp. 3–17. Princeton: Princeton University Press, 1995.

Pratt, Mary Louise. *Imperial Eyes: Travel Writing and Transculturation.* New York: Routledge, 1992.

Rafael, Vincente. *Contracting Colonialism: Translation and Christian Conversion in Tagalog Society Under Early Spanish Rule.* Durham: Duke University Press, 1992.

Richards, David. *Masks of Difference: Cultural Representations in Literature, Anthropology, and Art.* Cambridge: Cambridge University Press, 1994.

Rubin, William. "Picasso." In William Rubin, ed., *"Primitivism" in Twentieth-Century Art: Affinities of the Tribal and Modern,* pp. 241–344. New York: Museum of Modern Art, 1984.

Sahlins, Peter. *Boundaries: The Making of France and Spain in the Pyrenees.* Berkeley: University of California Press, 1989.

Said, Edward. *Culture and Imperialism.* New York: Knopf, 1993.

——. *Orientalism.* New York: Vintage, 1979.

Samuel, Raphael. *Patriotism: The Making and Unmaking of British National Identity.* Vol. 2, *Minorities and Outsiders.* London: Routledge, 1989.

Sandiford, Keith A. P. *Cricket and the Victorians.* Aldershot, Hants: Scolar Press, 1994.

Sanjek, Roger, ed. *Fieldnotes: The Makings of Anthropology.* Ithaca: Cornell University Press, 1990.

Semmel, Bernard. *Jamaican Blood and Victorian Conscience: The Governor Eyre Controversy.* Boston: Houghton Mifflin, 1963.

Shapiro, James. *Shakespeare and the Jews.* New York: Columbia University Press, 1995.

Sharpe, Jenny. *Allegories of Empire: The Figure of Woman in the Colonial Text.* Minneapolis: University of Minnesota Press, 1993.

Simpson, David. *Fetishism and Imagination: Dickens, Melville, and Conrad.* Baltimore: Johns Hopkins University Press, 1982.

Soyinka, Wole. *Akè: The Years of Childhood.* New York: Vintage, 1989.

Spivak, Gayatri Chakravorty. "The Burden of English." In Carol A. Breckenridge and Peter van der Veer, eds., *Orientalism and the Postcolonial Predicament: Perspectives on South Asia*, pp. 134–57. Philadelphia: University of Pennsylvania Press, 1993.

——."Imperialism and Sexual Difference." In Clayton Koelb and Virgil Lokke, eds., *The Current in Criticism: Essays on the Present and Future of Literary Theory*, pp. 319–37. West Lafayette, Ind.: Purdue University Press, 1986.

——. *Outside in the Teaching Machine.* New York: Routledge, 1993.

——. "The Ranir of Sirmur." In Francis Barker et al., eds., *Europe and Its Others*, 1:128–51. Colchester: University of Essex, 1985.

Stocking, George W., Jr. *Victorian Anthropology.* New York: Free Press, 1987.

——, ed. *Colonial Situations: Essays on the Contextualization of Ethnographic Knowledge.* Vol. 7. History of Anthropology Series. Madison: University of Wisconsin Press, 1991.

Stoler, Ann Laura. *Race and the Education of Desire: Foucault's History of Sexuality and the Colonial Order of Things.* Durham: Duke University Press, 1995.

Suleri, Sara. *The Rhetoric of English India.* Chicago: University of Chicago Press, 1992.

Taussig, Michael. *Shamanism, Colonialism, and the Wild Man: A Study in Terror and Healing.* Chicago: University of Chicago Press, 1987.

Thiong'o, Ngugi wa. *Homecoming: Essays on African and Caribbean Literature, Culture, and Politics.* New York: Lawrence Hill, 1972.

Thomas, J. J. *Froudacity.* Introduction by C. L. R. James. London: New Beacon Books, 1969.

Thomas, Nicholas. *Colonialism's Culture: Anthropology, Travel, and Government.* Princeton: Princeton University Press, 1994.

Torgovnick, Marianna. *Gone Primitive: Savage Intellects, Modern Lives.* Chicago: University of Chicago Press, 1990.

Trotter, David. "Modernism and Empire: Reading *The Waste Land.*" *Critical Quarterly* 28 (Spring/Summer 1986): 143–53.

Viswanathan, Gauri. *Masks of Conquest.* New York: Columbia University Press, 1989.

Ware, Vron. *Beyond the Pale: White Women, Racism, and History.* London: Verso, 1992.

Williams, Patrick, and Laura Chrisman. *Colonial Discourse and Postcolonial Theory.* New York: Columbia University Press, 1994.

Williams, Raymond. *The Country and the City.* New York: Oxford University Press, 1973.

——. *Culture and Society, 1780–1950.* Harmondsworth, Middlesex: Penguin Books, 1963.

——. *The English Novel from Dickens to Lawrence.* London: Chatto and Windus, 1970.

——. "Forms of English Fiction in 1848." In Francis Barker et al., eds., *Literature, Politics, and Theory,* pp. 1–16. London: Methuen, 1986.

——. *Politics and Letters: Interviews with "New Left Review."* London: New Left Books, 1979.

Zastoupil, Lynn. *John Stuart Mill and India.* Stanford: Stanford University Press, 1994.

Index